After, AFTER RAISING SUGARCANE

BOOK III

A memoir continued by,
BARRY RAFFRAY

Gotham Books

30 N Gould St.
Ste. 20820, Sheridan, WY 82801
https://gothambooksinc.com/

Phone: 1 (307) 464-7800

© 2024 *Barry Raffray*. All rights reserved.

No part of this book may be reproduced, stored in a retrieval system, or transmitted by any means without the written permission of the author.

Published by Gotham Books (May 8, 2024)

ISBN: 979-8-88775-489-5 (P)
ISBN: 979-8-88775-490-1 (E)

Because of the dynamic nature of the Internet, any web addresses or links contained in this book may have changed since publication and may no longer be valid.

The views expressed in this work are solely those of the author and do not necessarily reflect the views of the publisher, and the publisher hereby disclaims any responsibility for them.

DEDICATION

To My Stepsons

I dedicate this book to Jacob Elliff and Nathan Elliff. This is a continuation of my life during the time that I was married to their mom. I am hopeful that they will enjoy reading it and perhaps it will bring back some good memories of that time to them.

I am very proud of the men that these two boys became. They are good fathers and good providers to their families.

~ Barry

CONTENTS

DEDICATION III
CONTENTS IV
INTRODUCTION VIII
ACKNOWLEDGEMENTS IX

MY THIRD BOOK A NEW LIFE BEGINS

SUNSHINE COMES INTO MY LIFE 1
   TUBING THE GUADALUPE RIVER – SUMMER 1995 5
   MY 1st DEER HUNTING TRIP IN SOUTHWEST TEXAS 10
   MY 1st DUCK HUNTING TRIP IN SOUTH LOUISIANA 17
TRIP TO LOUISIANA IN 1995 24
   HUNTSMAN COMPANY GROWS 29
   MY 1st AND ONLY WILD BOAR HUNTING TRIP 33
   TRIP TO ARKANSAS IN RENTED VAN - 1996 38
   DUCK HUNTING TRIP WITH HOLLYWOOD MARINE 42
BUYING THE PLACE IN 1996 47
   THE PLACE THE DAY OF CLOSING JULY 19, 1996 49
   A HAIRY EXPERIENCE AFTER A DEER HUNT 58
   THE GRANBURY, TEXAS TRIP 1996 62
   GETTING MARRIED AGAIN 1997 70
LAS VEGAS TRIP JANUARY 11, 1997 72
   TRIP TO NIAGARA FALLS IN EARLY JULY 1997 80
   1998 86
   CRAWFISH BOIL AT THE PLACE 1998 93
   SELL OUT BY HUNTSMAN TO NOVA LATE 1998 99
NOVA TAKEOVER IN EARLY 1999 108
   2nd CRAWFISH BOIL AT THE PLACE APRIL 1999 112

SARAH GETS LAID OFF IN LATE 1999	122
MY NERVOUS BREAKDOWN IN 1999	125
MY STRATOSPHERE STOCK IS NO GOOD 2000	128
ET & C'D FROM NOVA JULY 2000	131
MY RETIREMENT PARTY	**136**
REBEKAH'S WEDDING DECEMBER 2000	140
SARAH, MRS. GRIFFIN, AND ME ON THE MOUNTAIN DEC. 2000	144
MY BEING LAID OFF BY NOVA IN JUNE 2001	150
HOT RODING WITH JAMES IN 2001	156
JACOB'S FIRST WEDDING MAY 2001	159
TRIP TO ARKANSAS AND MISSOURI MAY 2001	**161**
WORKING FOR HABITAT FOR HUMANITY	167
MEMORIAL WEEKEND HEART ATTACK	175
BEING SEVERED BY NOVA IN JULY 2001	184
SELLING THE LEAGUE CITY HOUSE IN 2001	189
RECOVERING FROM HEART ATTACK FOR BALANCE OF 2001	**192**
HOSPITAL STAY IN NASSAU BAY, TEXAS	196
VISITING WITH FAMILY	197
CASINO IN MARKSVILLE, LOUISIANA	198
THIRD CRAWFISH BOIL AT THE PLACE	201
GRAND ISLE LOUISIANA TRIP	205
MRS.GRIFFIN'S HEALTH PROBLEMS	207
MRS. GRIFFIN'S FUNERAL	**216**
AFTER MRS. GRIFFINS DEATH	222
THE FIRST 1ST COUSIN DIED	224
KENT AND MELISSA'S WEDDING	227
RITA HURRICANE	230
"BIG BEAR" PACKARD	236
CRAWFISH BOILS AT KENT AND MELISSA'S HOUSE	239
SELLING SARAH'S RENT HOUSE	243

TRIPS TAKEN. DURING 2006, 2007, 2008 AND 2009 248
BUYING THE 1936 OLDSMOBILE 252
HURRICANE IKE SEPTEMBER 2008 257
SELLING THE TEXAS CITY HOUSE 261
TRAGEDY IN MY FAMILY 265
ANOTHER TRIP 268
AND ANOTHER TRIP 279
OUR FRIENDS JON AND JIM JOHANSON 296
BUYING THE HOUSE IN RANDOM OAKS (PLAQUEMINE) ...299
JUST A FEW MORE PICTURES OF YOURS TRULY 305
SHORT STORIES THAT I MADE UP 308
HOW DEM CAJUNS GOT TO LOUISIANA (A CAJUN TELLING IT) 310
MY CANOE TRIP ON THE MISSISSIPPI RIVER 319
ULTRA CONSERVATIVE RIGHT-WING CONSTITUTIONALIST 328

SAM'S WOOD

LS AND U - WHAT WILL THEY DO 335
SHAKIN IN TEXAS CITY 336
PEOPLE DON'T WANT TO WORK NO MORE 337
WITH SLEEPY IN TEXAS CITY 338
BLUE'S IN THE WOODS 339
SICK COMPUTER IN THE WOODS 340
KEEPING COOL IN THE WOODS 341
IT WON'T BE LONG-NOW (APRIL 28) 342
CENTRAL SYSTEM FOR THE OLD HOUSE (APRIL 21) 343
U OF H CLEAR LAKE ALUMNI PARTY (APRIL 17) 344
57 YR. ANNIVERSITY OF TEXAS CITY DISASTER (APRIL 17) 345
PHI KAPHA PHI INDUCTION (APRIL 16) 347
NEW TEXAS CITY CONTAINER PORT (APRIL 16) 349
THE EASTER THAT WAS 350
BEEN GONE TO LONG 352

WAL-MART WOES (I got the) 353
BREAKFAST IN CLEVELAND, TEXAS 354
WHAT A TIMESHARE 356
ON THE ROAD AGAIN 357
ON THE MOVE 358

INTRODUCTION

This book is the continuation of the life of Barry Franklin Anthony Raffray.

This is the third book in the series of books depicting his life story.

This book covers mostly the second marriage of Barry to Sarah Ruth Elliff of Texas City, Texas. Again, relive the pain, enjoy the good times, and rejoice in his triumphs as Barry, at times, struggles his way through life trying to have a positive influence on the people around him.

This book was published in 2018 by another publisher that went out on business before making my book available.

- Barry R

ACKNOWLEDGEMENTS

I want to thank Sarah Raffray for her tireless efforts to correct grammatical errors and for supplying pictures and placing them into this book. Without her efforts, this book would not be as good as it is.

Thanks, Sarah, you are a great editor. I could not have completed the book without your help.

~ Barry R

MY THIRD BOOK

A NEW LIFE BEGINS

SUNSHINE COMES INTO MY LIFE

In 1994, just Kent and I lived in my house. I was still playing the field with the ladies. Kent was working at Blockbuster and taking communications courses at Alvin Community College. Kent moved back to Austin in late 1994 or early 1995 and got a job. This left me alone in the League City house.

Also in 1994, I took notice of this girl who was working in the accounting department which was across the hall from my office. During the past several years we did not communicate very much unless it was business related. I knew that she had gone through a divorce as I had several years before. She was and still is much younger than I. I did not think that she would be interested in an older fellow like me. I, on the other hand, was not looking to get into a long-term relationship with anyone. I was spending most of my time at work. It seemed that I was married to my job. What an awful thing to do.

Sarah Ruth Elliff was her name. She came into the accounting office working for Dave Hardy as a temporary employee. This was in late 1991. The accounting group was made up of three or four ladies who mostly stayed to themselves and did their work. As Virg Bodiker and I worked in the transportation and distribution of our product, we created a lot of the bills that the accounting group processed for payment. So, we interacted with this group very much. Virg handled most of the invoice approvals for my group, so he interacted with these ladies more than I did. I interacted more with the bosses and the other department heads at this plant.

Sarah and Virg used to play around with rubber bands. She would sneak up on him and use her finger to stretch the rubber band and let it go. It shot out like a projectile at him. He would retaliate. I do not know how or when this started. It had been going on for some time when I really noticed it. I wished that it was me interacting with Sarah in this way. I said or did nothing for a long time. Somehow one day, Sarah and I were shooting rubber bands at each other. This went on for a short time. One day she popped up at my doorway and let fly one of her projectiles. It hit me in the left eye as I was looking up from working at my desk. She quickly shouted that she was sorry and came and grabbed my head with both hands and pulled my face to her bosom to console me. I liked the way she felt. She then looked at my eye to check for damage. There was none. We decided to quit this rubber band shooting because someone could get hurt.

We started communicating more and more after this happened. Prior to this incident, the most communications we had was when her dad passed away in 1993. She was away from work for several days and I overheard her workmates telling someone that her dad had passed away. Upon her return to work, I happened to meet her in the hallway, and I offered my sympathy to her on the passing of her dad. She acknowledged me by saying, thanks. That was the longest conversation that I remember having with her until the rubber band incident in 1994.

Did I say that I was not looking to get into a long-term relationship? Well, guess what happened? I/we fell in love again. It did not happen this fast though. We went out off and on for almost three years. She had two sons, Jacob, and Nathan. I had three sons, Kent, Lane, and Todd. As you can see the names of my sons are easier to spell and they are all four-letter words. Her sons are as different as night and day. I did not know if I really wanted to participate in raising two more boys or not. Jacob was about twelve and Nathan about eleven at this time. After going through what I had with my three sons and the age I was at this time, I did not know what to do. But love is a great thing. If a person truly loves another person, they could accomplish great things together. When all else fails or succeeds you still have love for each other. You work all things out. It is not always easy, but love is not always supposed to be easy. Anyway, I wanted to help and have a positive influence on these boys' lives if I could.

We all drew closer over the next couple of years. Sarah and I got married on January 1, 1997. Jacob and Nathan had moved to live with their dad in the Fort Worth area. More on this part of my life to come later.

Sarah Ruth Elliff 1995   Nathan and Jacob Elliff 1995

TUBING THE GUADALUPE RIVER – SUMMER 1995

I again, made reservations far in advance for a campsite at the R & R on the Guadalupe River. This trip was with Sarah, Jacob, Nathan, and me. We made this trip in my 1992 Mercury, Grand Marque. It was a large four-door sedan. There was plenty of room in the trunk for my large canvas tent, Sarah's small tent, the ice chest, bed rolls, camp stove, lanterns, and other stuff.

It had been about ten years since I was last there. The place was really different. The Mechels family sold the place sometime during the last ten years. The new owners built a large office and grocery store at the entrance.

You could even get some hot food there. Across the entrance road was another wood building that housed men's and women's showers and bathrooms. This building also was where you could rent tubes, canoes, and other water supplies. This was also where you boarded the trucks for a tubing trip on the river after paying for such at the office.

The entrance road was blacktopped. I could not believe it. The outhouses were all gone. Every hundred yards or so were more modern, his and her bathrooms. These folks really cleaned this place up. They finally got into the modern world. We found our campsite unloaded all our stuff and set up the tents. We then locked up what we could, and all went to Canon City to have burgers and purchase ice and groceries. The groceries at this little store were way too high priced for me.

On the way to Canyon City, we decided that we would not use the jobbers at the R & R to test the river. We drove to the small building that I had last used with my sons some years earlier. I did not recognize anyone.

We rented the tubes and paid the fee, got in the large truck, and up the river they drove. We off-loaded at a location that I was familiar with. We each grabbed a tube and to the river we went. Jake and Nathan got into the water right away and did some yelling. They told me it was still cold. They had done tubing on the Guadalupe with their mom a couple of years before this trip. They been here and done that. They knew the pitfalls of this river. Sarah got in and yelled. I stepped into the water to my knees. Damn, the water was cold. I think it was the coldest that I was ever in. In the last ten years or so I think the water temperature went down one degree for each year. Of course, I was older now than back then and that may have had something to do with the coldness. As you get older you get colder.

They were ready to go, and I was still pissing around trying to get accustomed to the cold water. I finally lay backward on my tube. I did it without my butt touching the water yet. I was stretched out across the tube with my butt and legs and feet and hands out of the water. I guess I looked stiff as a board lying on the tube because Sarah and her boys started laughing really hard. Both boys tried to splash water on me and were making their way to me when I yelled at them to STOP and DESIST.

Sarah also told them to get away from me. Which they reluctantly did while still laughing hardily. We started drifting down the river. I made it to the middle of the river to get the most sunlight. I kept my position for over ten minutes while we drifted. Sarah would still laugh when she looked my way. The boys were drifting away from us. I could hear them laughing also. My muscles were now hurting, and I finally had to ease my butt into the water. I was not very happy, but I finally did it.

Before we knew it, Nathan was out of sight. He was being Nathan. I finally got wet all over and was almost accustomed to the cold water. After this first run, we made another one. After a break for lunch, we continued to play on the river until they shut it down for the day. We went back to camp, changed clothes, and Sarah and I started working on preparing supper or dinner as the city folks say. We just sat around after we ate until it was time to go to bed. Sarah and I shared the big tent. The boys had a small tent. When I got up in the morning, Nathan was sleeping on one of the picnic tables and Jacob on another. After they awoke, they both said that it was too hot inside the tent, so they slept outside.

After breakfast, we went to another jobber to rent tubes and try another section of the river. We tubed the river all day again without much excitement or unusual happenings that I can recall. We all had a good time on the river. After getting off the river, we did the usual driving around. We did the complete ride up and down River Road which is about twelve to fifteen miles long. We went to Canyon Lake Park at the Dam. We also did other sightseeing. We stopped and looked over the pump that fed the Guadalupe River from Canyon

Lake. This is where the River Authority controlled the amount of water being released into the river from the dam. They could release from twenty thousand gallons per minute to seventy thousand gallons per minute in a very short period of time.

The next day we went to The Schlitterbahn in New Braunfels. After paying and getting inside, Nathan disappeared. We saw him only two times during the whole day. One time he came looking for money to buy something to drink and the other time for something to eat. Nathan was all over that water park. They must have over twenty acres of water events. Nathan covered every inch of it. He located a parked train that went from one park to another. When I say he checked out the whole park-HE checked out the whole damn park. Jacob stayed in only one area of the park. He does not know anybody and does not make friends as easily as Nathan. Nathan is a get-in-your-face kind of kid. He likes to discover new things. He will meet a kid for the first time and in five minutes' time that kid will be his best friend. He has way too many best friends. Jake was in awe of what Nathan saw and talked about after we departed the park. So were Sarah and I. We did not know how to get to that other darn part of the park either. Jake did not know that there was another section of the park that could be seen or used, and one could get to it by park train. Goooooolly-Gleeeeeeeee wiz.

Jake had a good time doing the waterworks by himself. I believe we left the boys there while we drove around the area and saw the sites. We also spent a lot of time just hanging around the water park. I just love to watch the Tube Shoot. It was so much fun watching folks get themselves into predicaments as their tube lifted off the shoot and landed in the Comal River. The expressions on some of the faces were priceless.

We went back to the campsite that night and headed back to Galveston County the next morning.

MY 1st DEER HUNTING TRIP IN SOUTHWEST TEXAS

After several years of being invited to go deer hunting by barge towing company representatives, I decided to go. Hollywood Marine had what they called the Louisiana People Hunt when they invited their customers from Louisiana to come over to Houston. Then everyone rode to southwest Texas for a deer hunt. We were usually gone from home for about three days or so. This gave me the chance to see some of my pals from Louisiana that I used to associate with. We would all meet at the Hollywood Marine office off Memorial Drive in Houston. We parked our car in their protected parking area and boarded a large van. Sometimes there were two vans, depending on the number of hunters. Hollywood employees drove the vans. A couple of Hollywood sales representatives were always with us on these types of trips.

Sometimes the owner, Berden Lawrence, would come along also. He loved to hunt anything. We would hunt at a place called Rock Springs, Texas. I never did see any springs but there was a hell of a lot of rocks there. We may have had over twenty thousand acres to hunt on. The land was sparse there. Cactus, mesquite trees, brush, scrub oaks, and plenty of rocks- large and small. It was a rough and rugged country. How they raised cattle (and deer) there, I do not know.

The owner of the ranch came by the first night and gave us all the rules of his place. Hollywood would have a lease with landowners to hunt on their land- they paid them so much a head for each deer killed. He told us things like if you kill a cow, it will cost you one thousand dollars, a bull two thousand dollars, etc. This is something we did NOT want to do. He was telling us to be sure that we knew what to shoot at. He also needed us to kill does. He had too many females in this place and needed to thin them out. He, like most landowners in these parts, worked with the Texas Wildlife Department to better manage their property, leasing to deer hunters was a big business.

Most deer hunters want to shoot only big horn bucks. Everybody wanted a trophy buck. They shot does as the last resort. Some wait until the last hunt to shoot a doe or two. You shoot it for the meat. You shoot the buck for showoff and bragging rights and the meat. Every person that deer hunts like that will shoot a doe to get meat to take home.

The Hollywood folks were a great group to hunt with. After you shoot a deer or two, you just wait for the time to be picked up from the hunting stand. You hunted from a stand or box off the ground about twelve feet in the air. You did NOT go walking about. You could get your ass shot that way. Each stand was placed a good distance away from each other. After all, you are shooting high-power rifles. Rifles like the Remington 243. I used the camp gun until I purchased my Savage 30-06. Other hunters used 270s and other high-power rifles. You would only leave your deer stand to look for a deer that you wounded and ran off a bit. However, you did not go out too far from your stand.

One time I wounded a doe, and she ran off. I went to look for her by following the blood trail. It was a good thing for me that this was toward the end of a morning hunt. I lost the trail and decided to go back to the stand. I was one hundred percent sure that I knew where it was. I was wrong. I was heading in the opposite direction when I heard the van pull up. I went in the direction of the sound about twenty paces and the guys were getting out of the van. You just could not see very far with all the brush. If they had not shown up then, they would have had to send a search party for me. I met them and pointed to where I hit the deer and one of the guys was a really good tracker. Yea, you are right- he was a Louisiana boy. How in the hell he found that deer I will never know. Nevertheless, find it he did. She was dead. I hit her in the windpipe in the neck. By the time we found her, she had bloated. I did not know that they would do that. She was half again as big as when I shot at her. I found out from the guys that that was just air, and this is what happens when you shoot a deer or any animal in the windpipe. Four of us each grabbed a leg and carried it to the van and tagged it- this is a must and put it in the back area that was made for this sort of thing.

They say that these deer stands are placed in the air because deer do not look up. I do not know about that. On morning hunts, after awaking from a nap as it is just getting daylight, there were times when as many as a dozen does were within one hundred yards of the stand and as I look out the window-it looked to me that every damn one of them was looking up at me. You sit there and just look them over. You are looking for a buck. However, those suckers are much smarter than the does. They stay hidden in the brush and very seldom come out in the open. During the rutting season the bucks get crazy and forget about the hunters because they have the does on their minds and trying to get at one before another buck sees her. They are just like men when it comes to females. They forget everything that they learned in buck school.

These stands have open windows on all four sides so you can look all around you and not have a deer sneak up on your blindside. Therefore, there is not a blind side. You sit in a chair that is just the right height where you could place your gun on the window edge for support. Some stands have swivel chairs in them. They are really nice. It is a good setup.

There is usually a can of WD-40 in the stand in case the chair squeaks. They looked like old office chairs to me.

Now these Texans are not that sporty. About one hundred fifty yards or so is a deer feeder location. They put corn or other grain that the deer love to eat in these feeders. It looks like a fifty-gallon drum that has a hole in the bottom of it. At certain times of day, once in the early morning before the deer wake up and later in the afternoon after the deer take their nap; this feeder thingy goes off and a thing under the drum spends around and throws corn in a circle all around the feeder. It has a motor that runs on a battery. Of course, this is designed to bring in the deer to eat it. But that's not all. They also have a four-foot fence around the feeder. The fenced-in area may be thirty by thirty feet square with the feeder right smack dab in the middle of it. Now the poor bastards have to jump the fence to get into the feed area and jump the fence again to get out. Pretty smart huh? This is the time for a Great Deer Hunter to get his shot off. The fence slows the deer up coming and going. The fence also has something called hog wire all around it. This is to keep the wild hogs javelina and other smaller animals from eating all the grain before the deer get to it.

Now that I have given you the layout, this is my very first deer hunt. Since I had never been on a deer hunt before, my Hollywood sales representative friend, Mickey Bell, was going to sit with me in a two-seat deer stand. We were dressed up in our winter camouflage outfits and with our rifles ready to go in the stand before 5 a.m. You must to start early to be all settled into your stand before the damn deer wake up. A bunch of us got into the van. The driver starts out and drops off hunters at stands throughout the ranch. Sometimes you are in the van for a half-hour or more before you get to your stand. Therefore, Mickey and I got out where we were supposed to be. Of course, we have flashlights. We cannot see in the dark. We would never find a damn thing without them. We climb up the ladder and get into the stand. We each find a chair and sit. is still very dark outside. Mickey keeps telling me to be quiet while loading the rifle and be quiet while doing anything. We need our flashlight to load shells into our rifles. Put three shells into the gun. Be sure to put the safety on, and then lean the gun in one corner of the stand and wait and wait and wait. Now do not talk out loud because the deer may be eavesdropping and hear what you are saying, everything is dark, cold, quiet, and creepy- then Mickey have to light up a damn cigarette. Shit- now the deer stand is full of smoke, but it is all right, I guess. because we are high in the air and the deer cannot smell up this high.

After, AFTER RAISING SUGARCANE

It is getting a little lighter outside, but we still cannot see anything.

I still cannot see the deer feeder. I have an idea where it is but cannot see it. Mickey tells me again to keep quiet because it will be dawning any minute. It is so quiet that we could hear a pin drop if we had one to drop. I thought that I heard a noise outside. I was really concentrating on my hearing when it happened. My buddy, my dear stand mate, my friend, who had been on my ass since we got into the damn stand to keep quiet-started SNORING. He scared the shit out of me. I heard something, scurrying around outside and hauling ass. It was now daybreak and light enough to shoot but nothing was there to shoot at. I woke Mickey up. He did not know that he was sleeping. He asked if I saw anything. I said, "No, but I heard something BIG". However, somebody started snoring, and the big thing I heard has hauled ass. He said, "OH-SHIT, it may be back". We never saw that sucker again.

Right at daybreak the feeder thing went off. It scared us both again. I had never heard the buzzing sound before. That was the corn dropping on the spinning thing and being thrown off. We did not see the hide or hair of a deer for the rest of the morning hunt.

At about nine-thirty the guys picked us up. I told Mickey that I knew how it was done now and that I could be by myself for the rest of the hunts the next two days. Hell, I can snore by myself and do not need anyone else to accompany me.

I never shot at a deer on this hunt. I went with Hollywood to hunt deer every year for the next twelve years or so. I did not shoot a deer until my fifth year. I saw many, but I just could not shoot Bambie. Then on the sixth trip, I saw this eight-point buck and I wanted to kill it so badly that my rifle started bouncing on the window ledge. I shot three times and missed all three. It was a good shot, I just missed. There is this hunting rule, and it is DO NOT gut shoot a deer. Shoot them in the head, neck or shoulder. But never-never gut-shoot one. Well at the time I did not care if I gut shot it or not. I just wanted to kill kill kill.

After I quit shaking, I had a very bad feeling come over me. And it was that I wanted to kill the buck so bad - it made me feel bad about myself. I finally got over that feeling. However, I would never ever shoot any animal that I would not eat. And that is the truth.

On one of the hunts later, I got my nine-point buck. The horns are mounted and in my game room now.

MY 1st DUCK HUNTING TRIP IN SOUTH LOUISIANA

I was invited to go duck hunting by Denny Kokontis who was president of Arthur Smith Towing Company of Houston. Denny and I flew down to the area in a small airplane. There we met up with Chuck Sweeney who was my sales representative for the barge company and several other customers who were already there. We all were the guests of Arthur Smith Towing and Harris Cheramie, who owned Cheramie Towing Company.

The Cheramie's tugs and small push boats hauled many of Arthur Smith and other large canal and river barge company's barges to their destinations. Harris's company was headquartered in Golden Meadow, Louisiana. He and his family also lived there. Harris owned a large two-story fishing/hunting barge that he used for a camp. A camp hell I wanted to live on it. He kept it anchored about two miles out in the marsh from Golden Meadow. It was the base for excursions such as this one. It had a complete setup for spending a week or month on it. It had about eight bedrooms, several bathrooms, a large shower area, a kitchen, a very large living area, a large eating area, and a very large covered and not covered deck area where we spent most of our time when not hunting. You know, time like drinking beer and the hard stuff, playing cards, fishing off the deck, bullshitting, etc.

As I mentioned, the houseboat was built on a large barge. Therefore, it had a good supply of fresh water and potted water to take showers and flush the toilet and the sink dishwater. All the waste-water went into a tank below the deck to be disposed of properly later. It was set up with jack-up stands welded onto the barge base. It had one steel pole on each side of the barge near the corners. The steel polls had notches in them. This allowed the whole houseboat to be lifted out of the water if need be. But the jack-up polls were mostly used to go down into the mud to anchor the barge, so it does not drift or move with the tide or when boats pass by on the channel. If the houseboat needed repairs or Harris wanted to move it to another location, they would have the jack-up polls lifted hydraulically and connect a small push boat with cables to move it. It was set up really nicely.

As we were in the marsh, there was not much deep water. The canal that the houseboat was located on, and other canals that oil companies dug for transportation of workers and equipment, was the only deep water. They are only about ten feet deep if that much. We used small fishing boats to get us to the area where we were going to hunt. Then we would transfer into a flat boat. This was a wooden boat about five feet wide and about sixteen feet long with a go-devil motor on it. These boats are designed to go into just an inch or so of water if need be. The go-devil was a motor with a ten-foot or so-long shaft behind it. It went straight out behind the boat and had a propeller on the end of it. It was designed for the propeller to spin in the mud/water just a few inches and it would push the boat forward. It kind of went flop, flop, flop as it scooted the boat forward on the top of the marsh. The flat boats or pirogues got us to the duck blinds. The blinds were built on top of the marsh in a clump of weeds or marsh grass. These must have had stakes driven into the marsh and a wood platform or floor just above the water line because there was not any water in the blinds. You would get in the blind, and crouch down low so the duck cannot see you. When it was time to hunt, just after daybreak for morning hunting, you could call in the ducks. To call in the duck, I said, "HEAR DUCK, HEAR DUCK, HEAR DUCK". I am just kidding of course. Some guys were good at using their mouths to mimic a duck. Other hunters use a duck call. I cannot use a duck call so I just waited to see if any would just show up.

Hunting for ducks is the same as hunting for deer or hogs/boars. For the morning hunt, you had to get into the blind and be ready before the duck wakes up. For an afternoon hunt, we got into the blinds at about three p.m. Hunting is in the wintertime and the daylight is shorter then. you hunted for a couple of hours or so. You are not supposed to shoot at any birds or deer or hogs, etc., before daylight or after dark.

We only hunted one man to a blind. I do not know if all marsh hunting is like this or not since this was the first time and last time that I went marsh hunting. The blinds here were not set up for two people. They were too damn small. We did not have chairs to sit in them either. The weeds/grass to hide you was not tall enough. So, you either knelt down or squatted while waiting for the ducks to show up. I hunted with a twenty- gauge camp gun. What this means is that I did not own a shotgun at this time. Most good hunting camps will have a selection of shotguns for customers to use.

Well, I did not see any ducks on my first hunt. If I did, I did not know that it was a duck. One thing I forgot to mention earlier is - If you have to take a shit while you are in the blind, you are shit out of luck. You could be a stinky mess for the rest of your time in it and you sure in hell did not want to come back to that blind for your second hunt. You would swap with someone else after NOT telling them why you are swapping.

After one morning hunt, I did not understand why Harris came to pick us up in a pirogue after dropping us off in a flat boat earlier - but he did. I also do not know why he paddled out to get Chuck Sweeney first - but he did. Now here he comes with him and Chuck in the pirogue. After the sun came out, I could see where I was and there was no way that I could walk out to the little levee where the larger boats were located even if I wanted to. You were surrounded by water, mud, and weeds. You could not tell how deep the stuff was.

Well as Harris and Chuck approached in the pirogue, I could see that it only had about one inch or so freeboard. The freeboard is the amount of the top of the boat that is above the water. Harris, who did not want to make two trips, told me to get in. I told him that this pirogue would not hold three people.

He insisted that it could. I did not want to try but I already knew that Harris Cheramie was hard-headed, and I did not want him to get mad with me. He was one of the Hosts for the hunt and it is not good to piss the host off. And besides, Harris carries a grudge. So, I handed my unloaded gun (always safety first), to Chuck, took a deep breath, and put my left foot into the pirogue. The bastard went under the water. Chuck and Harris both yelled, "Get back". I was trying, but my right foot was in the air, and I missed the blind when trying to place it down and my leg went into the marsh. It went all the way to my crotch. "GOT DAMN", I said. I was able to get my left foot back on the blind and lifted myself out of the water. I was well pissed off. This marsh was cold and now I was wet to my balls on my right leg. After the pirogue bounced back up, Chuck and Harris were really happy and completely dry. They had a little laugh at my expense.

Harris said that he would come back for me. I told him that I would be very happy if he did. I still did not want to start any shit with him.

Now I want you to remember this about the marsh. What looks like dirt/mud about ten inches or so below the top of the water - IS NOT. That shit is black silt. I went down about three feet into this stuff. How I did not poo-poo as this was happening, I do not know to this day.

That evening hunt - no ducks again. I saw some but they were way too high for me to shoot at. I went out in my own pirogue for this hunt. From the little levee, Harris had shown his flashlight to the place where I was supposed to paddle. The pirogue was to go right into a long double row. of grass/weeds. This was my cover so the ducks could not see me. Well, I got there or so I thought, loaded up my gun, and waited and waited and waited. It was not until daylight that I noticed that I was not in the blind at all. In fact, I would not ever see or know where the blind was. One side of my pirogue and I was all exposed. No wonder I did not see any ducks. They could see me from a mile away. I paddled around to the other side of the clump of grass so any other hunters that may be in the area could not see where I was.

Ain't this some shit? That afternoon hunt, Harris had me and Chuckie, his oldest son, go out in a pirogue together. Chuckie was going to take me to the best blind and put me on some ducks. While in the pirogue, Chuckie told me to load my gun just in case since we were getting a later start than usual for what reason I do not remember. Just before we got to the blind, three ducks were coming in low. I was looking them in the face. They were heading straight at me only about fifteen feet over the open water. I lifted up my shotgun and BAM, BAM, BAM. It was automatic, so I did not have to pump it. You just pull the trigger and the lead flies. I turned to look behind me to see where they had fallen. The ducks were still hauling ass. looked over at Chuckie. He had his mouth open. Then he looked at me and said, "Maw, Mr. Barry, those ducks' shit all over you". He was right. I just hung my head, got into my blind, and did not say a word. I had to admit that his saying was really funny. Chuckie was about fourteen years old at the time and had already been working with his dad and mom on the push boats.

All that afternoon I was dreading getting back to the houseboat and Chuckie telling this story. My fears were misplaced because Chuckie did not even mention it. So, at supper with everyone in attendance, I told the story. Everybody got a good laugh out of this one.

I know that this may be unbelievable, but while pulling the trigger while shooting at those ducks, the thought occurred to me that if I hit one, he would land right on my chest and knock me and the gun out of the pirogue. I was really trying to hit them though.

By the way, these ducks happen to be Teals. They are almost one-half the size of a regular Mallard and fly about ninety miles per hour. OK, maybe not ninety but they are the fastest ducks alive - I believe. Good luck to you trying to shoot one if you ever get the chance. This was

After, AFTER RAISING SUGARCANE

our last hunt and we said our thanks and goodbyes. The next morning, we all headed home.

TRIP TO LOUISIANA IN 1995

Sarah, Nathan, and I took a trip to Louisiana to visit my brother and sister and their families. While there, we stayed at my brother's house in Random Oaks, just two miles South of Plaquemine, Louisiana. This very little settlement is located in a point of woods just off Louisiana Highway #1. The acreage is owned by one Vince Pizzolotta. He subdivided some of his land into lots back in the nineteen fifties or early nineteen sixties. My brother as well as other folks purchased lots there and had houses built for their residences. My brother had his house built in the sixties. There are also several lots with house trailers on them as well. There is one street coming from La.#1 into the subdivision. It makes a loop in the shape of a P. So, there is one way in and one way out. It is the same way out as in.

This was Nathan's first trip to South Louisiana. While there, we visited several places. One day we rode to Bayou Sorrell to site see and look at all the camps and houses that were built since my last trip there. These backwoods and swampy areas are all getting developed into residential and recreational homesteads. Houses or camps were going up at a feverish pace. Developers and landowners were dredging along the lake and building large canals. These canals were about a half-mile long from the lake inland. They used the mud and silt from the canal dredging to build up both sides of the canal to levels high above the floodplain. After the drying out of the mud and silt, they leveled this area and had a nice stretch of land on each side of the canal. They then cut roads into the land and either placed shells or gravel over the dirt. Then they partitioned the stretch of land into fifty foot wide lots. A lot could be fifty feet wide by fifty or sixty feet deep. They sold the lots to folks who wanted to build a house or camp on it. Some folks moved in trailers or campers onto the lots. The developers would have a water and sewer system as well as electricity and telephone lines available to the property. If you wanted gas, the lot owner would put in a propane tank. They developed a lot of low-lying land this way. Many people from the cities want to have camps on the water so they can get to the lake. From the lake at Bayou Sorrell, one could go to the bay and the Intracoastal Canal or even the Gulf of Mexico. Some folks actually retired and moved to this location to spend the rest of their lives and longer- if possible. If you like the water and water-related activities, this is as good a place as any. If you like clear clean-looking water, this is not the place for you. Any water location in South Louisiana is not clear. All the lakes have clay and mud-based foundations in this part of the country. If you want clear water, you need to find lakes with rock and/or limestone or other stone-based foundations. These are certainly not found on the US Gulf Coast. There is too much sediment from the Mississippi River and other rivers to find rock foundations in South Louisiana.

As folks-built dwellings and taxes were collected on the property, the shell/gravel roads were black-topped by the parish (there are no counties in Louisiana), making it more attractive to folks who want to live there and bringing up the price of the property also.

We drove all around this area. Nathan's eyes were big and wide open just taking everything in. The majority, if not all of the folks living in this area are Roman Catholic. So many yards had catholic statues in them. Many statues had shelters built over them that were painted white. After some time of seeing all of this, Nathan asked his mom why all these people here have statues of Jesus in a bathtub. We all got a good laugh out of that question. To Nathan, the shelters over the statues looked like the end of a bathtub sticking out of the ground. He thought they buried half the bathtub in the ground and put the statues under the remaining half that was on top of the ground. We all could see how a non-Catholic kid could make that assumption upon close inspection of the display.

My brother was driving. I was in the front seat with him. Sarah was on one side, Liz on the other side, and Nathan in the middle of the back seat. As we were heading back to my brother's house after just leaving the newest development area in Bayou Sorrell, my sister-in-law stated, "Look at those two black crows walking on the side of the road." Nathan popped up and was looking out of every window. So was his mom. They looked all around. Finally, Nathan said, "I don't see any black crows. Liz, my brother, and I all had a good laugh. My wife and Nathan did not get it. After I explained that the comment was about the two Negroes on the side of the road. Nathan still did not get it. His mom then knew what the comment meant. This is just an expression that some folks use to describe other more colorful folks. There are a lot of worse names than that used for these folks in this part of the country. Nathan nor his mom had ever heard of this expression before, and we have not mentioned it since until now. It was not meant to be sinister or evil - but that is just the way it is here.

We were sitting watching television one night after supper. Liz was sitting in her chair against the wall. On the sofa in front of her was Nathan, Sarah, and then me. My brother was sitting in his rocking chair directly across the room from the sofa. Nathan was sitting about four feet from Liz. It was fairly quiet sitting there in the living room. We were catching our breath and not saying anything and halfway listening to Liz who was talking about something when all of a sudden, she said, "GOD DAMN", louder than her normal tone. We all jumped. But Nathan jumped the highest. He left his seat and started looking all around. He acted like a gun had gone off in the room. His eyes were wide open and so was his mouth. She had scared the shit out of him. He thought something really bad had happened. He did not realize that this was just her way. Sarah and I had seen and heard this happen many times before and knew that it was just normal behavior. But poor Nathan, this was his first time to experience quietness being broken in such a manner. As time went by, he would experience more of this as the Raffray's get really loud at times when they think nobody is paying any attention. It is an attention-getter. In the few days that we were visiting, Nathan teamed up with this little boy from the neighborhood. They played mostly on the other side of the subdivision. The afternoon before we departed the little boy came over and got in the driveway and was talking with Nathan. Liz happened to look out of the window and saw him. She said that little bastard was in my yard, and she headed for her door. When she got to the carport, she shouted at the little boy and told him to get his ass away from her house. Nathan and I did not know what was going on. The boy quickly jumped on his bicycle and started pedaling away. She also told him to not bring his little ass near her property again. We all wondered what was going on. After making sure he was leaving, she turned to us and told us that the little bastard was a son of a bitch and always causing and getting into trouble. she thought or knew that he would steal things. So, she did not allow him around her house.

Sarah and I looked at each other and nodded as if to say we should have known that. Leave it to Nathan to mate up with the worst little bastard in the neighborhood. Nathan is attracted to these types of folks for some reason. We cannot figure out why, but he just is. It is the story of his life.

The next morning, we left for home. We had a great time. A lot of the fun was watching Nathan's reaction to these South Louisiana folks.

HUNTSMAN COMPANY GROWS

During 96, and 97, I continued to work for Huntsman Chemical Corp. The corporation really started to grow. Jon Huntsman purchased several companies and other plants along the way. Among them were Texaco Chemical Company, Rexene Chemical Company, a couple of polystyrene plants from Amoco Chemical Company, and several plants from Monsanto Corporation. The purchases may not have taken place in this order but take place they did. Huntsman had grown by leaps and bounds and needed to re-organize his corporation to keep pace with the growth. After the dust settled from the Texaco Chemical purchase our organization started changing. I stayed in charge of the distribution of styrene monomer to our internal plants, terminals, and customers for our division. I was no longer responsible for the transportation contracts anymore. This function was relocated to the Huntsman Galleria offices. Huntsman developed a corporate group for all transportation and terminal contracts that was headed by David Parkin. David was a member of the Huntsman family after having married the youngest daughter of Jon and Karen Huntsman, Jennifer.

David was a very bright and articulate young man. I enjoyed my association with him very much. He had an awesome responsibility and handled it well. His team was built around him. His department had a head of the marine group, head of the trucking group, head of the railway group, head of the leasing/purchasing of rail cars group, and a head of the DOT/hazardous materials transportation group who worked very closely with all the other groups and plant locations.

The old Huntsman Chemicals, Rexene Chemicals, Texaco Chemicals, and other purchased businesses made a very large corporation with many different plants producing many different products.

Some of the functions that I did such as the trucking, rail, terminals, and rail car leasing contracts were negotiated by other persons in the Galleria office in Houston. The corporate folks kept me in the loop when they negotiated new marine contracts - sort of. I was not always kept in the loop. My advice was asked for on several occasions. So, during 1996 and 1997, most of the representatives of these transportation service companies stopped calling on me. The marine folks are the only ones who continued to call on me. My friends in trucking (tank and Van), rail, containers, tank cars for leasing, and bulk liquid terminal leasing, all dropped me like a hot potato after I informed them of the changes in the organization and the proper contact for their particular line of business. I understood and accepted this. I had no choice. I heard from several folks from time to time asking me to intervene on their behalf with the Huntsman Corporate folks. I did so for some and did not for others. It depended upon my relationship with them as to how far I would go to try and get the corporate person to communicate with them. I also had to know that they did a good job for me over the years. If that was not the case, I told them that it was out of my hands which it really was and that's it.

I maintained a very good working relationship with all the department heads that my group worked with in Houston and Salt

Lake City (World Headquarters). They had a big job to do for the corporation, not just the division that I used to keep running on a daily basis.

I was given the opportunity to head one of the departments at Corporate. After being with Huntsman for about ten years and doing things my way, I could see the big changes in how business was done these days and I did not want to be involved in it. The first thing I would have to do was fire eight to ten people. I hated this part and just did not want to do that.

Driving from League City to the West Loop each day did not appeal to me either. But I just could not tell them no and leave it like that. So, I came up with this plan. It was a serious plan. If they accepted it, I would have moved to Houston during the week. I made a list of about nine different requests for me to take the job. When I went to work for Huntsman in 1986, Jon made promises to me through my boss, Brent Turkington. It was not unusual for Jon himself to promise certain things to folks he wanted in his company. These promises ranged from company cars to year-end bonuses, extra vacation time, pay for apartments, and so on.

One of the items on my list was for Huntsman to pay the full cost of an apartment near the corporate offices. Another was to give back my company car that they took away from selected folks to save money. I got a company car in 1989 in place of my annual raise after being promoted to Director of Supply and Distribution. The company car was good - I guess- and I was told that they never would take it away from me. I was talked into taking the car by two vice presidents of Huntsman. That car cost me a four thousand dollar raise in 1989 and a percentage of this amount every year thereafter through 1999 when Huntsman sold the business and ME to Nova Chemical Company. This car they took back from me in 1992 cost me many thousands of dollars in salary and therefore, cost me big bucks in my retirement due from Huntsman starting in June of 2008. Needless to say, I was very disappointed in the fellows that convinced me to take the damn car after I repeatedly told my boss NO - because of the salary and retirement issues. I was also disappointed in Jon Huntsman for allowing seventeen middle management hard-working folks to lose their cars while letting vice presidents and controllers stationed in Salt Lake City keep their cars. There is still no reason to have a car for business at the world corporate location. All business is carried on at plants many miles from the State of Utah. And these folks did not drive, they always flew to business meetings and plant locations. The only company business that folks in Salt Lake City could possibly use their cars for was to drive to the airport. Many of them used the limousine for this purpose. This was a very bad decision by Huntsman and showed a bias against middle management people. I know his shenanigans on the company car cost me over five hundred dollars per month in retirement benefits. This is like stealing from old folks. We are all being penalized in our old age by the Huntsman. And that is a fact, Jack or Jon as the case is.

MY 1st AND ONLY WILD BOAR HUNTING TRIP

I got invited by Lloyd Reihhart with Caleb Brett Inspection Services to go on a wild boar hunt somewhere on the other side of San Antonio, Texas. I do not know if there is such a thing as a tame boar hunt but anyway, I decided to go. Caleb Brett was one of the independent petroleum inspection companies that I hired to do the gauging and sampling when loading or unloading liquids at our terminal.

Inspectors detail a lot of things. Among them are gauging the storage tanks and vessels before and after loading/unloading, inspecting the vessel for cleanliness and drawing heal samples with loading, drawing samples from loaded vessels and transporting them to our lab for testing before unloading, issuing paperwork for all folks concerned, etc., etc. This type of company does an independent inspection and the measurement of quantity and quality that would hold up in court if necessary. All independent inspection companies work on facts and not fiction.

On the morning of our departure, a group of us met with Lloyd and loaded into a carryall -the SUV of that time. We headed west to Brady, Texas where a lot of wild game-hunting takes place. It was a very long drive. Upon arrival, we unpacked everything, had supper, and had a very relaxing evening getting to know each other. We were going to start the hunt bright and early the next morning.

All of these wild game and bird hunts usually have two hunts a day. One early in the morning and another in the afternoon until dark. Some counties had laws that prohibit the firing of a gun until after a certain time. It depended upon what you were hunting and what county you were hunting in. I think the time of day came up because all game has a certain pattern that they follow. All birds of a feather leave their perch in the morning and go searching for food and water. During the day they are usually not moving very much. In the afternoon they all start flying to get back to their perch area and stop for water on the way. So, one would normally hunt in grain fields and where ponds/tanks are located.

The land animal usually does the same thing. In the mornings they are on the move either looking for food, water, or females. In the afternoon they are heading back to their bedding down area which may be near water or not. And YES, looking for females. So, you look for an area where you see a pattern of traffic by the land animals and stake the place out.

I do not know if you ever saw a picture of a wild boar or not. If you have, you know that it is a very ugly animal. It is part of the hog family and has many features of the hog. But these things have very long noses/snouts. They have mean-looking teeth and tusks. One tusk on each side of their jaws. The tusks could be eight to twelve inches long and many are twisted or curly looking. They can do a lot of damage with these things. A one-hundred-pound boar can easily kill a three-hundred-pound man. A man that big cannot get out of his own way and the boar would just tear his ass up. These animals are very strong and wild. That is why they are called a wild boar.

After, AFTER RAISING SUGARCANE

The next morning, we get in the carryall and the driver delivers us one by one throughout the ranch to stand on the ground. I hate being on the ground. There were six of us actually hunting. As with all other hunts, we got out before daybreak to be ready for the animal if it decided to go on a stroll or just go nosing about. Did you get the NOSING ABOUT? OK, now don't tell me that's not funny. These are long-nosed hogs we are hunting. No one saw anything to shoot at. We were each picked up between nine and ten a.m. When we got back to the camp, we ate breakfast and milled around the camp until it was time to go for the afternoon hunt.

That afternoon, we left camp at three p.m. It takes over thirty minutes or more to drop every hunter off. The hunt covers a lot of area because of the high-power rifles. I was dropped off at a place where I had to climb a large wooden gate to get to my stand. It did not occur to me this morning but now I started thinking about this stand being on the ground. All the stands out here for hunting wild boars are on the ground. I do not like this one bit. Maybe I already said that and I just said it again. I cannot say it enough. Suppose the boar decides he wants to come inside the stand for shelter or to just nose around a bit. Nobody ever thought about that before they built these traps on the ground. Well, I sure have. And I am thinking about it a lot now. I hurry and load my gun. It only holds three shells. I wish that it could hold another three or four shells. I tried to jam a fourth one into it, but it just would not go. The boars are tough - it might take more than three bullets to knock one down. Now I am thinking too damn much. I am keeping my eyes peeled for anything that moves or makes a noise in the brush. You know what? This looks like land that BIG FOOT might like to hang out in. Oh, shit - I should have never thought about him. Now I know that I don't have enough bullets in my gun. I reach down in my pocket get three more bullets and put them where I can grab them in a hurry. Well, now I am sitting there worrying about a big wild boar and a big foot. I lock my little plywood door on my ground floor blind. Yeah, like this is going to help if I am attacked.

It is too dark to shoot at anything now. Where in the hell is the carryall? Oh good - I see the headlights. I got out of the stand and headed toward the gate. I climbed it and waited on the other side. It was really dark now. Of course, I had a flashlight. No moon out tonight either. I see the headlight turn to the left. What is this shit? I should have been next. I cannot see anything now. I think that I hear something in the brush on the other side of the gate. SHIT, I already took the bullets out of the gun before I left the stand. Back they went in as fast as I could load feeling my way with them. I could not hold the rifle and flashlight and bullets and stand up at the same time too well. But I managed to get all three-back in.

OOH-OOH, another sound. I climb on the gate. I was about three feet off the ground and straddling it. My butt started to hurt. I can take it though. I am not getting down until that damn truck gets here and they open the door.

There are the headlights again. HOORAY, what the hell- the bastard turned off again. I was disgusted. Finally, he is coming down my road. I waited for him to stop next to me before I got down off that gate. It was about forty-five minutes from the time I first saw the headlights until I was picked up. I was not a happy camper but did not say a word about it. I would prefer to be the last one to be dropped off and the first one to be picked up. But I did not tell anyone that. I did not want them to think that I was a sissy - which I was. I also kept that to myself.

One guy shot a boar on this hunt. After unloading it, I watch the guy who shot it cleaning it. It was one ugly hog. I tried to help but I did not know how. He skinned it, then gutted it. That is taking all the innards out. He kept the liver, heart, and other stuff that can be eaten from the innards. He then cut the feet and head off. He cut both hindquarters and forequarters off and placed them into a large ice chess with the innards that he wanted to keep. The carcass and guts were disposed of into a hole dug out for that purpose and covered up with dirt.

During the hunt, another boar and a turkey were taken, and I helped the guys clean their kill. It was an experience that I will never forget. If I would have seen a wild boar, I would not have shot at it. I may have hit it and be stuck with it. I shot a small deer once on a hunt like this and gave it away because I did not know how to gut and clean it. If you have to do it yourself, I will not shoot it.

The whole trip was nice and I enjoyed meeting and making new friends and drinking and eating and playing cards and such. But this was my first and last boar hunt. This is not for me. I did have the opportunity to go again - several times. It seemed that I was just too busy at work to take off, I had something pressing and just could not go. And as mentioned before, as it turned out, I never had the time to go on another WILD BOAR hunt.

TRIP TO ARKANSAS
IN RENTED VAN - 1996

It was the summer of 1996. For some time, Sarah and I planned to go visit her sister in Clarksville, Arkansas. We wanted to bring Nathan and Jacob with us. Jacob came down from Fort Worth to spend part of the summer with his mom in Texas City. Sarah and I both took one week of vacation time to make this trip. Clarksville was almost an eleven-hour drive from Texas City. Sarah's mom was in Arkansas and would be riding back to her home in Texas City with us.

Because we had to pack for four and had five coming back, we decided that I would rent a van instead of driving my 1992 Mercury Grand Marque. The car would be too crowded with five people for such a long trip. The van would have more room for the boys. They would not have to be stuck sitting together. Each had their own back seat if they wanted to. The luggage would be placed in the back. This van has three sets of seats and an empty space behind the third seat for luggage and or supplies. I had never driven a van before. The driver is almost sitting on top of the front wheel. It was very different than driving a pickup truck or car.

The morning we planned to leave, I left home early in League City and drove to Seabrook to pick up the van. I then drove to Texas City to pick up Sarah, Nathan, and Jake. We planned to depart Texas City at about eight a.m. When I arrived at Sarah's house there was a panic going on. Sarah and Jake were all packed and ready, but Nathan had hauled ass. He was nowhere to be found. He was gone out of sight- vanished, Sarah was really upset. We drove around the immediate area looking for Nathan but could not find him. After a time, Sarah decided to hell with it. She called his dad, Floyd, who lived in Fort Worth, and told him what happened and also told him to come down and find his son because she was leaving town now. We loaded the van and left. Had we known this would happen, I would not have rented a van.

We found out several days later that Nathan hauled ass because he thought that we were going to bring him to Fort Worth to live with his dad. It just shows how his mind works. He does not pay attention when you try to tell him anything. Why in the hell he would think we were going to Fort Worth on the way to Arkansas, I will never know. To me, that will be over four hundred miles out of the way. Nathan missed out on a lot of fun on this trip because he did not believe that we were going straight to Clarksville. We drove up through East Texas and West Arkansas to get to Clarksville which is between Fort Smith and Little Rock, Arkansas. While we were having fun in Arkansas, Nathan was with his dad in Fort Worth which is just where he did not want to be. Kind of ironic, isn't it?

We had a good trip going up without any problems. I drove the van like I had been driving it all my life. We had a lot of fun visiting with Sarah's sister, Alice Jean, and her family and her brother, Ronnie, and his family. Ronnie lived not very far from Alice Jean on Highway 103. He rented a house on the side of a mountain. We spent a lot of time at his house.

Alice Jean, and Chris (her husband) live in an older two-story wood frame house on about two acres. They live about four miles from the city of Clarksville. Highway 103 from their house goes through the campus of the University of the Ozarks just when you get back into town.

One day everyone decided to drive up into the Ozark Mountains to go to Ebenizzers Herb Shack. They are located high on this mountain. It was also decided that since the van could carry everyone, we would use it. And since I rented the van under my name, I felt compelled to drive it into the mountains. The departure from Alice's house was without fanfare. After all, we were on flat ground and no passengers had voiced any concern. But when we started up the mountain - well that was a horse of a different color. Yes, the roads were narrow. Yes, the roads had cliffs on one side and mountain walls on the other. Yes, it looked like a thousand-foot drop or more over the cliffs. Yes, there are hair pen curves on the mountain road. I was sitting in front. I had to be there because I was driving. I saw all of this and more. I did not much like it but there I was way up in the front.

There was this hair pen curve coming up to the right and a car was coming down the mountain while we were going up it. The cliff was to my right. I did not want to get in the middle of the narrow highway because the other car was approaching us. I made the turn to the right. I am fairly sure that the two front tires were on the highway. I heard all the screaming and yelling from the right side of the van. They were screaming to move over to the left. I acknowledged that the right-side rear tire may have been off the road in the middle of the hair pen curve, but I was over the road on my side of the van. I felt that everything was alright. But the bickering inside the van would continue as long as there was a cliff on this road. I did drive toward the middle of the road when not meeting any oncoming traffic which made everyone in the van happy. They all rejoiced when we saw Ebenizzers, and I turned into their very small parking area.

We all got out of the van and took deep long breaths. We could breathe easy again. Ebenizzers was an old frame house that was turned into an herb store. They had so much merchandise that you had to walk in the place single file. Each room and hallway were stacked floor to ceiling with stuff. They also had a big walk-in cooler inside one room. This was for the herbs that needed to be kept refrigerated. We spent over an hour there looking and buying herbs, pills, capsules, liquid, and gel caps.

On the way down the mountain, I did not catch much flak from my passengers because we were on the mountain wall all the way down. When we got to that very sharp hairpin curve, I could see how the rear tire on the passenger side may not have been on the road or on the edge of the road either. It was the sharpest curve that I have ever seen. Could the tire have been riding on air? I do not know. Some of my passengers think that it was. I know one thing for sure. and that is I was not eager to make another trip to Ebenizzers any time soon. In fact, I can wait until they make the road four lanes before I go back. Yeah- like that will happen.

DUCK HUNTING TRIP
WITH HOLLYWOOD MARINE

Mickey Bell of Hollywood Marine invited me to go duck hunting with a group of other customers In Louisiana. I had never been duck hunting before on land, so I decided to go. Most of us met at Hollywood's office in Houston. We loaded our gear into a large van then several fellows got into it and others got into another van and off we went toward Southwest Louisiana.

We traveled down Interstate 10 to the Vinton, Louisiana exit and made a right turn off the interstate into this area of Louisiana. After several miles, we came to a bayou and unloaded all our gear into a large cabin-type boat. After several more miles on the water traveling toward the Gulf of Mexico, we arrived at the Hollywood Duck Hunting Camp. It was a large barge with living quarters on it. It was pushed into the bank that was dredged out to get it out of the bayou right of way.

They had everything one needed to spend several days or a month or a very long time. There were sleeping quarters, lounging quarters, a game room, inside bathrooms, a kitchen with a cook, guns, shells, beer, liquor, and a live-in cook.

After arriving and getting settled, we walked off the barge into the backyard where a skeet shooting range had been set up. We were all going to practice our shooting ability. One of the guys operated the skeet machine. We took turns shooting at them. When it was my turn, I got my Winchester 12-gauge shotgun that I purchased from the Ohlmous Sporting store just for this trip. It is an automatic and not a pump. It has three chokes that come with it. The gun chokes are designed to screw into the end of the barrel. You use one choke for shooting at small birds like doves or pigeons etc. It allows for a spread-out pattern of the pellets. Another choke makes the pattern of shots not spread out as much and the third one makes a full pattern that is mainly for bigger games like geese and ducks where you need to reach farther out to get them and still have the knockdown power. I guess it could be used to hunt deer also if you shoot a slug. I never tried that. I used the camp guns. I liked to use the Remington 243 until I purchased my own Savage 30-06.

Most shotguns have room for six shotgun shells. The law states that you can have only three shells in it at a time when hunting. My gun came with a plug already in to take the room of three shells. So, I could not put six shells in it if I wanted to. If a game warden caught you hunting with more than three shells in your gun, you would get a citation and your gun would be taken on the spot. You would have to go to court or at least in front of a judge. You will pay a hefty fine and perhaps get your gun back at a later date. I do not know for sure because I never had any of my guns taken and checked by a game warden.

Back to the skeet shooting.

It is my turn to shoot at the skeet. These skeets are fast and are a red/orange color and four or five inches in diameter and round. I would shout PULL and the skeet operator would let the skeet fly. I got the first three that I shot at. I reloaded my gun and hit the next three also. The guys wanted me to keep shooting but I said no because my shoulder and arm would hurt, and I would not be able to shoot right-handed when we were hunting. I always had trouble when I shot getting my gun to my shoulder. So, I am shooting with the butt on my upper arm. My arm gets sore very quickly and I have to stop shooting because of soreness, so I did not shoot at any more skeet. Mickey and several of the guys said to me - I thought that you never hunted duck before. I told them that this was my first time doing this, but I never said that I could not shoot a gun. I used to headlight rabbits with my dad when I was a kid. I was and still am a good shot.

The next day we took the boat and went into the marsh where the duck blinds are. They are like wooden boxes buried in the ground/marsh. It was dry in all blinds and all of them we had to walk to. The boat was tied up a distance away. You stand up in the box with just your head above the ground and be alert for a duck passing by or coming to land on the water. Of course, you are going out there in the cold and damp, if not raining and smoggy so you need to be prepared for any kind of weather.

Hollywood kept dogs for hunting at their camp. They go and fetch the duck when you shoot it.

We had two or three guys in a blind. One would use a duck caller to call for any ducks that may be in the area. This duck-calling thing looked like a little whistle that the guy blew into. I do not know how that sound came out the way it did. But I was fooled, and I can see how a duck can be fooled also. Some male ducks may think that it is a female duck on the loose and just have to come for a closer look.

We did not see many ducks on this hunt. The next day we are back out there dark and early. Just at daybreak, I could see something flying into the land, I took aim and fired just before it hit the water. I got it. After my bird hit the water at the command, the dog took off. He swam out to retrieve the bird. When he got back to the blind, he had a young goose. It was beautiful. We thought that it was a duck and maybe it was. But it turned into a goose when it hit the water. Well, that was my first and only goose that I ever killed. Since it was my goose, I got to take it home. Nobody would take it from me. I offered it to everyone. I did not want it. I killed it, I had to take it home, those were the rules. I did not have the time to try and clean it because we left for home right after breakfast after this hunt. Hell, I did not know how to clean a goose anyway.

During our stay at the duck camp, the cook fed us breakfast, lunch, and dinner. The eating and drinking were really good. Except for one dinner meal. The cook, who is a black man and a great cook, made a duck gumbo. I like gumbo but found out that I did NOT like to eat DUCK. All I thought about now was that my duck turned out to be a goose and I wondered if it would taste like the duck. My answer to myself was probably yes. I still did not want it.

I took the goose home with me, and it sat in my ice box (refrigerator) for a week. It still had the feathers on it. One day I took it out of the ice box wrapped it up in a trash bag and placed it into my trash can. I did this before I went to work. It was the day of trash pickup so I knew that it would not be out there long enough to start stinking the place up. When I arrived home from work that day, I checked the trash can and sure enough – it was gone. I have never tasted what goose tastes like and have never tried to eat any more duck for that matter.

BUYING THE PLACE IN 1996

During 1996 I had this opportunity to make a bid for a place in the Country to go to on weekends. I had been looking for something for several years but could not find anything to my liking or that I could afford. Early in the 1990s I purchased a timeshare at Lake Conroe, but I was not even using up my one week a year. I bought it to make sure I would at least have one week away from work. My thought process was that if I paid money for something, I would certainly use it on a regular basis. Well, it did not happen. I still have the timeshare. We used the benefits of having it several times. One day I look forward to really taking advantage of the plan I have and utilizing the benefits by visiting the seven different locations that we have available to us.

We will.

Susan Ambler worked for me at Huntsman Chemical. Her maternal grandparents passed away a couple of years before 1996. Their estate got tied up in a family dispute. The old folks had a will, and everything was set up properly. They had one son and one daughter. The son sued over the probate of the will. This action tied up the estate for a couple of years. The old couple lived on thirteen acres in San Jacinto County. The heirs placed this property up for bid. I was one of the people to bid on it. I was informed by Susan's dad, who was the executor of the estate, that I won the bid. When I was waiting for him to get back to me as to when and where the closing would be, he called me back and said they wanted to look at some more bids.

This was after the bid time closing date. This is not right. He talked about the value of the trees and so on. I don't know about all this. I think this was bullshit. I guess I could have sued for breach of contract on a completed deal, but out of respect for Susan, I just decided to place another bid and went five thousand four hundred ten dollars more than the other bid. Susan's dad called me again and said that I had the high bid again. I did not know whether to trust this asshole or not until the family lawyer also called and verified this. I actually contacted him after getting his name and telephone number from Susan.

I sent the goodwill money to the lawyer. I got a loan from my savings and loan and made the arrangement to be at the closing to do whatever was required to be done at that time. This bidding back and forth and winning the bid and not rebidding took several months to do. It was now July 1996.

THE PLACE THE DAY OF CLOSING JULY 19, 1996

The Place is about twelve miles Northwest of Cleveland, Texas on Farm to Market Road 1725 in the Sam Houston National Forest in San Jacinto County. It has about thirteen acres of woods and is on the left side of the highway heading northwest. It is located between Highway 59 (Cleveland, Texas) and Interstate 45.

Farm to Market Road 1725 is twenty-two miles long, stretching from State Highway 105 at the south end to State Highway 150 on the north end. It is a very nice scenic drive in the country. It is also a single-lane road that is traveled heavily by loggers and eighteen-wheelers. It is used by the truckers and is a cut-through from Highway 59 to I-45.

On July 19, 1996, at midday Sarah and I arrived at The Place. It was weird. The seven hundred feet or so of overgrown driveway entrance from the road to the house had to be negotiated very carefully. After you drive through the double gate, the road/driveway curves to the right then the left. Trees and brush are all around you rubbing and scratching the car. We proceeded going downhill for the first three hundred fifty feet or so then crossed a small culvert going over Bear Creek, then proceeded uphill for another three hundred fifty feet or so to the house. As you are going uphill, you can see the old wood frame house sitting on pillars where the hill crested.

We parked in front of the old house. We had the car loaded down. The back seat had stuff and the trunk was full and I mean full. Things such as shovels, rakes, hoes, cutting tools, fans, axes, saws, ropes, hammers, mauls, and much more.

We opened the front door of the house and went in. We raised the windows to air the place out. It had a very musty smell. We raised windows in every room. The back porch, which is enclosed in and is part of the living quarters, has thirteen windows in it. As the house was airing out, we went outside to start doing some work in the yard. We started picking up trash in the yard around the house. I had a little time before I departed for the two--p.m. appointment in Cold Springs, the County seat, for the closing. Cold Springs was only twenty miles away by taking Tony Tap, a red dirt road cut through road, cutting off about fifteen miles of blacktop highway driving.

So, I had plenty of time to pick up limbs and pile them up to be burned later. Sarah got busy with the broom and a rake.

After a short time of working, I told Sarah that I should be back about three p.m. It should not take long to sign the papers. I departed there at 1:10 p.m. heading for Cold Springs. I left a little later than I had planned.

I got busy doing things and just forgot about the time. I went south on FM- 1725 for a little over two miles and made the left turn onto Tony Tap. It was very dry and dusty, red dust. I went about one mile when it happened. I was driving too fast, and I came to a high rise in the road, and off to the right was a ranch that I had never seen before. I looked back to see the name on the fence which a first glance seemed unusual - it was. Boot Hill Ranch was the name of this ranch. When I looked back at the road, I was coming down the incline and the roadway went to the left. I hit my brakes and steered to the left. That was when I went into a slide. I hit the ditch on the left side of the road for about fifty yards. Thank God it was very dry. Fence posts were flying by. I was hitting bushes but did not hit any fence posts or barbed wire. I got the car out of the left ditch only to go across the road to ride in the right ditch or about forty more yards. My car was moving sideways for a while in the ditch on the left side of the road and sideways for a short time on the right side of the ditch also. I could feel the frame/chassis of my car dragging on the road as my tires/wheels were in the ditches. I straightened out the car then hit an embankment which was a pile of red dirt and gravel and came to a stop just five yards from a rather large culvert and ditch. It felt like the rear end of my car came off the ground when I hit the embankment. As it turned out the pile was there because the culvert had been recently drugged and the dirt/gravel mound had not been removed yet. After I stopped, the red dirt was still flying all about for a minute or so.

I got out of my car. It was covered with red dirt. My car, which is dark blue, looked red. I stood back in the road to look at what I just did. A driver in a large pickup slowed down to look but did not stop to help me out. Then I noticed another pickup truck stopped some short distance behind me. He pulled up and parked behind my car with his flashers on. It was a service guy. You know, the kind of pickup that has side panels on each side of the truck. The driver got out and asked if I was all right. I was. I asked him if he knew if there was a wrecker company nearby. He did not know; he was just taking the shortcut like I was doing. Now I started to worry about not making the closing appointment on time. I checked my front end. It did not look too bad. The bumper was pushed up a little and the chrome was pushed up a little above the bumper. I felt pretty good considering what had just happened. The right side front-end of the car was in the dry ditch. The back end was still on the road but at an angle. I got back in my car, it was still running because I forgot to cut it off. I put it in reverse and lightly gave it the gas. My back drive wheel/tire started spinning. It was barely touching the road and could not get a grip. I asked the repairman if he had a rope to pull me out. He did not. Along came a Chevy Suburban; it really looked good. They went around the pickup and me but did not stop, although they passed really slowly and had a good look at us.

The repair man, a bearded, big gut man said I can try to push you out. I did not see how he could get the truck in a position to push my car with the culvert there in front and the back end up in the air. Then he said that he would move his truck from behind my car. He drove past me pulled to the right side of the road and parked again. The plan was, he would push, and I would try to back my car out. He bent down with his back to the hood of my car, grabbed my front bumper, and tried to push back. I tried to back out, but the tire would just spin. The big guy said that he would try one more time. He then started rocking the car by lifting it up and down in a rocking motion. I waited until he got the car at its highest point and the back right tire got traction and I backed out. I tried to pay the big guy, but he said, no way. I thanked him and he drove off. I followed him doing about twenty miles per hour until we got off the red dirt road and onto FM-945, which is a blacktop. I then opened her up again because I thought that I would be late for the closing.

Even after all of this ordeal, I made it to the office in Cold Springs before my appointment time of two p.m. I had to wait my turn. I signed the papers and was heading back to my car before two twenty. I noticed that my left rear tire was almost flat. I opened my trunk, GOOD LORD. It would be a big problem getting to the donut because of all the stuff in the trunk. No way was I going to put all this stuff in the street while I put the donut on and then have to reload it all again. I went back inside and inquired about the nearest garage. There was an auto repair shop just one-half mile away. I drove to it very slowly. Waited to be waited on. They had a lot of work to do since this was Friday and they close on Saturday. They did not want to take on any more jobs. I pleaded that I was in trouble and was from out of town. They told me that they would put air in my tire for me. They came to the car, got an air hose, and pumped up my tire to fifty pounds of pressure. It was leaking out. They told me where a tire repair shop was, and I headed out.

After about five miles. I found Lonnie V's shop. They took the tire off and checked it out. It was not punctured. It had small gravel between the wheel rim and the tire. The pressure of the tires when I was going sideways in and out of the ditches on Tony Tap Road forced the gravel to lodge there. Some pressure huh?

After twenty more minutes, I paid Lonnie V and was off. It was way past three p.m. now. I could not get in touch with Sarah because we did not have a telephone at the old house yet and we did not have a cell phone then either. Instead of taking the shortcut back, I went the long way. I was just too afraid of driving on Tony Tap Road again. All the way to Shepard then another twenty-two miles to Cleveland then another twelve miles back to The Place.

I traveled over fifty miles to get back to the house using this path.

I made the trip in due time and at about five p.m. I pulled up to the gate of The Place. As I drove down the driveway, the steering became difficult. I crossed the creek and started up and could see Sarah on the roof of the house getting the pine needles and leaves off. I could tell she had been working very hard. She was red in the face and sweating. I parked the car in front of the house and Sarah started telling me about my right front tire being flat as I was getting out of the car. I was so upset and disgusted that I did not even tell her what a great job she had accomplished since I left over four hours earlier.

I started throwing stuff out of my trunk. I finally got to the donut. I got it out and could not find the car jack in my trunk, I had never had a flat or even had to change a tire since I bought the car. I had this car for four years and could not find the damn jack. I was really pissed-off now. I retrieved the owner's manual from under the front seat on the passenger side and started looking for the section for changing tires to try and find out where they stored the damn jack. If I bought a new car that did not have a jack, I do not know what I would have done. I may have hurt myself. I was upset for a very long time that Mercury would have the gall to put a donut in their Grand Marquis. I did find the section in the book and found the car jack in a side panel in the rear fender wall. I set it up and worked on changing the tire. I got the flat tire off and put the donut on. "OOH SHIT," said I. The donut was half flat. I was really disgusted now. Sarah had gotten off the roof of the house and helped me with the tire ordeal. She was a calming influence on me also. If not, I guess I could have given myself a heart attack right there on the spot. Thank God for Sarah. By now it was getting close to six p.m., and I was afraid to wait until Saturday to go into Cleveland because the donut might go completely flat by then. I did not have an air pump at the time. I now have two of them. We got in the car and headed for Cleveland twelve miles away. I did a top speed of twenty-five miles per hour. People coming up behind us were really upset. Farm Road 1725 is a single-lane winding road and some of the log trucks and other big rigs just seem to want to run over the top of us for going so slow. People like to speed on this road. Well, we needed to put air in the donut, and we needed it now and I was afraid to drive any faster and that was that.

We made it to Cleveland and went to the first filling station we came to on the side of Highway 59. We waited and waited for a woman to leave the air pump. She finally left after several trips in and out of the store part of the station. We pulled up and found the air pump was not working, got back in the car and drove to another station. No air there either. What the hell is going on? Cleveland is having an air shortage. This is ridiculous. We drove around the corner on Highway 105. We found a station/tire repair shop about to close. There was only one old lady in the place putting things away for the night. She told me that she was closing the shop, and nobody could fix my tires. She did let me put air in the donut and I left the tire off to be fixed on Saturday. We said we would come pick it up on Saturday morning. I was afraid of not having any spare if the donut would not hold up. But we did not have a choice in the matter. All shops were closed by this time. We went back to the place with a full donut. I punched it up to forty miles per hour heading back to the woods. That big car must have looked really silly with that donut on it.

As I recall, our first night in the house was hot. I did not sleep very well. The house still had a strong locked-up mildew scent. We did use the attic fan, but it was hot and sticky nonetheless. Boy, what a day. I never want to go through this again. I just do not know why I did not catch a heart attack then. I had every reason to catch one. I was just lucky - I guess. Ha! How could all this mess be luck? Well, maybe it was. I don't know.

Saturday morning, we got up. I rushed out to check my car and the donut was still pumped up. Thanks be to the Lord. It was still pumped up. It finally looked like things may start going my way. We went to Cleveland to retrieve our full-size tire. Upon arrival, the service center was open and working but they had not even touched my tire yet. We waited another hour or so until they got to it. It had the same problem as my other tire. There was no puncture in the tire. It had gravel lodged between the wheel rim and the tire sidewall. All that sliding sideways on the red dirt and gravel road caused gravel to get in there. They just cleaned the gravel out, put air back into my tire, took off the donut, replaced my full-size tire on my car and we were off.

HOORAY!!

As I look back on this incident, I can count my lucky stars. God had to be watching over me to protect me on Tony Tap Road. The first tire that went flat was the left-side rear tire. The second tire to go flat was the right-side front tire. Sliding sideways as I did cause a tremendous amount of pressure to force gravel between the rim and tire sidewalls.

I am also lucky because of the heavy car that I owned. I believe a light-model car would have flipped over several times. I must have been driving about fifty miles per hour when the accident happened. Since that day, I have not driven over thirty-five miles per hour when taking these types of roads. I am just happy to be here. Praise the LORD.

A HAIRY EXPERIENCE AFTER A DEER HUNT

One time at band camp - just kidding. I never went to band camp. It is just a saying that I heard and saw in an old movie, and I love it. I always wanted to put it somewhere in my writings. One time, when we were driving back from Southwest Texas after a deer hunt at night, we had a harrowing experience. We were again, with a Hollywood Marine group. We all decided to leave the hunting camp and head back to Houston after the afternoon hunt instead of the next morning, Mickey Bell, the Hollywood salesman said that he would drive. He always did. Hollywood had this very nice van that held about nine people comfortably with a storage space behind the last seat. First, we loaded the guns in their cases in the back of the van and placed all of our luggage on top of them. It was piled up high but did not block the view out of the back window. In the van was Mickey, Pee Wee Pitman from Mississippi, two guys from the New York area, another fellow, and me. There were six of us all total. Also on this trip was Mickey's brother-in-law, David Tauber of Tauber Oil Company, and the president of Sea Lion Company whom I cannot remember his name. This is very unusual for me because I did business with this fellow also. His company supplied us with a product that we needed to produce styrene monomer. Anyway, the Sea Lion guy was driving a sub-compact car and David was riding with him, so he did not have to drive back to Houston alone.

After, AFTER RAISING SUGARCANE

We departed the hunting camp sometime after dark for the several hundred-mile trip back to Houston. Mickey had a heavy foot when driving. He liked to do about eighty miles per hour and make good time on the highway. We headed east on Interstate 10 then got behind two eighteen-wheelers. They were driving side by side so we could not pass them. They had been chit-chatting back and forth on the CB radio for what seemed like forty minutes or more. We were doing about sixty miles per hour all this time. This action by the driver of the big rig in the passing lane was slowing us down. Mickey had a lot of patience and not flashing the headlight at him or anything. We were just listening to their chit-chat and waiting for the driver in front of us to pass the other truck so we could pass them both. Finally, the driver who was blocking us told the other driver that he was going to back off a bit because a four-wheeler had been behind him for some time. He decided to get back into the right lane behind the other truck and let us pass. Mickey was the only one who was really alert as the rest of us were sort of dosing off and on.

After the driver got back into the right lane behind the other trucker, he was jaw jacking with, we started passing him. When we got past him and started passing the lead trucker, Mickey got on the CB and spoke. "It is about time your mealy mouth cocksucker moved over". Why did he say that? Well, we heard a yell on the squawk box. That driver was telling the other driver to cut us off. Do not let him pass, he yelled into the CB. The other driver told him to just let us go on about our business. He shouted back, "HELL NO, I'M GONA KILL THAT SON OF A BITCH". No one is going to talk to me like that. I am going to run over him. Man - we are all awake now. Mickey had the petal to the metal. We were really hauling ass. We all looked back and saw the big rig swing into the left lane and pass the lead truck. I wondered just how fast the van could go. The driver of the first truck was still trying to settle him down. But he would have none of it. He again said that he would run over us and kill everyone in the van. We could all tell that he was picking up speed since he was leaving the other trucker behind. Mickey said that he thought that the trucker son of a bitch was going to kill us all. He said that someone should get one of our rifles ready just in case. Since I was in the front seat with Mickey, I could not do it. Pee Wee leaned over the seat he was sitting in and started digging to try to get to the gun cases. After several minutes he said that he and the other guy digging could not get to the rifles. By this time the other truck driver was still trying to talk the hot-headed one out of trying to kill us. But this fellow would still have none of it. I am going to kill them he said again. And the big rig just kept on coming.

Mickey had us doing ninety miles per hour in the van. That was as fast as the sucker can go. As we passed both big rigs, our buddies in the little car were right behind us. They did not know what was going on. They did not have a CB or phone.

For over fifty minutes everyone in the van was wide-eyed and kept looking back. We could see the headlights on the small car in the distance. They were trying to keep up with us. After an hour and a half later, we needed gas. Mickey turned off the interstate and into a station. While he was filling up the van, we got a rifle or two out of the back just in case. The small car followed us into the station and David jumped out of the car and asked, what the hell is going on?" They were on fumes with the gas tank showing empty. They really needed gas. After we told them the story, everyone was watching the interstate for eighteen-wheelers. We noticed that several drove past the turn-off. No one could tell if any that passed was the one chasing us or not. We were all ready to poo poo our pants if one did.

After filling up both vehicles we started out again. We were pretty sure that the killer trucker went on by. Nobody and I mean nobody got any sleep the rest of the way to Houston. We were all alert and watching in case he was just up ahead of us. We did not pass any more eighteen-wheelers from this point on into Houston. I am so happy to still be here.

THE GRANBURY, TEXAS TRIP 1996

Also in 1996, Sarah and I planned a trip to Granbury, Texas. We picked Granbury because it was close to Fort Worth where Sarah's sons live with their dad. There was a time when her boys lived with her, then their dad, then her, then their dad, then oh, you get it. At the time of this trip, they were both living with their dad in Crowley, Texas. Crowley is a suburb of Fort Worth.

I had purchased a timeshare on Lake Conroe in 1990.

I did this to force myself to take vacations. I figured that if I spent this kind of money on something surely, I would use it. I would not want to lose the time and space available to me. So, I would take a vacation from work and use my timeshare. During this time in my life, I was not taking most of the vacation time due to me and just losing it. In later years we were able to carry a week or two vacation forward and even sell back a week or two when I worked for Huntsman. I loved this deal. I sold weeks back to Huntsman the last several years that I worked for them. The extra cash came in handy. I really wish that we had this option in the early years that I worked for them. I would have put many thousand dollars away if they did.

With the timeshare, I had the option to exchange locations. So, for this trip, I swapped my Lake Conroe week for a week on Lake Granbury. We had made plans to pick up Jake and Nathan in Crowley on a certain date at a certain time. When we arrived at their house, Jake was almost packed and ready to go. But Nathan was nowhere to be found. It was during the summertime and Nathan had spent the day before at a friend's house and was not back yet. We waited while his stepmom called around for him. She got a few of his clothes packed together while we were waiting to hear back from his friend. We finally heard back, and Nathan was not at his friends anymore. He was out and about. Perhaps on his way back home - who knows what Nathan is up to?

We decided to load up the car and go look for him on the streets in the area. As we were driving around, we spotted him. Sure enough, he was still playing and was not heading back home yet. Nathan was being Nathan. He had forgotten about our planned trip today. This is the same old Nathan that we know and love alright! We pulled to the side of the road and picked him up. He was really red-faced. He was not feeling well at all. He was red all over. He was sunburned and thirsty and tired. Nathan has a light complexion and he looked really bad now. He got in the car, and we took off towards Lake Cranbury, which is only about seventy miles. Nathan did some complaining about not feeling well but there was nothing we could do for him. Just tough it out, we told him. You knew we had plans to go to the lake. You should have stayed home and not played in the sun all day he was told by his momma. Well before long he had to throw up. We told him to try and hold it. But it was getting serious. We did not have a container in the car. We did have some groceries in the car. Sarah took two plastic grocery bags put one inside the other and handed it to Nathan. Just in time. He upchucked into the plastic bags. After he was finished, he wanted to throw the bags out of the window. I said - NO. I told him to tie a knot in the top of the bag. Maybe his mom did it. We kept the puke in the car with us. Before too long, Nathan got to feeling much better. Waiting and looking for him had delayed us a couple of hours and now it was getting dark. I was not happy about all of this. So, what else is new? We finally found the entrance to the resort where we were to spend a week. The office was shut down. Nathan came with me to the porch of the office and tried the doors. They have closed all right. They did leave a note informing us of where to pick up the keys to the condo that we would be staying in. I told Nathan to get his bag of puke. I planned for him to put it into a trash can nearby. I wanted to get it out of the car now and not take it into our living quarters. He got it and we could not find a trash can on the porch. There was a tall container that was used as an ashtray. He placed his puke bag on top of it. We left for the apartment that had our key.

We retrieved the key and unloaded everything from the car that we needed into an upstairs condo. It was a two-bedroom one and nice enough for us. The note with the condo keys said to come back by the office in the morning and sign in. We made ready for sleep.

The next morning after breakfast I told Sarah that I would go up to the office and sign in. Nathan wanted to tag along with me. Since it was a good distance, we rode in the car. When we got there, the office lady was sitting on the porch smoking a cigarette. I told her good morning and that I had come to sign in. OK, just a minute, she said. She wanted to take another drag or two on her cigarette. At this time Nathan picked up his bag of puke and said, "Look Barry, my puke is still here. I could have shit right there on the spot. The lady looked at the bag and then at me. I then noticed a dumpster about one hundred yards away in the complex. I told Nathan to go throw the bag into the dumpster. He took off running in the direction of the dumpster with his bag of puke. The lady snuffed out her cigarette in the spot where the bag of puke was, got up and we went inside. I signed the paperwork. She followed me out and lit up another smoke and went back to the bench where we found her. Nathan got back and we went back to the condo. Although the lady never said anything about the bag of puke, I was still embarrassed about the whole situation.

While at the condo, we played tennis and other games. We also went fishing. We walked to the lake and fished. We did not catch anything but it was fun. I flashed back to when my sons were younger and the things we did together as a family.

On the way to the lake, we had an exciting experience. We decided to walk to the lake. It was about one hundred yards or so from where we stayed to the lake. We had to take a right out of our front door walk sixty or seventy feet in front of the tennis courts and then take another right and walk down the black-topped ramp to the pier on Lake Granbury. Nathan and Jake did not have any shoes on. Jake and I were walking in front. Nathan and Sarah were behind us. I was carrying the fishing tackle box and a rod and reel. Jake had a rod and reel and so did Nathan and Sarah. Unbeknown to me, Nathan was playing with the rod and real. He was casting the line out and then reeling it back in. We hear Sarah say something. Jake and I stopped and turned around. Sarah and Nathan were about thirty feet behind us. Nathan had his fishing line wrapped around two power line wires about thirty feet over his head. I was pissed again. Somehow, he flung the lead up in the air and it circled the two lines. Sarah and Nathan were just standing there looking up. Someone said to pull it down.

Nathan started pulling on the fishing line. Someone said to jerk it. Nathan pulled harder. The two power lines came close together. Then they touched. Then all hell broke loose. Sparks and crackling and fire were shooting overhead. The filament fishing line burned all the way down to the rod. The fishhook with a red plastic worm still on it fell to the blacktop. While all this was happening, I was out running Jake down the ramp. Nathan and Sarah were catching up to us. When the sparks and crackling stopped, we stopped. We all looked around. We did not see anybody. We then slowly walked up to where Nathan had dropped the rod and reel. The worm, hook, and lead were just lying there. Nathan reached over with his big toe pushed it and jumped back. Nothing happened. He picked up the rod and reel. I picked up the worm, hook, and lead. We all looked around again to see if anybody was watching us. I then said," Let's get out of here". We hurried down the ramp and set up to fish and tried to pretend that nothing happened. I know that we must have knocked all the electricity out at the facility. We stayed down by the lake for a couple of hours. When we went back to the condo, we had lights. I was happy. I was also glad that nobody saw what happened. The things kids do. Boy oh boy. No, we did not catch one damn fish.

We spent one whole day in the small town of Granbury. It is a historic and unique place. We just toured the town square. We visited several stores and shops. Granbury has a history from the early eighteen hundreds. One restaurant where we spent a lot of time had reprinted newspaper articles on the walls inside. It was a two-story building, and all the walls were in print. Many articles had to do with John Wilkes Booth. He is the fellow accused of killing President Abraham Lincoln. The articles claimed that Booth lived in Granbury for five years after Lincoln was killed. He used another name - of course. There were many articles stating that Booth died many years later as an old man and was buried in another town in Texas. The articles almost seemed believable to me. They could be true. Who knows for sure? I've been wanting to revisit Granbury for a long time. Maybe one day I will go back there.

On the last day at the resort, we walked down to the lake again. We wanted to let the boys ride the jet skis. After seeing the prices, I was not sure that they should take a chance of getting hurt or even drowning. The prices were kind of high. After talking with the guy running the operation for fifteen minutes or more, he offered me five free minutes to try the jet ski out. I did not want to do it. Sarah, Jake, and Nathan tried to talk me into doing it. I still said no. The guy offered me ten free minutes now. I still said NO. I could have done it if I wanted to, but I just did not feel like it that day or any day since for that matter. I did get the guy to take a more reasonable amount for thirty minutes of riding for Nathan and Jacob. Hell, all of his jet skis were riderless. This happens a lot on weekdays. The boys did not want to ride together at the same time. We decided to let each one ride for fifteen minutes. After the first fifteen minutes, the guy there would blow his horn and the rider would come back to base and the other rider would get on.

Nathan was the first to ride. We should have known better. We were watching from the dock area. He would ride in a large circle. Then he opens it up and darts across the lake. He was supposed to stay in the general area. But you should know Nathan by now. Before we knew it, he disappeared on the lake. We think he rode to the dam which seemed over a mile away. Then all of a sudden he was back running wide open. He made a sharp turn and off the jet ski, he flew. It is a good thing that the jet ski manufactured has an automatic cut-off set up on the ski. There is a key attached to a cord that is attached to the life vest that the driver wears. The rider is not allowed on the ski if he/she does not wear a life vest. If the driver gets thrown off, the key is pulled out of the switch and the jet ski shuts down on the spot. After fifteen minutes the rental guy started blowing his horn for Nathan to come in. He did not seem to hear it. The horn blew and blew and blew. Jake and I were getting pissed because Nathan was abusing the deal. Finally, he came in and Jake did not waste any time getting into deep water. It was now his turn to have some fun. And boy was he having fun. We watched as Jake opened it up. He also made a turn too sharp and went flying head over heels and made a big splash. Sarah and I jumped up to see if he was alright. We saw his head pop out above the water. We were happy to see that little pointed head. Back up on the jet ski, he climbed and off he went. We had chastised Nathan for riding out of our sight when he came back in. Well, it did not take Jake long to ride out of our sight too. He went toward the dam. Before too long the guy blew the horn for Jake to come in. Since there was not much going on today, he had let Jake ride a little longer than what we agreed on. The guy was still trying to get me to take a free ride. I think that it became a challenge for him to get me on those damn skis. They all wanted to see me ride one. But as I stated earlier, not me, not today, not any day. I would never give them the satisfaction to laugh at my big ass flying head over heels on this contraption. My eye, hand, and foot coordination were never that great and I knew that I might make a fool of myself. I've done that before but not today and surely not on a jet ski.

Much to everyone's disappointment, I did not ride the jet ski. Not even for free, you ask? That is right - not even for free.

GETTING MARRIED AGAIN 1997

Sarah and I and her sons took vacations together. We also went to Austin to visit my sons and other folks on a number of occasions. As we ended the year of 1996, we had planned to get married in Baycliff, Texas on January 1, 1997. It was to be a very small wedding.

We were married by Judge Mark Foster in his office. In attendance were Jacob, Nathan, and Mrs. Griffin (Sarah's mom). Judge Foster performed three or four other marriage ceremonies that day. He had to work that day to swear in several folks who were elected to public office whose term started on January 1.

SARAH RUTH RAFFRAY, JUDGE FOSTER, AND ME

After walking out of the building, Sarah and I were hit by rice thrown by two lady friends who worked with Sarah in the accounting department. They were Debbie Patton and Linda Cox. We enjoyed seeing them there. Later that day the wedding party went to The Flying Dutchman restaurant for dinner.

For several months prior to our wedding, we were repairing repainting and, otherwise fixing up Sarah's house in Texas City to rent. Jacob was in the tenth grade and living with his dad. Nathan was in the ninth grade and started attending Clear Creek High School after moving to League City to live with Sarah and me. He had lived with his dad in Fort Worth until they tore their britches and then he moved in with us. Nathan was and is a little different and marched to a drummer who was high on something. He was very high-strung and restless all the time. He was always on the go and got bored very quickly. He had to be doing something all the time and do something he did. Nathan seems to always be in trouble. Getting into something that he shouldn't have. Making friends with the wrong people. If there were ten kids hanging around on a corner, the cops would pick out Nathan to arrest. I think the cops in our area picked on him a lot. We bailed him out of jail numerous times. Thank God as the years passed, he finally grew out of that getting into trouble mode. He just had a knack for being in the wrong place at the wrong time. Maybe he realized that after he turned eighteen, he would serve a hard time and not an easy time playing with the cops in these local jails. I am not sure what it was, but he became a fine young man and paid us back much of the bail and lawyer money we put up for him over the years.

LAS VEGAS TRIP JANUARY 11, 1997

Before getting married, we arranged to take a trip to Las Vegas for our honeymoon for a couple of days. I used a timeshare that I had at the time to swap for a room at the Sahara Timeshare section of the hotel by the same name in Las Vegas. We invited my brother and his wife to come along with us. We arrived in Las Vegas on January 11, 1997.

LIZ, PUT AND SARAH RAFFRAY

We had a fun airplane ride from Houston to Vegas. My sister-in-law, Liz, had never been on an airplane before. It was fun watching her. She was a big smoker at that time, and she could not smoke on the plane. We changed airplanes in Albuquerque, New Mexico. While waiting for the next flight, Liz and Sarah spent their time in a bar. I believe they each had beers and cigarettes in both hands. They were trying to get in some relaxation before the next flight. The cigarette smoke was heavy all around them in the bar.

Before long we boarded the airplane and took off for the last leg of our flight. I was sitting across the aisle and two rows behind Sarah and Liz. My brother was sitting a row behind them - I believe. There were several lady passengers and a stewardess sitting next to them also. They all were laughing and having a grand ole time. They were all trying to keep Liz from thinking about flying. The stewardess found out that she and my brother had a bunch of grandchildren and started giving her bags of peanuts for the grandkids. When we got off the plane in Las Vegas, Liz had over five pounds of those little bitty bags of peanuts. She had found a plastic bag to hold them all. The loaded bag was larger than a basketball. Other than being cold and wet, we had a great time in Vegas. We also went to Hoover Dam and drove across the dam into Arizona where it was an hour later than the Nevada side of the dam. We also visited a marsh mellow factory and learned how marsh mellows were made. Also, how they bagged them for the different companies that they were sold under. They made marshmallows for every company that sold them in the country. They just used a different container/bag with a different company name on it. We planned to visit a cranberry canning facility also but had to get back to a casino to get our free meal before we ran past the time slot. All the food was just great everywhere we ate. If you played the slots a lot, you would get points and trade them in for meals at the casino you gambled in.

Before playing the slots, we went and signed for our slot cards that identified us. You just stick the card into a slot and start playing. The card figures how much money you spend and gives you credit in points. You then can redeem the points for free meals and other items or tickets for events or things like that. Sarah and I used some points to ride the elevator up to the one-hundred-eighth floor in the Stratosphere Casino. Liz and put did not care to do this. They just stayed on the ground floor and played the slots some more. After we got off on the one-hundred-eight floor, we then walked up to the one-hundred-ninth floor where there were shops and an observation deck. We could see for many miles. This casino is over seventeen hundred feet tall. There is actually a roller coaster on the top of the building. Hell NO, we did NOT ride it. The only person that comes to my mind that might want to ride this ride is Beverly Curtice who Sarah and I both worked with at Huntsman and Nova Chemicals. Beverly likes to ride these wild roller coaster-type rides. Not me - no way. I don't even like the baby roller coaster.

We went into a number of the casinos but really did not see much of Las Vegas. Sarah and I went to the old downtown casinos. We went into all of them. They were much smaller than the monstrosities down the strip. I enjoyed playing the dime slots in one of the old casinos. We watched two of the three laser shows shown on an overhead screen about one city block long. One show was a parade with horses and band and dancing girls. The other was showing jets flying in formation. It was incredible and looked and sounded real. I was ducking for cover. They waited one hour between shows. It was just too damn cold to wait for the third show, so we went back to our casino and found Put and Liz. They did not venture out very much.

They just wanted to stay in one place and play the slots and try and make money. It was hard to get them to move about after they found a slot to their liking. The weather may have had something to do with them not wanting to venture out. But when I think about it, they are not adventurous folks.

We walked to the Circus Casino. It was like an amusement park inside a large building. As we were walking around, Sarah wanted to ride the roller coaster. I do not like roller coaster rides. They look too dangerous to me. Put and Liz did not want to ride it either. We told her to go get a ticket and ride it and we would wait for her at the spot where we were. We thought that we were where you get off the ride. We sat down at that spot and waited. We waited and waited and waited. We saw the roller coaster go around a number of times but did not see if Sarah was on it. After fifteen minutes, I got concerned. I wondered if someone abducted her. We left that spot and started looking for her. We walked the complete amusement park section looking everywhere. No, Sarah. We then went into the casino. Put and Liz checked the front of the casino while I walked all over the back part. We almost lost each other. We went back to the amusement section and looked some more. It was now over thirty minutes since we last saw Sarah. I was really worried, and I was getting pissed off as well. We planned to be somewhere else at this time and here we are still looking for Sarah.

We decided to come back to the spot where we last saw her again. We waited there for several more minutes. I was thinking of how could I do a missing person's report. I did not know who to call or contact. Then all of a sudden, there she was. She was looking as frightened as

I was. She said that she was looking for us while we were looking for her. I was really happy to see her. Then I got pissed off. We spent almost one hour trying to find her. To this day we do not know where each of us was or why we could not find each other sooner. This just goes to show you that you can be in the same area and get lost. So always stay close to your loved ones. when you don't know where in the hell you are.

We left Circus Casino and went to another casino. I did not even want to play the slots there. I just wanted to get out of there. And we did. We went into the MGM Grand. While they played the quarter slots, I went looking for a certain dollar slot machine that was in a section near the escalators. Several friends back home told me about a certain dollar slot that always paid off well when they came here. I did find the row of dollar slots where I was told they would be. I counted them in the order that I was told to and found the good paying machine. The only problem was that someone was playing it. There were twelve slots in a row. Ten were being played. I sat at one that was not being played. I put a twenty-dollar bill in the machine and got twenty credits. I like to play one at a time. I also like to pull the handle and not press the button. I make one pull then wait a minute or two before I pull again. I was keeping my eye on the machine that I wanted to play. I could see and hear it paying off. Shit, I thought, as long as it pays off, that asshole, is going to play it. You know, that asshole is acting just as I would if I had a machine that pays off like that. Ain't that a coincidence?

After about forty-five minutes, I had lost my twenty dollars the machine that I wanted was still going K-ching, K-ching. It took me this long to lose my twenty dollars because I played that slot slowly. I do not remember hitting over two dollars at any one time. I finally left that area. I did notice other folks milling around in the area. They would put a dollar in a slot but were not really playing the slots there. I believe that they were doing what I was doing. They had heard about that one slot machine and came over to play it too. Some of them would leave then come back a little time later and look around. Several people did this while I was there. Yeah, they were after my slot also. There are too many big-mouth gamblers telling folks secrets that were meant only for me. Over the two days and three nights, we were there, I came back to this casino and dollar slots three or four times and never got the chance to play it. There were times when only two of the slots were being played and my slot was one of the two.

After getting back home, my two friends told me about this slot and asked if I played it. My answer was a resounding NO, I never got the chance. I told them that I tried but it was always busy and still paying off. They both said, I told you so.

I mentioned earlier about the little plastic card that was used to get points for free meals and other stuff. I will elaborate more on that now. On this trip to Vegas, we learned what those little plastic cards on a string that everybody had around their necks were. These cards had all kinds of information on them. Information like your name and address and how much you played the slot machines. It kept track of each pull or push you made on a slot and registered it. After it counted so many it gave you credit in points. After so many points you could get a free meal or a free pass to a show a ticket to a special event or other gifts. Upon arrival at the Stratosphere, we all signed up for these little plastic cards. You place it in a special slot on the slot or gaming machine that you play. As long as you play that machine it will register points. Put and Liz ate for free on their points. Sarah and I used some of our points to ride the elevator up to the top floor of the Stratosphere. We wanted Put and Liz to come with us, but both said, "hell no, we don't want to go up there." I already mentioned how high we were and about the roller coaster even higher than we were. This is one big and tall building. The folks on street level looked smaller than ants. We looked through the telescopes and even saw farther away. Since we did this in daylight, we could not tell where the other cluster of casinos were. At night I bet we could have seen a lot of bright spots. But I do not think that I care to go that high up at night. I like to think that I can see more in the daytime and be more aware of what is around me.

On the way up the elevator, we noticed where the large meeting and convention rooms were. This was a large building. Have I mentioned that before?

We stayed up there quite a while just enjoying the view and being in awe that there was a roller coaster above us and in further awe that some crazy folks wanted to ride it. It takes all kinds to make up the world, I guess. There are some crazy bastards out there. I may be crazy, but I am not that damn crazy to ride a roller coaster that is one hundred nine stories in the air.

I think that is over eleven hundred feet up.

When we got back downstairs, we told Put and Liz that they should go up and take a look. Both again said, "HELL NO". And that was that. They rather sit on the ground floor and lose all their money than go up to the top. We did use our own money on this trip, but we surely did not spend a lot of it in the casinos. We traveled around quite a bit. We still did not see everything that the Las Vegas area has to offer but we enjoyed what we saw.

We did get a telephone call from Nathan while we were in Vegas. Nathan was being Nathan. He was up to no good and enjoying himself by cutting his arms. Sarah made a couple of telephone calls and when we got back home, we visited him in a special ward of the hospital in Texas City. He was placed in a ward where the nurses and doctors could keep watch over him.

They gave him pills that calmed him down a bit for a little while.

Up until the call from Nathan, we had a good time in Vegas for the most part. We plan to go back one day and spend more time visiting the casinos that we did not see and sightseeing the sites in the area that we did not see.

TRIP TO NIAGARA FALLS
IN EARLY JULY 1997

In July of 1997, Sarah and I flew to Buffalo, New York. We went out one night to eat at Duffy's which is the original home of Buffalo Wings and is located just out of the city limits of Buffalo.

One day we drove to Lockport, New York. We took a tour of the Erie Canal. I really enjoyed this ride on this historical waterway. We went through locks that had to displace thirty feet of water while heading toward the Niagara River. We went under the widest bridge in the country in Lockport. We also went under an upside-down railroad bridge. The railroad company put the strength structure at the bottom of the bridge instead of on top of it. This was to inhibit the passage of barges loaded down with cargo. The railroad company blocked larger barges from utilizing the waterway by building the bridge in this manner. Pretty smart, isn't it?

We also saw the passageway where the mules walked to tow the barges. They were very narrow. Every fifteen miles the passageway was made wider in the rock/stone bank. This is where the mules would stop, and rest, and another set of mules would take over the towing of the barge. The mules could make fifteen miles in one day. I believe the Erie Canal ran from the Hudson River on the far eastern side of New York state to the Niagara River on the far western side of New York state. The Niagara River ran from Lake Erie through Niagara Falls and into Lake Ontario.

After, AFTER RAISING SUGARCANE

ERIE CANAL LOCKS AND THE TOUR BOAT LOCKVIEW

The next two days we visited Niagara Falls on the Canadian side. Upon arriving at Niagara Falls, New York, we were freezing, parked the rental car, and went into a mall to shop. We each purchased long-sleeved jackets because we did not bring any with us because THIS WAS IN JULY. When we left the mall, I had a parking ticket on my windshield. I was pissed because we were only gone a few minutes. We went on to the Canada side where we spent time looking at the sights. We drove to the Whirlpool but did not take the cable car ride across it. It did not look that safe to me. I do not like to ride on cable cars anyway. Later we visited a gambling casino and Sarah won a jackpot of over two hundred fifty dollars American on a quarter machine. When the machine started making funny sounds and the lights started flashing, we almost ran away from it because we thought that she had broken it. It did not react like the slot machines that we play in the good old U. S. of A.

A worker came by and told us that we won some money. This machine did not pay any coins as I recall. It must have given us a piece of paper that stated the amount. We turned the Canadian money into American money right there in the casino. We later found out that if we had made the conversion on the street, we would have had more American dollars. The conversion ratio in the casinos there was less than the real conversions. I guess it is another way that they screw the Americans that don't know better. Yes, that means us. We got screwed by the casino Canadians. We were OK with it until we found out about it. Then again, I got pissed. It seems like I get pissed a lot. Well, maybe I do - I don't know.

One time we drove on the Canadian side from Niagara Falls almost to Buffalo and back to Niagara Falls before crossing back into the United States. Our motel was just outside Buffalo, so we went back and forth to Canada each day. We spent one-half day in a small village on Lake Ontario. This lake is beautiful. We walked to the edge and put our hands into it, but it was too cold to walk in. We visited small towns in the area and saw cherry trees full of cherries. This must be the area where Wash Gorgington errrrrrrr I mean George Washington cut down the cherry tree with his little axe that his dad gave to him. Doooogh, if you give a kid an axe you should expect this sort of behavior. I would never give a hand axe to Nathan unless I wanted him to use in on me.

We were in Niagara Falls on July 4. The Saturday fireworks that we saw while in Canada at Niagara Falls were far better than anything we could see on the American side. This was the fourth of July. We expected large fireworks show from the city of Niagara on the American side. We were very disappointed with the small display put on at a distance from the falls. We were very excited and happy that Canada would have such fireworks display for us on an American holiday. We just could not believe that they would do such a thing, being as close to the British as they are. This was very nice of them to do especially since the Americans kicked the British asses and won independence. Canada still under British influence was honoring the American Independence Day celebration. What a great country thought I. We were so glad to see this that I mentioned it to another person near us.

The Canadians doing this for the American tourists. Wow, this is just great. Well, again my bubble burst. I was informed by this person that the Canadians have the fireworks display each and every Saturday of the year. It just so happens that today was the fourth of July. They did not do it to celebrate our holiday. Those bastard Canadians. I knew that we could not trust them. Trying to make Sarah and me believe that they were having fireworks show for our holiday. That just shows you that you cannot trust the Canadians. You should always keep a good eye on them. The fireworks display was still a great show.

NIAGARA FALLS ON THE LEFT AND THE MAID OF THE MIST ON THE RIGHT

The Niagara Falls is just awesome. We enjoyed it very much. The flower gardens, boat tours near the falls, the walking tour under the falls, everything we did, or saw was great. We would recommend to anyone who can afford it to go there. It is all awesome. But Horseshoe Falls from the Canadian side is the most awesome site. We enjoyed our visit to the Falls very much.

Several weeks after returning home, I received my credit card bill that I used to pay for the usage of the rental car. It had an extra charge on it. I had wondered how the city of Niagara, New York was going to make me pay for the parking ticket I got when shopping in the mall there. Well, they had a plan. Those bastards notified the rental car company and charged them. The rental car company charged me by placing the fine amount on my credit card that I used to pay them. So, they got me. I wonder what they would have done if I had paid cash for the rental car. So, trying to save five or ten dollars in parking fees for an hour in the mall cost me forty-five dollars. I am happy that we both made exceptional low-cost purchases of the winter jackets we purchased. Perhaps everything came out even. My free parking and the huge discounts on the winter jackets evened us up for that day with the parking ticket. We came out ahead considering that Sarah won that small jackpot in the casino. That paid for all our sightseeing, tickets purchased, and some of the meals as well.

Overall, we had a good trip. When we got back home, we had a lot of stories to tell and pictures that we took to go with them. I could do this trip again someday.

1998

In 1998 things were running along. Sarah and I were still working for Huntsman Chemical in Bayport, Texas. Nathan was living with us and getting in and out of trouble. Jacob was still in the Fort Worth area living with his dad and stepmom and her kids. My sons, Kent, and Todd, were in Austin and I think that Lane was in Chattanooga, Tennessee at this time.

I remember when Sarah and I drove to Chattanooga to pick him

up and haul all his belongings back to San Marcos, Texas. Lane had been in a major car accident on the freeway in Chattanooga and had totally wrecked his car. No one was seriously hurt in the accident. He was hit from behind and sandwiched between other vehicles. After seeing his car, I don't know how he came out of there alive. But he did - thank God. The car that Lane was driving was Sarah's old car from before we were married. Before I go on, let me tell you about how Sarah got this car.

Before we were married, back in 1995, Sarah had a nice little nineteen eighty six Buick two-door hardtop Skylark. She purchased it from Ron and Maureen Sikora who are friends of ours. In fact, Maureen worked for me for several years with both Huntsman and Nova before I was let go. When Ron got another vehicle, he sold this one to Sarah. The car was old but was sharp looking. We both liked the shape and style of the body. The only problem was that the paint was flaking away. As hard as this is to believe she got a letter in the mail from General Motors stating that they will pay to repaint the car. The company acknowledged that there were faulty paint jobs on many cars that were made that year and was making offers to repaint all the vehicles still in service. She dropped off her car at the Buick dealership in Clear Lake. It was David Giles Buick. When they finally finished painting the car, I went with Sarah to pick it up. It looked just great. It was a new maroon color and looked much better than the old maroon. She continued to drive this good-looking car. It was still running great and without many mechanical problems. It seemed that it wasn't very long until she wrecked it. Jacob was visiting her, and they were driving on Fourteenth Avenue coming from Nathan's Alternative school back to her house. She leaned over to change the radio station and BAM. A large pickup truck with one of the big pipe rear bumpers backed into the street from a school parking area and she rear-ended him. His truck was fine. He hardly had a scratch on his big rear bumper. But Sarah's car was a mess. It was hit on the front passenger side. I think that Jacob got bruised a little but he and Sarah were not hurt badly. Sarah's car had to be towed away while the other guy just drove off.

The pickup driver was in the wrong because he backed up into them. Several days later the guy's insurance company notified Sarah that they totaled her car. I was really surprised. The damage did not look that bad but the chassis or frame had been bent. They offered her what I thought was a very good settlement. It was over forty-five hundred dollars.

Sarah asked me to go with her to pick up the check-in in Houston. It was raining while we were driving on Interstate 15 toward Houston.

As we approached the NASA Road One exit, we decided to stop by the David Giles Buick place and see what they had available. Sarah could not afford a new car, so we were looking at used ones. A young Mexican American came out in the rain to help us. Of course, we were just looking. But he was persistent and would not leave us. We looked at two used Buick Skylarks. Sarah liked the style of the car she had as did I. We looked at a nineteen ninety and a nineteen ninety-one. Both were white and both looked very good. I wanted her to have the newer one, but the price was about sixty-two hundred dollars. They came down on the price but not enough for Sarah to buy it with the check she was going to get from the insurance company.

We settled on the nineteen ninety models. It looked good also. I really could not tell the difference in the year models. They listed this car for over five thousand dollars. Sarah and I talked it over away from the young sales guy. She left the dealing up to me. I told her to not let the salesman know how much money she would be getting from the insurance company. They tried to find out several times, but we skirted the questions.

I told them that Sarah would/could not pay five thousand or even forty-five hundred dollars for this car. I think she would have taken it for forty-five hundred because she could cover that much with the check she was going to get. But I had other plans. They had been trying to get us to test drive the car. I kept putting them off by stating that we could not test drive a car that she could not afford. That just did not make any sense to me. Besides, it was raining and nasty outside and we just stopped to look around. We had other dealerships to visit. This was my hooker. By their reaction, I knew that I had them where I wanted them to be.

During all this talking, Mr. David Giles came by several times and talked with us. It was a very slow day at the dealership. In fact, on rainy and nasty days, it is always a slow day for car sales. Most folks just don't like coming out and shopping for vehicles on days like this. These types of days are the BEST time to shop for a vehicle. This is something that I knew, and it made sales folks more aggressive in pricing when there were fewer people at the dealership. I wanted to take advantage of the weather and we did.

The salesman said that he was pretty sure that we could come up with a deal and just kept dangling the car keys in our faces and trying to get us to go for a test drive. We finally agreed to do it. We took off from there and went to Houston and picked up Sarah's check for over forty-five hundred dollars. I pretty much knew that we could buy this car for less than that thus leaving Sarah with money in the bank.

The car drove really well. We could not find anything mechanically wrong with it. I checked the motor oil, the automatic transmission oil, the power steering, and the brake fluids. I checked out the back seating area and into the trunk to make sure there was a spare and a jack. It had everything. The air conditioner heater and radio all worked. It only had a loose handle on the door and a plastic clip on the seat belt. This was nothing. The ashtray was loose, but I fixed it and the inside doorknob later after she purchased the car.

We came back to the dealership and told them that Sarah liked the car. The only problem was that we only had four thousand dollars TOTAL to spend. The salesman hemmed and hawed and went back and forth to talk with Mr. Giles. Each time he came back I again said four thousand dollars TOTAL. I think that Sarah really wanted this car now and would have gone up a couple of hundred dollars, but I stuck to the plan that she and I decided when in the car.

I believed that they were getting ready to take my deal when I told them that we wanted to test drive the car again. They agreed to it if we put in a fifty-dollar deposit before we departed with the car. These fifty dollars would keep them from selling the car to someone else while we were out test-driving it. Yeah, sure, that is going to happen. I gave the guy a fifty dollar bill.

We knew that we were going to get this car now. We took off in their car on their gas and went to Texas City where Sarah deposited the insurance company's check into her checking account. I believe that was the most money she ever had in her account up the that time. It was short lived though.

When we arrived back at the dealership, everybody was ready to deal. We all shook hands on four thousand dollars even for the car. While the salesman was writing up the sale and doing the paperwork, I went upstairs with Mr. Giles to get my fifty-dollar deposit back. He had placed it in the safe in his office. I waited in the hall while he went into his office to retrieve my deposit. When he came out, he counted two twenties and a ten and handed them over to me. I said wait a minute, I gave you a fifty-dollar bill, I want MY money back. He looked at me in astonishment with his mouth open. He stated that he may not find the fifty-dollar bill. I told him that I could find it because I knew the serial number on it. His mouth opened again, and an even more astonished look came over his face. Well, he said as he looked toward his office door and started to move that way. I then interrupted him and said that I would take the notes that he gave me. I had made my point about how I was about money - especially my money. This would come in handy in the minutes that followed.

I followed Mr. Giles back down the stairs. He still had a puzzled look on his face. As we approached the sales office, the young salesman was just finishing up the paperwork and handing it over to Sarah to sign. I walked over and looked over the paperwork. "OH, OH", I said, this amount is over four thousand dollars. It was for nearly forty-three hundred dollars. I told them that this was not going to fly. The price was four thousand dollars TOTAL. They said yes and then we added taxes, licenses, and fees. No way, said I, four thousand dollars TOTAL includes taxes, licenses, and fees. They could have shit right there on the spot. We still had a deal but spent another twenty minutes while they corrected the paperwork and recalculated the car sales price and other fees to come out to four thousand dollars even.

Sarah drove this car for several years until after we married. In 1997, Sarah and I spent about eight hours dealing back and forth with sales folks at Star Toyota in League City. We finally bought the T-100 pickup truck that we were dealing with. Not long after we purchased the new truck, we gave my 1992 Mercury Grand Marque to Sarah's mom and took her old 1978 Ford Crown Victoria and gave it to Nathan. We then gave the 1990 Skylark to Lane who later drove it to Chattanooga when he got the job with the state of Tennessee.

This is how the Skylark got to Chattanooga, Tennessee, and a year or so later got totaled in the freeway accident. I am happy to say that Buick must have made this style of car very sturdy. Two different-year models were in two different car wrecks where both cars were totaled and all passengers received just minor injuries. These were two great little cars.

CRAWFISH BOIL AT THE PLACE 1998

From time to time I had boiled crawfish or crabs or shrimp for my family and a few friends. I did it several times when my boys were little and when they were young teenagers when we lived in the big house in the Clear Lake Forest subdivision in the city of Taylor Lake Village.

After I moved to League City in 1990, I boiled crawfish

several times. My brother, Put, and his wife, Liz, came for a visit once or twice and they boiled the crawfish. He actually brought them from Louisiana with him. This is something that I was raised with. We had crawfish/crab broils every year for as long as I can remember. If we did not go out and catch them, my parents, or friends purchased them. These were great times and I still remember them very well.

On Easter weekend in 1999, we had a crawfish boil at our house in the woods near Cleveland, Texas. Sarah and I planned it two months in advance. We had to make a lot of preparations. The first thing I did was to write instructions on how to get to our place in the woods. I issued several instructions based on the direction the person would be coming from. I typed these up and made several copies of each. We then made a list of whom we would invite. We invited my department from work and their families and Sarah's department from work and their families. We also invited my sons and dates or friends and Sarah's sons and dates or friends. We also invited John and Carol Beeson, friends from my American Hoechst days.

We started buying the supplies that we needed for the boil. I went to Sam's Warehouse and purchased over ten pounds of sausage, forty-eight years of corn, ten pounds of potatoes, five pounds of onions, two boxes of mushrooms, four pounds of lemons, eight pounds of crab boil, four boxes of salt and some cayenne pepper. We also purchased hamburger patties and hot dogs and buns for both for those folks who do not eat crawfish. There were several who did not eat the crawdads. I also got my propane bottle filled and checked out my boiling equipment. Everything was ready to go except the available parking space.

I cut many saplings and cleared out enough of an area to park eleven or twelve autos. I tied three onion/crawfish sacks on our gate at the highway as a marker for the folks coming to the boil. Our house is over seven hundred feet off the highway and cannot be seen from the highway. The drive entrance is narrow and winding and lined with trees. The house is in the Bear Creek area and the creek runs the width of our property. The creek has to be crossed about three hundred feet before you get to the house.

I told all invited guests that eats would be ready between one and two in the afternoon but they could arrive anytime they wanted to. They were also informed to bring drinks and chairs for their family. We had horseshoe, bad mitten and some other games available for kids and adults to play.

I had placed my order for three sacks of crawfish with a seafood house in Seabrook a week or so before our event. Since I had to get everything set up, I went to our place in Cleveland the day before the boil. I brought all the stuff with me when I came up. Sarah was to pick up the crawfish in Seabrook early the morning of the boil. She also had to go and pick up this little girl that Nathan wanted to have come to a boil. I did not like this idea. She was a wild thirteen-year-old and I thought that we might have to keep an eye on her and Nathan. That would be hard to do with all the work we had to do. I was also upset because Sarah would have to drive all the way back to bring this girl back home since she could not spend the night with us. We could not have any of that. I was pissed because I would be alone and also would have to clean up everything all by myself. Boo hoo hoo. The day of the boil I got all my equipment ready to go. I set everything up behind the old house. I placed the boiling equipment the tubs and cooking pot and the water hose where I could get to them easily. I brought out all the ingredients and stuff that I was going to use. I wanted to have it all ready for when Sarah got here with the mudbugs. My biggest fear was that Sarah would arrive without the crawfish for some reason or other. My mind made up many reasons why she would not have the crawfish.

I dug a large hole in the backyard away from any trees. This was to be where I would bury all the peals and trash from the boil. If you have ever been to a crawfish boil you know how much trash that it can make.

I would empty the boiling water into this hole too. You really have to be careful where you empty the water. It has much salt in it and will kill grass or roots of trees and trees for that matter. That is why I dug the hole away from any trees. The hole was about four feet deep and four feet wide. After digging the hole, I waited for Sarah. She arrived about ten in the morning. I unloaded the crawfish sacks into my wheelbarrow and hauled them to the backyard. I needed to get things going fairly quick.

After the water came to a boil, I placed a packet of crab boil and a box of salt into it. I added four or five lemons cut in half and squeezed into the pot also. I then placed about five pounds of potatoes. You need to boil the potatoes longer than anything else, so you start them out first. Boil them for about ten minutes before putting in the crawfish.

When you add a sack of crawfish to boiling water, the boiling comes to a stop. Crawfish only takes about seven minutes to boil - after the water gets to boiling again. When I think that they are about done I cut off the fire and place ice cubes on top of the crawfish. After being boiled the crawfish want to float on top of the water. The ice weighs them down and they soak up more seasoning. After fifteen or so minutes I take the boiling basket out of the pot, let the water drain back into the pot as much as possible then spread out the crawfish and boiled potatoes on a large table to get ready for the feast. Some folks like to stand around the table and eat. Others prefer to place the crawfish in a container or tray and sit and eat.

It was a little after twelve noon when folks started arriving. I did not have a lot of time to greet people, Sarah did that. I told them hello when I got a chance. Since some food was ready, I told them to go at it which they did.

My job was just starting. I had two more sacks to go.

When the pot is boiling water is evaporating from it. When the ice melts it replaces water lost. You then add more seasoning and salt cut up and squeeze more lemons back into the pot. You do not need as much seasoning this time around. I again put in another five pounds of potatoes and got it going. After seven or eight minutes I added another sack of crawfish and followed the same procedure as last time. When the water came to a boil again, I timed it again.

I did this three times that day. I also boiled corn, onions, mushrooms, and sausage. You can do this separately or add it to the crawfish. Corn and mushrooms only need about three or four minutes of boiling time to be done. Be sure they are not still frozen. Sausage takes about five or six minutes to boil. You can also boil okra, bell peppers, and anything else that you have a taste for with crab boil.

We had thirty-two folks including the kids attend our first crawfish boil at our place in the country. Everybody had a good time. That is what they told me anyway. Although it is a lot of work, we enjoyed doing it.

I did not get a chance to eat any until after the last batch was done. It was after four in the afternoon when I had the chance to eat. Everybody was finished eating by the time I could start. That is always the way it is when you are the cooker of crawfish in this manner. I think Sarah cooked several hamburgers and hot dogs for folks who did not eat crawfish.

Everyone had something to eat.

It was getting dark by the time our last guest left. Then Sarah had to bring Nathan and his little girlfriend back as well. I got pissed off all over again. I would have to stay up here all by myself. The next morning, I burned any boxes and trash that would burn. I emptied all the peals into the hole and covered it back up with dirt. I had rinsed my pot out after the boil but now I washed it with soap and water. I cleaned off the tables with water and a hose. I got all my equipment cleaned and in good shape to be used in the future. Cleaning your equipment is the life of your equipment. All these seasonings and salt are corrosive on any metal. So, if you want to use it again and again, it is best to clean it thoroughly after such use.

My burner, regulator, and hose were over twenty-five years old at the time of this boil and still in very good shape. I purchased them in Baton Rouge in 1977 or 78. They have served me well.

Oh, did anything happen between Nathan and the little girl, you ask? Hell no. They sneaked off into the house several times when everyone else was outside. I ran them out a couple of times. I believe that Sarah did also and one or more of our guests did too. We had everybody keeping an eye out for them. And it worked. They were really frustrated which made us feel really good.

SELL OUT BY HUNTSMAN
TO NOVA LATE 1998

In early 1998 we began the hear rumors that Huntsman was looking for a buyer for the Styrenics business. This meant the styrene monomer, polystyrene, and derivatives businesses. This rumor persisted all year. We heard names such as Dow Chemical, BASF, and even Mobil Chemical to name a few. When I looked over who should buy us and who needed styrene monomer, I came up with BASF. They were purchasing a very large volume of styrene monomer from us and from Lyondell Chemical located in Channelviewn, Texas.

Channelview is located just up the Houston Ship Channel from the plant facility that I worked for. BASF was a company that needed more monomers to keep up their production of polymers in Brazil and other locations in the world. Well, I was wrong. So were many other folks who thought the same as I did. It turned out that several companies made bids for our businesses, but the highest bidder turned out to be Nova Chemical. This surprised us all. We did not think that Nova was even in the running. But in the running they were. They offered over 100 million dollars more than BASF or thereabout. After we found out the offer amounts, we thought the BASF offer was more in line with what this part of our business was worth. But those crazy Canadians added another 100 million to the mix. This was a windfall for the huntsmen who laughed all the way to the bank.

I was familiar with Nova. In the old days, their name was Polysar Limited. I had many dealings with the folks at Polysar. We had a very good working relationship over the years. We exchanged and traded styrene monomer and also purchased the product from each other. My dealings with them went all the way back to my early Foster Grant days. As time went on, in the mid-1970s, Foster Grant Chemical became a Division of United Brands, then American Hoechst Corp, and then in the mid-1980s became Huntsman Chemical Company. Now in the late 1990s, we were having discussions about becoming Nova Chemical Corp.

For many years I had dealings with Mr. Wayne Hyatt of Polysar Limited.

They may have had another name before Polysar, but it slipped my mind. They were named Rexene Polymers for a number of years and maybe another name before Nova, which slipped my mind also. I know that this is a lot of minds slipping going on here but that is the way it is. Wayne had a long career and went through several company name changes just as I did. After Polysar became Nova Chemical, it was a much larger corporation. We still made exchange agreements and continued to purchase products from each other.

At one time there were nine styrene monomer producers in the world. We all knew each other and for the most part, traded and exchanged and purchased from each other. Of course, we had our favorite folks and companies that we liked to do business with. For me, it was always a people business. People doing business with people. The company name was never of any importance unless they were in financial trouble. As mergers and acquisitions took place and company names started changing, we still did business with people. If the guy or gal had a great reputation for being honest straightforward and trustworthy, we continued to do business regardless of the name or who the major shareholder was. If you trusted the person, you would let him or her borrow/exchange product on their word that they would pay it back at the agreed to time frame.

I was very fortunate to have some good relationships with competitors in the styrene monomer business. We all worked together to help each other out. Yes, we were in competition but us distribution folks did not let this get in our way. The distribution group at each company had the responsibility for keeping products flowing to all of their internal usage plants as well as into the merchant market customers. We did not let our marketing and business folks dictate who we swap products with. There were and still are very good reasons to swap/exchange products with your competitors. Every plant facility must face a turn-a-round in their facility. All production plants must shut down for catalyst change maintenance and repairs. The time interval between shutdowns depended upon the type of catalyst that the facility used. Shutdown intervals could be from one year of operation to just over two years of operation. Other factors may figure into how long a plant can run before repairs and catalyst changes are necessary. So, to keep your plant operating at optimum capacity and purity, one had to replace the catalyst when it had wand down. Because of knowing that your production plant will shut down sooner or later, our distribution folks lent/exchanged/swapped products with other manufacturers so they would owe us a favor and lend/exchange/swap products back to us when our plant was in shutdown. It was just good business to do so. You do them a favor now, and they do you one later. This was a tremendous amount of work just keeping up with exchange balances. We had to keep records of all transactions. I always had my team keep records within our department although the accounting department was supposed to be responsible for this work. We had to know where we stood on exchange balances before we made other deals with other folks looking for products. Many times, we had to correct the accounting department numbers and furnish them with the correct information from our records. After computers came into play this record keeping was supposed to be easier. Well, I don't know if it was or not. But we continued to do it and the accounting team leaned on us for copies of our spreadsheets because they would have loopholes in their system.

After Polysar Limited became Nova, I continued doing business with Wayne Hyatt until he retired. Jim Swingle took his place, and we continued as in the past for a couple of years. Jimmy ended up going to another division within Nova. I really missed working with him. He was such an honest and straightforward young man to do business with.

As we got into the decade of the 1990s, business practices started changing. As the old timers in the businesses started retiring, new folks started coming into the distribution jobs. Some were young and aggressive and wanted to make names for themselves. They tried to structure deals where they would have an advantage. Some even tried to screw you in order to make themselves look good at their company. Before long we had to have written exchange agreements between companies stating the requirements of the exchange. The next phase was the drastic curtailing of exchanges altogether. Several companies refuse to exchange but would sell you the product outright at a producer discount. Then after several years, the producer's discount disappeared also. Large producers paid the same price for the monomer as a small company buying the product on the open market. It was sad to see this happening.

I had come through a period of years when I could call a competitive producer and borrow/exchange/swap products on my word only. I borrowed over 100 million pounds of styrene monomer in anyone-year a number of times to cover a turn-a-round at our production plant. All I had to do was call around and promise to pay back in the time slot that we agreed upon. Usually, the payback was to be over several months starting after our plant was up and running again for some time.

Those reading this who are not familiar with this sort of business may not realize what they read above. I will explain further. The reason you need products from other companies when your plant is shut down is because your plant is not producing it. Duh. We still had to run all of our internal user plants (polystyrene business) and contractual commitments to customers. We could not just take a vacation because our plant is shut down. We had to make the arrangements to keep all the other customers running their businesses as if nothing had happened. Our workload really went up every time we had a turn-a-round or an unexpected outage. This is when your plant crashes down because of any number of reasons. It is unexpected because no one knew it would before it happened. There was always a big scramble to find products during these times. When we were planning for a turn-a-round, we at least had eight months or more notice to start looking and planning on getting the estimated product we needed to take the place of the product we would not produce. How much product did I have to go out and find, you ask? Well, that depended upon how many days we expected to be shut down. Let's say that we produced 3 mm pounds of styrene monomer a day. The plant folks planned to be down for 21 days. This equated to 63 mm pounds of lost production. But if you worked in this business and had one turn-a-round under your belt, you knew to figure far more lost production than the plant operations folks told you. The plant operation and maintenance/repair folks always estimated the most positive situation. They are optimistic that the plant will be running in the shortest amount of time. I am pessimistic and thank God that I am. I believe in Murphy's Law. And I was right eight out of ten times.

No plant manager wants to tell his higher-ups that his plant will be down for a longer period of time. These shutdowns/turn-a-rounds cost millions of dollars and the pressure is always on to do it in the shortest amount of this is 24 hours a day seven days a week work. Rain, shine, storm, fog, or whatever else happens, the work must continue. It calls for up to 500 extra folks working in your plant at one time. It is not an easy task to get this set up or to accomplish. But it all gets done over time. The plant operation folks as well as all other departments want everything done yesterday.

When planning for a turn-a-round, I got in the habit of adding two or three days to the official time that they gave to us. As mentioned earlier, I was right eighty percent of the time in doing so. I would borrow more product than the estimated production lost. Now getting all this product into our system was another problem. When our production plant shut down for any reason, my group's workload increased by several hundred percent. We had much more work to do. When operating normally all of our loading was scheduled at one or two loading facilities. However, during a shutdown, I had to plan on saving products in our normal storage tanks at our normal loading facilities and schedule loadings from our exchange partners' locations. The possibilities of loading locations on the Texas Gulf Coast were eight or nine. We also had three or more loading locations in Louisiana between Baton Rouge and New Orleans.

So, where we had one or two loading locations before shutdown, we now had eleven or more during a shutdown. This took a lot of coordination with a lot of different folks in different companies. We had to schedule and inform the carriers where to load and then set up the inspection companies, so they knew where to go to witness the loading. After the operation was completed, we then had to gather the shipping information, record it, and notify customers of such. The detail work was horrendous. But it was also fun and kept us on our toes all the time.

Bad weather played havoc with our schedules just as it was the main cause of delays in estimated shutdown time. Those were the good ole days - who am I kidding - me?

Now back to the Nova acquisition.

As co-producers started getting away from exchanging to cover a turn-a-round, we started having to purchase products to take the place of exchange products. Polysar Limited, which became Nova, planned a joint venture with Lyondell Chemical at Channelview, Texas. When this was completed, Nova stopped exchanging with us. For years they have given us styrene in Canada to run our polystyrene plant in Mansonville, Canada. We paid them back on the Texas Gulf Coast in the Houston area. After the venture with Lyondell, they had products on the Gulf Coast and did not need to exchange for our product. We worked a deal with Mr. Rick Sequin, who had taken the place of Jim Swingle, who had taken the place of Wayne Hyatt, to purchase the styrene for our Mansonville plant. We hated to buy it but did not have a choice at this time.

Nova changed their way of doing business. At one time I had several exchange locations where we swapped products. After Jim Swingle moved on, it became extremely hard to work exchanges with them. They became hard-nosed about everything. They wanted to charge us and all other exchange partners a premium for exchanges with them. It was like they thought that they would never need to borrow products in the future. My other exchange partners were having the same reaction as I toward Nova's new way of screwing us errrrrrr I mean doing business with us. We really missed Mr. Wayne Hyatt and Jim Swingle and their easy-going direct way of doing business. It got so that we could no longer exchange with Nova. They wanted us to pay a premium on every pound we did and were hardnosed about it.

I did not trust or like them very much. Was I in for a rude awakening when Rick Sequin later became my boss at Nova?

As acquisition talks continue with Nova, I was called upon by Huntsman to compile the plan for our distribution system to present to Nova representatives in joint company meetings being held at our Chesapeake, Virginia polystyrene facility. I did so and had several high-level meetings in Chesapeake. I gave my presentation to the large group there. At the last one that I attended, I gave a slide presentation on how our distribution system worked and the transportation modes involved. After a question-and-answer session before the group, I had one-on-one meetings with the Nova transportation representatives. I then returned to Bayport to await our fate.

The Huntsman family finally finalized the deal with Nova at year-end in 1998. I was very disappointed with the family. I thought that they should have protected me after all I did for them. I felt that they abandoned me. They left me to forge my way with the damn Canadians. I helped give the Huntsman family some credibility and now they cut me loose. Those bast— errrrrrrr, I mean rascals. Although I did not know that I was really upset with the Huntsman family at this time, it was something that came out of me a little later after we became Nova.

NOVA TAKEOVER IN EARLY 1999

The Nova folks came in like gangbusters. They were everywhere interviewing and talking with everyone. Before long they started culling out the folks that they did not want and replacing them. I was interviewed several times. It never occurred to me that they might not want to keep me. It just never occurred to me until I received a telephone call at our place in the woods one weekend. The call was from a guy that I had most of my interviews with. He informed me that I had a job with Nova. I thanked him hung up the telephone then got weak in the knees. I don't know why I did not consider all those interviews as me trying to jockey for a position with this company. Hell, I didn't even like that company because of the way that they did business. And here I am working for them and not thinking that it had to be official.

My distribution team was placed under Rick Sequin's group. Rick had supply and distribution, and some traffic and transportation contract negotiation responsibilities. He was also in sales and marketing at the time. Everything was in transition. Everything was changing. Nova was in the market for a product sales director, a distribution director, and other middle management personnel.

Before long I received a telephone call from the president of our division. We talked for over 30 minutes. Again, I did not realize that I was being interviewed for a higher position. It just never occurred to me at the time. I told this guy something that I should not have.

But I am just a regular guy. If I have something to say, I say it. If anyone asks me a question, I will answer it. It did then and does now, not make me any difference whether you care to hear it or not. Some things just had to be said. How else is the boss going to know what the hell is really happening? At the time of this conversation, I must have said too much because Les cut me off and said that he had to go and hung up abruptly. It seemed sort of strange at the time. I did not realize this until several days later I was interviewed. There was no way in hell I was going to get a middle management job now. This was all right with me. They would have made me move up North and I did not want to do that. I would have to do things that were against my nature and this I surely would not want to do.

Rick Sequin and several other Nova employees had an office near The Woodlands, Texas. They had been there a year or two when the buyout occurred. Nova had set up an office in Gun Point Mall- I mean Greenspoint Mall off Interstate 45 north of Houston several years before. That office had several Nova groups working in it. Rick was in Sales and Exchanges at the time and Hermina Harper and Jlynn Stout were in Distribution and Inventory Control and they had two other ladies helping them also.

When Nova decided to reduce the workforce there, Rick decided to change the location of their office. They chose Kingwood because Rick, Hermina, Jlynn, and the rail car lady all lived there. The other lady quit working for Nova rather than drive to Kingwood. She must have lived very close to the Greenspoint office and just did not want the extra drive to Kingwood. In the last several years that we purchased styrene from Nova for our Mansonville plant, we did it with Rick at the Greenspoint Mall location.

Things were really starting to get very hectic now. Nova started placing people into new positions. Hermina went from distribution to inventory control. Jlynn went from traffic and scheduling to customer service. Rick and Nova were pushing me to hurry up and take over all the supply distribution traffic and transportation of the Nova/Lyondell styrene monomer production. This was over 800 million pounds of product. I had 1.5 billion pounds of product at the Bayport location to start with. This entailed the scheduling of their contract barges and tanker movements and rail car and tank truck shipments as well. As mentioned above, this was the movement of an additional 800 million products annually. I also had to take over the schedule of benzene and ethylene into the Lyondell plant to produce the styrene that we were getting. The Lyondell folks were just great to work with but this was a large task to accomplish given that I was moving over 1.5 billion pounds of styrene already. Most of it was produced at Bayport but a couple hundred million pounds came from other locations.

The pressure was really building up in the early months with Nova.

They were also trying to change my way of doing business with my exchange partners and all the other folks that I did business with. I did not like their cutthroat way of doing business. I knew this before I started working for them. I did not want to treat folks the way that the Nova folks did. It was and is still not my way of doing business. Or better yet, it is not in my nature to treat folks that way.

I was really feeling the pressure. I would go home later than usual. My usual time for going home was already late. I did not sleep. I stayed awake and worried about what the hell I was going to do tomorrow. I was always the go-to guy. If there was any job that needed to be done, I would do it. It did not make any difference whether it was my responsibility or not. If it needed to be accomplished, was the guy. Everybody came to me for everything. Somehow, I would get it done. But not being able to pull this together as quickly as they wanted was getting to me. We had unusual distribution problems where we were making tank car shipments when barge loads were usually done. This put extra work on my folks, and they could not help me with the new computer system that was to be used now since we merged the businesses. I felt alone and overwhelmed. The pressure was just too much to endure much longer.

2nd CRAWFISH BOIL AT THE PLACE APRIL 1999

Early in 1999, we decided that we would have a second crawfish boil at the Cleveland property. We started making plans accordingly. Again, here we were making a list of who to invite what we were going to have when to have it, and so on and so forth.

We decided to do it the same way as the first one. Both of our departments from work and their spouses or friends would be invited again. Our five boys and dates or friends and the Beesons and the Amblers. Susan Ambler had worked for me and had transferred to the Huntsman office in Houston for a better-paying job. It was Susan's family that I purchased this property from in July 1996. We always enjoy visiting with her and Curt, her husband.

We also invited Chip and Toni Howman. Toni worked at Huntsman with us but not in either department. They are close friends of ours. Toni helped me out many times when I really needed it. They just so happen to be Susan Iulzwig's parents. Susan worked for me in my department.

Everyone on the list this year knew how to get to our place in the woods.

I had placed my order for three sacks of crawfish with a crawfish farm in Winnie, Texas. They had advertised that they already purged the crawfish before selling them. Purging is the term used for washing off mudbugs inside and out. The way I do it is to empty a sack of crawfish into a number 3 tub. Then fill the tub half-full with water. Have another tub available nearby. I let the crawfish soak in the clean water for several minutes while I picked out the dead ones and foreign matter. I then dip them out of the first tub and place them into the second tub in water. The first tub of water is usually black now. I pour it out and put fresh water back into it and give the crawfish another round of washing. During the time that they are in the water, they are taking in water and spitting it out. This helps to clean them inside. This is the long way to purge them. Most of the time I use the short purging method.

The short method is:

Empty a sack of crawfish into a number three tub. Fill the tub with about half-full of water. Have another tub nearby. Pick out the dead ones and any twigs, leaves, trash, or foreign matter. Place the live ones into the other tub. Fill it half full of water. Then pour a quarter to a half box of salt over the crawfish. Stir the crawfish around in the salty water. Since they are freshwater critters, they will burp after being in salty water. After a few seconds in the salty water, they spit up all the mud and such that is inside of them. It is like they are throwing up. This really cleans out their insides while their outsides are being cleaned too. After several minutes in the salty water, dip them out and place them into the number three tub or into the strainer basket, if you have a crawfish boiling outfit. You must be ready to boil them fairly quickly after purging them with salt. Salt will kill them, so you don't want to purge them until you are about ready to place them into the boiling water.

You must always remember to never eat a boiled crawfish that has been dead a long time before boiling. If the tail is straight out on a boiled crawfish - DO NOT eat it. As live crawfish are boiled, the tail curls up under the body.

If you eat an already dead one you will know it in a hurry and probably will never eat another crawfish again. Which would be fine with me, because the more folks eat these mudbugs the higher the damn price get that I have to pay for them. Eating a crawfish that has been dead a long time before boiling will be like eating a bad oyster. Eat one and you will never ever try and eat another.

I drove to Winnie the day before our boil and purchased my three sacks of crawfish. I then drove back to League City. The next day I drove to our place in the woods early in the morning. I will not purchase crawfish that far away again. I drove over 250 miles to get these damn mudbugs- all totaled. That is ridiculous. I am counting the miles from League City where I lived and back then the drive to Cleveland. While at the crawfish farm in Winnie, Texas, I saw firsthand how they purge their crawfish. I liked the way that they did it. They had a very large oblong tank. It was about thirty feet long eight feet wide and five feet deep. As the crawfish was harvested straight from the field, the sacks were emptied into this large tank. The tank had water streaming into it from above the tank at several locations. This kept the water fresh and bubbling. This added oxygen to the water as well.

This agitation kept the crawfish in the tank moving.

The large tank had several sections in it. You could work in/on one section at a time. Each section had a hydraulic lift basket inside the tank compartment. The crawfish actually were inside this basket inside the tank of water. After the crawfish had been agitated for several hours. The operator lifted a section up out of the water and refilled the sacks with clean purged crawfish. As one section of the tank was empty the workers went to the next section to do the same while sacks of crawfish waiting to be purged were placed into the section of the tank that was just emptied. They kept the process going all day.

As the purged crawfish was re-sacked, the sacks were weighed and a tag with the weight was tied to the sack and then it was placed into a very large, refrigerated cooler. All retailers of crawfish have them in coolers. Cold crawfish don't try and move. To store them you must tie the sack tight and keep them as cold as possible without freezing them. If they can move about inside a sack, many will get smashed and die. You do not want this if you are selling or buying crawfish. You must keep them from squirming around as much as possible. After I purchased my three sacks, I wetted down some large beach towels that I had in my truck and placed them over the three sacks for the ride back to League City. It was a very hot and sunny day, and you must keep the direct sun off the crawfish. This will suffocate the crawdads. I used the wet towels because I did not have anything else to cover them with. The towel was almost dry when I got home. Winnie was just too far to go get crawfish without large ice chests and ice or a refrigerated cooler. When crawfish are moved from the grower to be sold commercially, they are always transported in refers otherwise known as refrigerator trucks. This goes for all seafood as well as citrus and vegetables, meats, and most fruits.

Upon arrival at home, I unloaded the sacks into my garage. I wetted down the towels again and placed them over the crawfish. I did this again before I went to bed that night.

We made another trip to Sam's Warehouse and purchased most of the stuff we needed. We got ten pounds of potatoes, five pounds of onions, ten garlic cloves, six lemons, eight pounds of sausage, five bell peppers, forty-eight ears of corn, two boxes of mushrooms, and five packages of crab boil. The other supplies were purchased from Kroger. Things like hot dogs and hamburger patties and the fixings that go with those things. The Sam's hamburger patties were just too large a pack. We ended up letting many of them get freezer burn the last time we had a boil, and I did not want to buy that many and just throw them away later. That is just money wasted and I am a money saver, not a money or food waste.

We started out for our place in the woods early the next day bringing everything with us. I started boiling at about eleven in the morning. Curt and Susan arrived shortly after and gave me a hand until other folks showed up. We had another great time in Sam's Woods. That is short for The Sam Houston Forest which is where our property is located. I made it up - I think.

One of Sarah's co-workers and friend, Sharon Montgomery attended with her husband, Herman. Herman gave me a hand and helped me do the last two pots of crawfish. I like to keep a list of what needs to be done and how many ingredients to add to each batch. Herman noticed me looking at my list. He was outdone. He shouted, Barry, you are from Louisiana, and you have a recipe? Oh no, I cannot believe it, he continued, you got a recipe. I could not deny it. I told him, yea I have a sheet to go by because I may not remember how much of each indigent to add. He just shook his head from side to side and grinned. Did I mention that our friends Sharon and Herman were black? If not, they most certainly were and still are.

By the time I finished the last batch of crawfish, everyone was finished eating for the time being. At a crawfish boil what usually happens is this. The people eat as much as they can then take a break and let the food go down a little and then eat some more later. I have known some folks to eat three or four times in this manner. I went to the table and started pealing and eating some of this good stuff. Ron Sikora got up from his easy chair and joined me. He started eating again.

I had the table, which was a sheet of four by eight plywood, on top of two 35-gallon trash cans turned upside down, placed near the area where I boiled the crawfish. I had plastic and two shower curtains (as tablecloths) over the plywood so as not to ruin it. The guests were sitting in their lawn chairs in a semi-circle about twelve feet away from the table and closer to the house. We had a boom box in one of the windows of the house facing the backyard playing music with a rhythmic beat.

I combined some of the five-gallon buckets that I had around the table for peals and trash into one almost full pail. I ask Sarah's boss's eleven-year-old son to go empty the pail into the hole further behind us. He did and came back, placed the pail by the table, and kept on walking toward where everyone was sitting and talking, I looked at the ground about four feet behind him and saw a rattlesnake slithering along. I was frozen for a couple of seconds. I yelled snake about the same time that Ron did. The snake went right in the middle of the people in the two half-circles. Everyone was just staring at it. I had walked around the table toward the snake but was well behind it. It seemed to be on a straight path toward the boom box which was blaring in the window. The snake went to a trash can that I had near a small tree for aluminum cans to be placed into.

I was thinking about going to get a shovel to attack it with. But before anyone else moved, Herman jumped out of his chair and was on top of the snake before you can say Jack Robinson. He was moving the trash can with one hand and reaching toward the snake with the other. When he stood up he had the rattlesnake by the head or neck just past the head. It had six or seven rattles on it.

While all of this was going on, Sharon, Herman's wife, was over on the side of the house in a hammock that I had tied between two trees for folks who wanted to rest or take a nap. Herman told us that he used to catch rattlesnakes when he was a kid. He showed the kids and us the fangs of the snake by squeezing its head slightly. He told us several other things about the snake. The kids were petting it, which I did not like although Herman had a good grip on it. I just do not think that small kids should pet a rattlesnake under any circumstances.

By this time the crowd had moved closer to the back of the house. Sharon had noticed all the commotion and was trying to lean forward and lift her head up to see what was going on. At this time, I was standing to Herman's left. We were about thirty to forty feet from where Sharon was in the hammock. Herman looked up and saw Sharon lifting her head to see what was going on. I could almost see the light go on above Herman's head. His eyes lit up as well. He just got an idea. He started walking toward Sharon.

Now she was sitting straight up in the hammock and yelling at him to not come any closer. She could now see that he was holding a snake in both hands. Sharon had the hammock rocking back and forth. Her feet could not quite touch the ground. She looked like she was in a swing. About her fourth time swinging forward, her feet hit the ground and she came out of the hammock like a cannonball shot out of a cannon. All the time she was still yelling expletives at Herman. She finally hit a card and he stopped in his tracks halfway to the pump house which is the direction that Sharon was running.

Now, everybody was standing around Herman and the snake. He wanted to know what to do with it. This was only the second snake that I have seen out here. I did not want to kill it, but I could not let a rattlesnake run loose on the place. Not with all these kids around.

Maureen and Ron Sikora's son, Blake, and his friend also named Blake, were there dressed in their camouflage outfits with boots and the whole outfit. They came dressed to go hiking in the woods, which they did. They each had a machete to cut a pathway and any vines that they came across in my woods. Blake and his friend wanted to cut the snake's head off with his machete. Herman placed the snake on the ground as everybody backed away. Blake made a swing at it. He missed. He tried again, but he missed. He tried a third time and missed again. He was pulling back as he swung the machete toward the snake on the ground. I told him that I would kill it.

After Herman had picked up the snake, I retrieved my shovel. I had it with me since that time. I placed it over the snake's head and chump. I cut the head off. You still have to be careful with a dead rattlesnake's head. The eyes and mouth were still moving as was the rest of the snake. I dug a hole in the ground right there and buried the snake's head. The boys wanted the skin. Herman skinned the snake for them and told them how to care for it. I got some old newspaper and Herman had the boys place the skin on the paper and we poured salt over it and coated it well then rolled the paper up tight and tied it with string, Herman wanted to know if I wanted to cook the snake. I said that I would if anybody wanted to eat it. We had no takers. I had heard from my brother and other folks that rattlesnake meat was good eating. It was a white meat. I was not going to fry it if none wanted to taste it. I buried it with the crawfish peals.

Well, this was certainly exciting. I am very happy that nobody got hurt. We all kept our eyes peeled after that. We all were looking down at the ground everywhere we went after that.

Toni Howman was taking pictures during the day. Several weeks later she presented me with a collage of pictures in a nice frame. Most of us. were in the pictures and so was the snake. All three of my sons had departed for Austin, their home before the snake event occurred. They missed out on all this excitement.

We offered the guests crawfish and other leftovers to take home with them when they were ready to leave. We do this at all of our crawfish boils. We always have leftovers. Some folks would take some home and others would not.

We always had several of us peeling all the leftover crawfish and placing the peeled tails in the freezer for later use. I always placed a container of tails in the ice box for use over the next couple of days. I loved making an egg omelet with crawfish tails the next day for breakfast. I might eat that for the next couple of days to use up all the meat not frozen. Sometimes I cook a crawfish etouffee with the tails the next day also. You eat an etouffee over rice. I use the left-over boiled potatoes to make a potato salad. It tastes so good. There is nothing like a cold boiled potato salad and hot crawfish etouffee. Hummm, hummm, good. The next day we cleaned everything up and put it away until next time. We had about 30 folks attend this time.

SARAH GETS LAID OFF IN LATE 1999

Late in 1999, Sarah was notified that she would be laid off from Nova because of the new computer system called SAP. This system was supposed to eliminate the need for Sarah's accounts payables job. I do not think it actually did that but after extending her stay several times she finally was laid off along with her co-worker Sharon Montgomery. As mentioned, because of glitches in the computer system, Sarah was asked to stay on beyond her first departure date. She worked for several months after her original discharge date was announced. Sarah did not mind the continuing moving by Nova of her departure date. This gave her more time to decide what she wanted to do in the future.

After several months of thinking about it, she decided to take the severance package from Nova that would allow her to get a four-year college degree at their expense. Nova's severance package is the best one that I ever heard of. There are seven options. The person getting laid off can choose which one they want. Three of the top options are as follows:

1. A four-year college degree

The laid-off person goes to college full time which means they take at least 12 semester hours each semester. Their books and courses will be paid for by Nova after passing grades are made for each class. The student must pay for all books and classes and submit an itemized list and proof to Nova after the semester is over with the passing grades. Then Nova will reimburse them by check. Also, while the student is in college, Nova will pay them one-half of their former salary during the time that they are in school. They do this for eight semesters or what is considered four years.

After completion, there is no severance pay with this plan.

2. Entrepreneur severance plan

This plan calls for Nova to pay the former employee up to $25,000 to go into business for themselves. They must put a real doable plan together and have it approved by the severance committee at Nova's Corporate office. Nova supplies professional help to the person working up a feasible plan. The former employees will get their severance pay when this plan is approved, and they are severed to begin their new careers. The severance pay was figured at two weeks' pay for every year of service with Nova plus one week for each year of age you are over 55 plus any vacation weeks that you have coming to you. Some folks did very well on this. I know I did. But I had more years with Huntsman than anyone else at our plant.

3. Volunteer work for a non-profit organization

This is a great opportunity to do work for a charitable organization and get paid by Nova for it. The former worker volunteers for an approved nonprofit organization for one year and Nova pays the person one-half of their former salary for 20 hours of work per week. After the end of one year, the former employees will receive their severance payment from Nova. I will have more to say about this plan later in this book.

All of the seven severance plans offered by Nova are offered after your active employee time is over. Nova may continue to pay you but your tenure with them is over. They no longer pay any retirement or 401-k benefit for the employee. They will cover you with medical insurance and deduct the cost from your half paycheck but not for all the plans they offer. It depends upon which severance plan the employee chooses if they will be eligible for the medical insurance or not. I think that it is just great that Nova Chemical has so many plans to pick from.

It was a long haul, but Sarah got her bachelor's degree in early May of 2004. She finished the University of Houston Clear Lake with a 3.89 grade point average and is in an honor society. I am so proud of her, as are her brothers and sisters and sons and stepsons, and aunts and uncles, and everyone else we know. We are very sorry that her mom did not live long enough to see it. Sarah graduated one semester later than she was supposed to because she skipped the spring 2003 semester to become the full-time caregiver for her mom who was fighting cancer at the time. Her mom actually beat the cancer and was cancer-free when she passed in mid-August of 2003. It was a very sad time for all of us who loved Mrs. Griffin. She fought so long and hard, and we thought that everything would be alright. We believe it was a blood clot that took her life.

I thank Nova for giving Sarah the opportunity to continue her college education and for paying for it. They were the worst company that I ever worked for and the best company to leave and not be working for.

MY NERVOUS BREAKDOWN IN 1999

Things were not getting better or easier at Nova, and finally, everything came to a head. I had this feeling of impending doom coming over me. I felt jittery all over. I felt funny inside. I was in my office at about 2 p.m. when it all came to a head. My wife, Sarah, was still working in another wing of this building. I burst out of my office and ran down the hall took a left and went into the men's room. I got into a stall and started crying. I tried to compose myself. I dried my face off and walked hurriedly into the other section of the building and into Sarah's office. As soon as I sat in the chair in front of her desk, I started balling all over again. I told her that I just could not take it anymore. She got up and closed her door and came by me and let me cry on her. We stayed in her office for maybe fifteen minutes or so. I don't remember. She took my hand and said to me - for us to get out of there. She opened the door, and we went out of the back door into the parking lot. We drove around a little until I calmed down and stopped crying. We talked a lot about what I do not remember. After some time passed, we drove to the barbershop where I got my hair cut. We both went in, and I got a haircut. I was feeling a lot better. It was close to four p.m. now. We decided to go home. I do not remember if we went back to the plant to get my vehicle or not. I do not think so.

The next morning, we got up at our usual time and got ready for work. Sarah kept saying that maybe I should stay home. Are you sure that you want to go to work today and things like that? I am going to work was my reply. We were ready by seven a.m. We just sat there and waited. I usually leave by this time. It only took fifteen minutes to get to work.

Sarah just sat there with me. I was in the big wooden rocking chair and rocking back and forth. Sarah was waiting for me to say let's go. Before too long it was seven fifty-five and we had not left the house. She could see the change in my face, and I broke down again and started crying and told her that I just could not go to work today.

Sarah called into work for me and told my team that I would not be in today. She also called our nurse at the plant and notified her as to what was taking place. I did not go in the next day either. Through our plant nurse, Linda, arrangements were made for me to see my doctor. I get in to see him very quickly. Sarah came with me. After the doctor's visit I had several pills to take that would help me to fight depression and make me feel better. Through our nurse, arrangements were made for me to see a professional psychologist. Sarah came with me for the first several appointments. I visited with the psychologist several times a week for eight weeks. Each week I was making progress. I was in denial that I was having a problem at first. Then it came out that Nova was the problem. Then I was the problem. Finally, it was Huntsman that was the problem. They sold me down the drain. They left me for dead. After everything that I did for their family, they did not take me to work for them. I took this harder than I realized at first. I tried to communicate with my friends at work but just could not. I would break down on the telephone. I was seeing my medical doctor on almost a weekly basis. Sarah came along with me for the first several weeks to see my doctor. This went on for a couple of months or so. As I started to feel better, I had steps that I needed to do to keep progressing. I finally got to the place where I called Virg Bodiker and Maureen Sikora (my team) and apologized to them for the added workload that I put on them for not being there. This was very hard to do but I did acknowledge this to each of them. They were very understanding. I talked with my boss in Houston who wanted me to come back to work as soon as I could but not before I was ready.

I think that I missed almost three months of work. My family and friends were very understanding and sympathetic during my trying time. Depression is something hard to explain. My youngest son has bouts with it, and I continue to fight it although I have been off medication for several years. I don't like taking medicine. But this depression medicine really works.

I finally went back to work. A computer system had been put in place and was in use somewhat. The organization was changing over to a new computer system that was going to cost some jobs. No jobs were lost in my group, but other departments were going to lose employees. This is not true. Our department secretary lost her job and another in our group would lose their job later on.

MY STRATOSPHERE STOCK IS NO GOOD 2000

Back in 1993 when my brother and I first went to Las Vegas, we noticed the very large building being built near Vegas World Casino. Bob Stupak, the owner of Vegas World was building the tallest structure West of the Mississippi River right on top of his already large casino. The building was to be known as The Stratosphere. I picked up information on it while in Las Vegas.

After arriving back home, I purchased 300 shares of The Stratosphere stock for about $10.00 per share. Within a year, I purchased another 300 shares for the same amount of money. I also purchased 300 warrants which I lost when I forgot about them, and they expired over time. I had a little over six thousand dollars tied up in this company. Bob Stupak got into financial trouble and had to take on partners. These partners eventually took over the company; then it all went into bankruptcy. This took several years to happen. After hearings and notices and more hearings, I received a letter that the Stratosphere was bankrupt. I forgot about it for several more years. I still had my stock certificates tucked away in a safe place. In early 2000, I noticed the name Stratospheres in the news. This guy, Ichan, pumped many millions of dollars into it and it showed up in the stock market reports. I checked the call letters on my computer. Sure enough, it came up and had a price of over $45 per share. I was elated. Can you imagine what I thought? If you cannot, I will tell you. I thought that after seven years, I had turned my $6000 into twenty-seven thousand dollars. I was walking with a hop in my step and feeling good about it. I checked the stock each day for several months. It would go down to about $41 per share then back to $47 or so. Well, when Sarah was going to get laid off from Nova, they paid for her (and me) to go and see a financial advisor. We did just that. We liked what we heard and signed up with the fellow. I closed out some of my accounts and transferred the money to this guy to manage. We did the same with Sarah's 401-k and IRAs. During this process, we rediscovered my Stratosphere stock. The guy said that he would check to see if my shares were still good. I signed the paperwork for him to do this and sent my shares to him. Over time I got an answer as to the worth of my shares. It was a big zero. My shares were bankrupted and of no value at all. But Mr. Ichan's shares were worth over forty dollars a share. I had in fact lost all shares. My finance guy sent my stock certificates back to me. I still have the worthless pieces of shit papers put away in a drawer somewhere.

Getting this financial guy may have been the worst thing that I have ever done. We have been paying him to lose our money. In the past, I have lost $7000 here and $6000 there, but I have never lost the amount of money that this guy lost for me and Sarah. And I paid him to do it too. I had always saved on my own. And did a fairly good job of it for all those years. I am very conservative. I stated that in all the papers and forms we filled out before this guy took our money to invest. I would prefer to make two percent on an investment instead of a chance to make ten percent if that chance may have cost me money. I don't like to lose or risk my hard-earned money.

I transferred money from fixed annuities getting five percent to him so he could put them into variable annuities. We lost over 45% of our annuity and it is still 40% down. It will never come back to what I transferred to him in my lifetime. A hard lesson was learned. Well, maybe it was not learned since the guy still managed the money we had left and still took his 1.5% per year.

ET & C'D FROM NOVA JULY 2000

I now had the same options that Sarah had almost two years before. I had to decide which of the seven options I wanted to take. I knew that I did not want to go back to school. But I checked out how much money it would mean to me if I did compare it to the other options. And I also had to consider the volunteer option at half my salary plus my severance pay. I was making much more money than Sarah. So, any severance money would mean much more to us. I also had more years of service with Huntsman/Nova than anyone else at this location because I was with Huntsman for three and a half years longer than the other employees when Nova purchased us. Later I had to remind the Nova Corporate folks of this fact. They tried to screw me out of seven weeks of severance pay.

After all was said and done, I decided to do the volunteer severance package. This would benefit us the most financially. I decided to volunteer with the Bay Area Habitat for Humanity in Dickinson, Texas. I took several weeks to get the paperwork done because the Habitat folks had never had such a situation happen before. So, we had to have several meetings and go over what I would be doing put it on paper, and present it to the Nova Corporate folks for approval. We finally completed the paperwork and forwarded it to Nova and missed the Board meeting by a couple of days. I had to wait until the next meeting which was in two weeks. This meant that I would miss a half paycheck for one month which put a little strain on our finances at the time. I was overextended because of lending/giving money to one of my sons and to a nephew to help them out. The following month my plan got approved by the Board for laying off people at Corporate and I started working for the Habitat near the end of July.

The volunteer severance was to work for a maximum of one year of service. It could not be more than that because Nova would not pay for more than one year. Boy, I wished it could. Of course, I could have volunteered longer for no pay. I considered this but we moved from League City to the Cleveland, Texas area just when my year was over. This severance would get me one-half of my pay for one-half of the normal forty-hour work week. To put it another way, I would get one-half of my former pay for volunteering twenty hours per week with Habitat for Humanities. I could put in more hours if I wanted to, and did on many occasions when I only had to but in 20 hours minimum per week.

After completing my year of volunteer work, I would get my severance check from Nova. They sent me a recap of my severance. As I mentioned before, they shorted me by seven weeks or so. They had my start day of going to work for Huntsman wrong. Our retirement and time served with Nova were tied to the years of service we had with Huntsman Chemical. I went to work for Huntsman in Bayport in early 1986. The rest of the folks at this plant came on board in September of 1989. I had almost three and a half years more service with Huntsman than the other folks here.

After I notified the Nova folks of the error with my severance time of service, they corrected it and sent another sheet for me to go over. It looked alright and I gave my approval that it was alright. I was due 42 weeks of severance pay. Nobody else can come close to this number. I bet some of the Nova higher-up folks must have shitted after they saw what I was going to get. I wish I could have seen their faces. I was almost making six figures at the time they laid me off. I had over 30 years of service. During my Huntsman years when I received my promised bonuses, I made well over six figures. Not too bad for a hard-working kid from the sugar cane fields of South Louisiana with only a two-year degree that he received in 1986, huh?

I did all right. But there were many times when I thought that I should be making a lot more for the sixty to seventy hours a week that I was putting in at the office and being on 24-hour call the rest of the time and all those hours spent at the terminal and other locations taking care of Huntsman business working my ASS off to keep all the Huntsman businesses running.

I was trying to finalize my paperwork and get it returned to the folks in Leominster, Massachusetts who were handling all of Nova's severed employees when one of the ladies who handled the severance packages asked if I was going to retire or what. These folks at the location were not Nova employees but were contracted to them to process all the paperwork for all the different severance and retirement packages that Nova offered. It was during our casual conversation that this lady asked if I was going to retire. I told her that I didn't think I could retire. She said, "Aren't you over 55 years old? Yes, I said. Then you very well can retire, said she. I was really pissed off at my boss and the little bastard at the plant in human resources who NEVER mentioned this to me. I had not even considered it. The lady asked what I would do for insurance. coverage. I don't know what to do and I did not think about that.

Well, you should think about it. This office had handled Sarah's severance and knew that she was not paying for any type of insurance whatsoever.

Health insurance will cost you an arm and a leg if you are not covered by a company insurance plan. She suggested that I say that I will retire. I was eligible for Nova's retirement insurance for me, and Sarah and I did not even know it until now. Without medical insurance, we would have been up shit creek without a paddle. I wanted to delay telling Nova that I would retire until after my volunteer year, but I had to declare before July 1, 2001, or I would not get it.

I was so pissed off at Nova representatives for not telling me that I could retire and get medical and dental insurance coverage from them at a reduced cost. I filled out all the new paperwork and called it retired. I did not opt to start drawing it, which was a mistake. I filled out paperwork to roll it over to this financial guy that Sarah and I hired the year that she was laid off. We rolled the money into my IRA, and it was all promptly lost several months later with a lot more of our money. As for the insurance, we still have it, thank God. I used the hell out of it.

I worked with the Habitat for Humanity for one year. When I completed my agreed commitment, Nova sent my severance check to me and washed their hands off me. When you are going through your severance choice, you are no longer a Nova employee. They send you money and take out the applicable taxes and insurance costs, but your time of service has stopped as did any of your funds going into a 401-k, and certainly no matching funds into any savings plan. At the end of your severance choice, you get a W-2 from them stating all the information that W-2s state and then it is over. You are done with them forever or longer.

MY RETIREMENT PARTY

In June of 2000, Nova Chemical Company allowed me to use the lobby of our office building for a small "retirement" party. I was being laid off, but because of my age and years of service, I was able to retire from Nova/Huntsman. This is because of the type of deal that Huntsman had with the Nova folks when they acquired the Company. I was grateful to Nova for letting us use the lobby of our Port Road office to do it here.

Maureen Sikora and Toni Howman were very much involved in setting all of this up. They did a wonderful job along with Sarah and Janie. There were about thirty or so folks invited, I guess. Many of them I had done business with for years. My very good friend, Bill Noak of Shell Chemical Company was the first on my list to invite. Bill and I worked together from my Foster Grant days in Baton Rouge. While I was working for American Hoechst and Huntsman Chemical, he and Shell Chemical were my number one supplier for our raw material, benzene. At one point, they received almost thirty percent of our Bayport's plant production of styrene monomer.

He is my pal. We had other folks from our plant of course and Petro United Terminal my largest terminal. Jerry Tuttle, traffic manager, and Mike McKenny, President of Petro United were there also. I had barge company representatives, one in particular was Jeff Ponthier with Hollywood Marine. Jeff had many years with them, but we worked together even before that when he was with Gulf

Chemical/Chevron Chemical Company and we used to swap/trade styrene monomer with each other.

I had a friend for Petroleum Services, Brian Haymond. His company ran our docks in Baton Rouge and provided tanker man services to load and unload barges for many years. And Justin Mauskjen of Baytank/Terminals and later of Odjfell Tankers, who are tank ship owners.

Several inspection companies' representatives were there. I enjoyed seeing my friends for Unimar, Charles Martin, and Caleb Brett there to see me off. A friend of mine came all the way from Kansas who is with Koch Industries. I was happy that he came that long way. We all had a wonderful time. I just could not believe it, but they all brought gifts. There are a lot of really good folks in this business that I was in.

I would have loved to have a larger place and for more folks to come but we were limited because of lack of space. When people work for over thirty-three years in one industry, they get to know and deal with many people, and more often than not, many of us become very good friends for life. It is a wonderful life.

VIRG BODIKER, JERRY TUTTLE, AND BILL NOAK

ME, TONI HOWMAN, AND MAUREEN SIKORA

TOP: JOHN BEASON, ME, BRIAN HAYMON, AND CHIP HOWMAN

BOTTOM: TERESA SIMON, BILL NOAK, JEFF PONTHIER, VIRG BODIKER AND BILL BISPECK

REBEKAH'S WEDDING
DECEMBER 2000

Alice Jean's daughter, Rebekah, planned a December wedding in Northwest Arkansas. She had attended college there and met the guy there and then decided to get married there. She attended John Brown University in Siloam Springs, Arkansas. It is a small Christian school. This small town was located on the Oklahoma border and about forty miles from Fayetteville, Arkansas. We had a very exciting drive as we neared Northwest Arkansas. There was snow and ice everywhere. Why would anybody pick this time of year and this place to get married is beyond my comprehension. I would never have done it. But that is just me and I do not follow the crowd. I drove my old 1992 Mercury Grand Marque which was now Sarah's mom's car. We made it to the motel where all the out-of-town guests were staying a couple of hours before the wedding party dinner. We barely had time to check in then we were meeting in the lobby to form a convoy to drive 50 miles into Oklahoma to some desolate spot where we were to be served dinner. During the short time we had, I tried to scrape the ice from our windshield but could not do the job with the coin that I was using. I wanted to get some hot water at the motel, but the water pipes were frozen. It was still daylight but was going to be dark in less than 30 minutes. I was really irritated when I could not get any family members to help me with cleaning my windshield. I had a windshield scraper in this car when I gave it to Mrs. Griffin but could not find it now. I bet she threw the damn thing away because she did not know what it is used for. You just don't have to use this sort of tool very often when you live in Texas City, Texas. Perhaps once or twice in ten years would be all. So, who needs it? I do - damn it.

Before I knew it, folks were piling into cars and hitting the road. In our car we had Sarah, Alice Jean, Mrs. Kotter, (Alice's mother-in-law), and in the front was Mrs. Griffin and me, the chauffeur. Rebekah and her to-be husband, Chad, and a few others were in the lead car followed by a number of cars then us. It was getting dark, and I was already having problems seeing out of the windshield. As soon as we got out of the city limits, they gunned it. I was afraid of driving that fast on the ice and snow. Within five minutes, we were all alone on the highway. I was trying to see through the small area that I scrapped with my quarter before we left the motel but it was icing over. The heater and blower in the car were doing nothing to melt the ice buildup on the windshield. Thank God we had directions before we left the motel. We also had the name of a road that we had to turn right on to get to the place we were going to. I had no idea how far up the highway it was. We had to pass through several toll booths and pay a toll. I did not know where in the hell we were. By this time we were in Oklahoma, but where? No one in this car knew. Now there was not even a tail-light in sight.

I drove and drove. I had to pull over on the shoulder and try to scrape ice off the windshield. I just could see one damn thing. I got the ice scraped about seven inches square and could see out of that spot.

After some time on the highway, I decided that we must have past our cut off road and did a U turn in the middle of the highway and headed back from hence we came.

Since there were no traffic on the road, (we were the only fools out here), I drove with my bright lights on. I noticed a road sign on the left side of the highway and turn onto it. In due time we found the place of the dinner. We were late and all seats near Rebekah and Chad were taken by their friends. We had to sit at another long table that had folks with another wedding party. This really sucked for the two Grandmothers of Rebekah as far as I was concerned.

Shortly after we arrived, dinner was served. It was a homemade type dinner. The folks serving looked to be Amish. They prepared and served the dinner and waited at both tables. The parents of the bride and groom used this place because it had the cheapest er, I mean best price.

I do not know how far we drove from the motel in Siloam Springs. It seemed like fifty miles or so. The trip back to the motel was much better and far less exciting than the trip over. At least it was for me. I could see where we were going. I still did not drive as fast as the other folks. I do not like driving on ice and snow. We arrived back at the motel and disbursed to our assigned rooms for a good night's sleep. The next morning, we got up and met family members for breakfast. We then putted around the motel and visited with family and friends of the family until it was time to go to the place where the wedding was to be held.

The wedding was held in the college chapel on campus. It started on time and ended on time. I do not remember anything unusual happening during the ceremony. One young man played the bagpipes during the wedding. A friend of Rebekah's was supposed to play the violin but did not get enough practice time in and she refused to play. The boy did a good job with those bagpipes and did it on short notice too. Although he did not wear the kilts, he did a creditable job.

It was a cold and rainy day. We went to another building for the reception. We stood by and watched the events as they took place. When the cake was cut, we had some cake and punch and had a good time. After the wedding reception was over, we loaded into the car and headed to Alice and Chris's house in Clarksville, Arkansas.

SARAH, MRS. GRIFFIN, AND ME ON THE MOUNTAIN DEC. 2000

After Rebekah's wedding, we caravanned to Clarksville following Alice Jean, Chris, and Christopher (their son), who was in one car, and Ronnie (Sarah's brother), his wife, Judy, and their children, Tiffany, and Joshua, in their car. In due time we arrived in the Clarksville area. We went to Alice's house and dropped off Mrs. Griffin, who was going to sleep there. We then proceeded to Ronnie's house where Sarah and I were going to spend the next couple nights.

For the next several days, we visited with each family at both houses. During the day we drove around the area and looked at houses and property as if we were again thinking of buying something in the area. The nights were spent playing cards, watching home movies, and just watching television at either Alice's or Ronnie's house.

Because of the snow and cold weather, we did not do any outside activities except look at the stars at night. The sky is so clear there that every night one could count and look at the stars.

After several days we were ready to head back home. I checked the map and wanted to try coming home by a different route than in the past. I thought that we could take Highway 103 west to the small town of Ozark and then catch a highway south toward Texas. After we all got into the car, I announced my plan to Sarah and her mom. They said that this was just fine with them. After leaving Alice's house, I took a left on Highway 103 heading west. When looking over my map of the area, Ozark looked to be ten to twelve miles from where we were. So, I figured that we would get there in twenty minutes or less. The state of Arkansas, or the county, or whomever does a great job of keeping the highways clear of snow and ice. This is one nice thing that I noticed while in this area. The local folks get around very well in conditions that would bring traffic to a halt in the Houston area. So here we are driving on a fairly nice highway heading west. Until this day I still do not know what happened. After about twenty minutes, we were in three or four inches of snow in an isolated area going up a damn mountain. What in the hell is this I thought to myself, not wanting to alarm, or let my passengers know that I was lost. I decided to continue to drive a little farther. Surely there must be a town nearby. Because of the conditions, I was going maybe twenty-five or thirty miles per hour. The passage got narrower. I was driving in the middle of the passageway or at least I thought that I was driving in the middle and there was not very much room on either side of me. It now looked like we were on a levee and we could see down both sides of us. The trees were thick and none of them had any leaves on them. I really started to wonder where in the hell we were now. I stopped the car several times to look over the map. But I still could not figure out where we were and neither could Sarah, my co-driver who was riding in the front with me, I think. We were now more than thirty minutes into the trip back home. The slops on the side of the levee we were driving on began to become cliffs. We could not see the bottom from where we were riding. All this time we had not passed a car coming or going or seen any house or anything moving at all. I was already nervous. Sarah wanted me to turn around and backtrack.

I could not find a place that I thought was wide enough to turn around in. Mrs. Griffin, who does not see very well, was enjoying the pretty white snow and the scenery that was all around us. Sarah and I were cutting buttonholes. Let me interject here because you may not know what cutting buttonholes means. Well, it means that our assholes were so tight that they could cut something to perfection like buttonholes. Yes, we were afraid. I also had my asshole so tight that it could drive ten-penny nails into two-by-fours. Now that is tight.

We finally came by a house that was about fifty yards off the road. It was on the built-up ground and had several large sheds that you raised chickens in behind it. There was a ramp that led to the house. There was so much snow I was afraid to try and drive on the ramp/pathway. I stopped on the levee and looked at the house and area for a couple of minutes. We did not see any activity whatsoever. We did not even see smoke coming from the chimney. I thought that it might be abandoned for the winter months. Who in the hell would live way up here anyhow? We could not see any type of tracks in the snow around the place. I was afraid that I would drive off the ramp/pathway trying to get to the house. So, we decided to continue forward.

I took it as good news seeing those chicken houses. That meant that someone raised chickens up here for Tyson Farms. Tyson is the largest chicken grower and supplier in Arkansas. It also meant that folks had driven up here during better weather to get the chickens. And if this was still a chicken business then someone would perhaps find our remains in the Spring after the thaw. I knew that if we went over the cliff on either side of this road none of us was coming back up alive. We would all be gone pecans, a southern saying for dead.

After about fifteen more minutes of driving and worry, Mrs. Griffin made a statement that Sarah and I did not want to hear. She said, "This reminds me of the movie, Misery". Sarah and I looked at each other with grim looks on our faces. Mrs. Griffin was enjoying all this scenery while Sarah and I were scared shitless. The old lady had no idea what the hell we were going through. We tried not to let on to her because she was having too much of a good time for the situation, we were in.

Yea, scared shitless. You know what this means. I will tell you anyway. Scared shitless is when you are so afraid that the only reason you don't shit on yourself is that you forgot you had an asshole.

Look up ahead. There was a large white pickup heading our way. It was a dual pickup truck, I think. I pulled over to the right side as much as I thought was safe to do and stopped. As the guy got near, I pushed the button to lower my window to ask him where in the hell we were. He just drove on by. I could hear his motor revving the engine. It seemed that he was sliding a little. I am sure that he passed within two inches of us. It was very close. I could not believe that he did not hit us, that bastard. Shit, I said as I watched him keep on going from my rear-view mirror.

Within less than a mile here came another big white pickup truck. It was a four-door but not as wide as the other one, thank God. I stopped and had my arm out of the window when they pulled alongside of us. He put his window down. I yelled; can you tell me how far to the next town? He could not hear me. His damn truck was a diesel and making a hell of a lot of noise. He shut off his motor. I asked the question again. He answered that the state highway was about a mile up ahead. He and his passenger were laughing, I must have said something like thank God. I thanked him as he cranked up his truck and pulled off. The two guys in that truck were having a good laugh. When he stopped his truck there was about a foot between us.

This was much more room than the truck before this one. We drove a little farther. I started thinking that those guys were full of shit. We have not seen anything yet. I kept looking in my rear-view mirror to see if they turned around and were coming after us. The hell with this Misery movie, shit, I was now afraid of Dueling Banjos in the Wintertime.

We could see a slight curve to the left up ahead. With all the woods we could not see beyond it. As we were approaching the curve a small white car came toward us. What is this business with all these white vehicles on a damn covered mountain about? It looked like a family of folks in the car. I was waving my arm out of the window before they got to us. I believe that they noticed our Texas license plates as did the other truck that stopped and when they stopped, they were already smiling. I asked how much further to the road. The whole carload started laughing. The guy told us that the highway had just passed the curve up ahead. HOORAY! They were shaking their heads side to side and laughing out loud as I pulled away. As soon as we came around the curve, we could see the state highway. We made a left turn onto it. Right, there was a sign stating fifteen miles to Ozark.

I checked my odometer. I always write down the miles before I start a trip or use a trip meter. The odometer on this car does not work. We started out about eleven miles from Ozark. Drove over thirty miles and were still fifteen miles from there. We arrived in Ozark very quickly. I found the highway that we needed and headed south. After checking the time, I discovered that we spent over an hour and thirty minutes trying to get eleven miles. I was really mad at myself but for only a very short time. I realized how lucky we were to get off that damn mountain alive. And I thanked God again for our safety.

Until this day, I do not know what mountain we were on or how we got on it. We have been back to Clarksville several times since this trip but never bothered to try and retrace our steps or tracks as the case may be to find out how it happened. No, not even during the summertime. And that is all I will say about that.

MY BEING LAID OFF BY NOVA IN JUNE 2001

After a little over a year with Nova Chemical, in mid1999, they decided to reorganize the Corporation again. I was offered the job of distribution something or other. This meant that I would travel to Europe on a quarterly basis to look over the terminal operations. I would be in charge of marine transportation terminal operations and some other stuff like rail car shipments in Canada. My boss gave me several weeks to think about it. I could have told him on the spot what I thought but the extra time was good. This way I could talk it over with Sarah who had already been laid off and was attending the College of the Mainland in Texas City, Texas. We were still living in League City at this time.

After talking with Sarah, we decided that I did not want to become a world traveler by air. I notified my boss of this about two weeks after our original meeting. I was never crazy about flying in the first place. I have flown inside the United States but never over its borders. And at fifty-seven years of age, I did not want to start now. I started enjoying the work that I had been doing for them for the last three years. But this last year and a half with Nova were the pits. I did not like the changes already made by them. I also did not like going without a raise for the last three years that I worked. One of those years was with Huntsman who was trying to sell the company, so he wasn't giving out raises, and two plus years with Nova who thought that I was making too much money for my thirty-plus years of service in this business.

After the nervous breakdown from stress brought on by the Nova acquisition, I did not care to work for them long-term anyway, I really knew when we found out that they were going to buy us that I would not last very long. I did not like the way that they did business and I told them so. But it went in one ear and out of the other. I guess in the final analysis it was to be their way or the highway. They gave me the highway. Which was only one way and that was out of there. After I told Rick Sequin that I did not want the job, he stated that they had a decision to make then about my future with them. I indicated to him to go ahead and make his decision and that I was still not going to quit the company.

Rick got back to me several weeks later and asked me to participate in getting someone else to take my place. He and someone in corporate wrote up a new job description for the new person and the search to fill the position was on. After several more weeks, they had a candidate. He was someone who had worked at Lyondell Chemical and was well familiar with styrene, benzene, toluene, ethylene, and other products that we were involved with. He was also familiar with the storage and transportation of them as well. He was a very good candidate. After another couple of weeks, Rick asked me to contact this guy. He was not saying yes and had some reservations. This guy had worked very closely with the Nova folks running the show in the Kingwood office for years. I had known of him but never worked directly with him during my time at Hoechst or Huntsman because we were not doing any trading or purchasing from Lyondell during the time that he was there. I called the guy to get a feeling for what he was thinking. We rehashed some old-time stories that we were both familiar with and then talked about the direction that Nova was going in the future. We had a good conversation, but I could not get a commitment from him one or another. We decided to talk some more a little later in the month. I notified Rick that he was non-committal and that we would talk again in the next week or so after he got back from a trip.

A week or so later he called me. We were both much more candid about the job duties. He inquired about my past. He had heard of me also but did not know me. He wanted to know why I did not want the job. I was very candid with him. I don't like to fly is the main reason. But another big reason is I have been a hands-on guy in this business for over thirty years. Now they want me to be the boss and travel the world and have/let other folks do what I loved to do. This really struck a chord with him. He told me that he was the very same way. He also loved to roll up his sleeves and get in there and do what it took to make things happen no matter how long it took. Traveling all around the world and going to the required meetings all the time was not for him either. This guy and I were two peas in a pod. I believe we would have made a great team if we ever worked together. Although I had been part of some great teams in the past. Like back in the 1960s and 1970s with my boss, Harvey Bourgoyne. And in the early 1980s with Nell Davis and me and the early 1990s with Brian Parsons and me. And in the late 1990s with Virg Bodiker, Maureen Sikora and me. Those were some good teams.

After, AFTER RAISING SUGARCANE

As we were wounding up our conversation, I mentioned to the guy that he should notify Rick that he did not want the job. He did that the next day. We were all disappointed. They had to start looking for a replacement all over again. Which shickled the tit out of me or another way of saying this, is tickled the shit out of me.

After several weeks two more persons were interviewed. One really looked good in the interviews. He knew what styrene monomer was. He had worked for Dow Chemical for a couple of years. All were impressed with him except Virg Bodiker. But Virg went along with the rest of us when we recommended to Rick to bring him on board so we all could get back to work doing our jobs. In due time he came on board, I was asked to work with him and help train him and give him guidance - which he did not want. He was an asshole from the start.

I was told that I could work on special projects for two years as long as I did deals that saved the company more money than I cost them. I think they wanted to be sure that the new guy, Eric, was thoroughly trained before they turned him loose completely. I tried working with Eric for some months. We traveled and I introduced him to our marine carriers and our terminal operators in Texas and Louisiana several customers and rail car leasing companies a few truckers' inspection company representatives and others, etc.., etc.

This guy had a different type of personality than the rest of the folks in our group. The job had been expanded and now had folks in Sarnia, Canada, and in Europe reporting to him. He spent most of his time traveling and did not want to be back up for Virg and Maureen in the movements of all marine vessels and tank truck and tank car shipments as I did for all the years that I worked. He could not set up a marine vessel to load if the life of the plant depended upon it.

Rick gave me some guidelines as to what kind of savings he expected and where I could try to get some of them. We put a computer program together to compile and accumulate the totals. I had about nine categories. I started with Petro United Terminals and renegotiated several items and eliminated testing four storage tanks every day and a number of other items that saved us many thousands of dollars each month. I got discounts from inspection companies barge cleaning plants repair shops and the terminal in Louisiana, and barge transport companies as well as others.

I was making Nova money. I had to issue weekly reports to Rick who looked them over and added my numbers to a master list for Corporate to see. I was also working on several major projects and helping other team members with problems. My big project was making a booklet on the polymer problem on barges and how to identify a suitable barge to load. This booklet also identified all the equipment and gave the definition of the usage of such. It came with pictures and everything. It took many months to complete and many trips to the barge cleaning plants climbing into barge compartments and taking pictures while doing inspections of such. After over thirty-one years of hiring and shipping barges, I was finally finding out what made them tick. Of course, many new apparatuses were added to styrene monomer barges after the Coast Guard regulations changed to include them in the enclosed loading rules. Equipment like enclosed gauging and sampling devices, high-level of liquid alarms, emergency cutoff automatic valves, etc. I had not finished one year of my two-year assignment when Rick and Eric took me out to lunch and dropped the bomb on me. I was informed that they would let me go a year sooner than he said. This was a little hard to take but what could I do. I had a lot of plans to work and spend the money on our place in the country in that last year that I was going to work for Nova. Well, that all went by the wayside. I was planning on using part of my full-time salary to do great things for the country house and property. Well say la vee say the old folks- it just goes to show you never can tell what will happen.

I had about two months to decide which severance plan I wanted to be served with. This goes back to what I said about the folks earlier in these writings. I just did not trust them and did not like the way that they did business. They certainly did not keep their word with me.

HOT RODING
WITH JAMES IN 2001

Sarah and I was visiting with my relatives in south Louisiana. We went to visit my sister and brother-in-law in Addis. They are Bobbie Jo and Gene Bertrand. Two of their six kids live next door to them. They have two girls and four boys. David, their third son lived around the corner toward the back of their house. He usually cuts across the yard in the back fence area which is a shortcut to get into his mom and daddy's yard. James, their second son lives next door. Gary, the oldest son lives on Bayou Plaquemine about ten miles away. Mark, the youngest of all the children, lives in Corpus Christi, Texas. The first two born are girls, Carol Jo the oldest, and then Windy Gale, my godchild, was the second born. Both girls live in the Holden, Louisiana area.

Since James was a young teenager, he worked on and owned hot old cars. He liked fast cars. As a teenager, he worked on one car for years and had it looking and running great. He went to a tractor-pull truck show in Baton Rouge and his car was stolen from the parking lot when he was attending the show. The police never did find his car or any trace of it. He never was compensated for his loss because he was not insured. In those days you did not have to purchase auto insurance. Jim lost this car forever. He speculated that it was pulled up inside one of the large vans that were there participating in the program. What a bunch of damn crooks.

After, AFTER RAISING SUGARCANE

Not long after Jim got another car. Over the years that followed he stripped it down to just a shell. As he got money, he had work done on the new project. What he could not do he paid other folks to do.

Jim should write a book on the circumstances that led to him getting this car project going and the trials and tribulations of building his second car which is an old 19-something Trans Am. This one took him over five years to get it to where he wanted it to be.

On different visits over the years, I would check on the progress of the car. There were a number of times I looked over the car when Jim was not available. For years he stored it and worked on it when he could at his dad's shed. So, on visits to see Gene and Bobbie, I would check to see if anything more was done on the project.

On this trip, Sarah and I walked over to his house. He was outside working around in the yard. He showed us his car. He had it almost finished. It only needed some work on the interior to complete it. He said let's go for a ride. Sarah and I said o k. Sarah got in the back seat. I got in the front with Jim. He cranked it up. It ran great. He had a four-speed on the floor. Everything on this car had been completely rebuilt. He drove out of the subdivision and went on a blacktop road through the sugar cane field nearby. We came to Sid Richardson Road. This was a blacktop road that went from La. #1 for two or three miles to get to the plant.

There was no traffic out there on this day. There is never much traffic on this road unless you are going to or from the plant. As soon as he made the right turn onto Sid Richardson Road, he opened it up. Our heads lurched forward and then backward as he hit the gas. I could hear and feel the power of the engine. Before we knew it, we were cruising along at 110 mph when Jim shifted into third gear. Since we were not ready for this, our heads bopped back and forth again. The car jumped when he shifted into third gear and hit the gas. Then he shifted into fourth gear. I was holding on and did not notice what the speedometer was showing but I know that this was the fastest that I ever went in a car in my life.

We came to a stop and turned around in the middle of the road. On the way back Jim wanted to show us how well the stabilizers worked. We took a slight curve in the road at about 90 mph and made a left-angle turn at about 45 mph. This car was very stable. It did not swerve or sway at all. I told Jim that. I had enough and we could head back to his house. I was hoping that we made it without running out of gas. We left his house empty and returned empty. He never did tell me but perhaps the gas gauge was not working properly. He still has some work to do on this car. Sometime after our ride, he purchased two other old Trans Ams that he hopes to rebuild someday. On a later visit, when I asked him why he purchased the cars now when he still had some work to do on this one, he said that they were available at that time, and he could not take the chance that they would be available when he was ready to work on them. Other folks in the area are into restoring the older Trans Ams also.

JACOB'S FIRST WEDDING MAY 2001

While attending college at North Texas State University in Denton Texas, Jacob met this girl at the Local Church he attended. They were both members of this church and became close friends. This friendship grew and sometime past a year later, they were planning their wedding. The wedding was planned for May in the year of our Lord 2001 in a small-town Northeast of Denton. They got a leading Brother in the Local Church to marry them. All the attendants were their friends from the church and family members.

Sarah, her mom, and I rode together to attend the wedding, Sarah and I and Jake's dad paid for the rehearsal dinner which was held in Fort Worth with family, friends, and other guests the day before the wedding day.

Sarah's sister and her family came from Arkansas. Sarah's brother from Fort Worth and his family also attended. It was a really nice wedding. Everybody had a good time and had a lot of fun at the reception which was held in the same hall that the wedding ceremony took place in. We spent two or three days in the area then departed for Clarksville, Arkansas.

Alice Jean, Sarah's sister rode with us back to her house in Arkansas. Her husband, Chris, and son went to visit his brother in the town of Granbury which is west of Fort Worth for a couple of days.

Jacob has been going to college in Denton since the fall of 1999. This is the year that he graduated from Crowley High School in Crowley, Texas. which is near Fort Worth. Sarah and I made a number of trips each year up there to visit with him. Jake was very much involved with the Local Church during these days and years. His involvement was such that during his first two years in college he lived in one of the church's houses. The cost was less than a dorm or an apartment and this helped us financially. We were also happy that the brothers from the Local Church were also involved with all the kids that lived in their houses. There were regular meetings and gatherings. The kids had to live up to certain standards to be allowed to live in a church house. We liked this aspect of the arrangement.

For some time, we had been making plans to attend Jake's wedding then go to Arkansas, then also visit Branson, Missouri. I had exchanged my week in Lake Conroe Texas with my timeshare for a week in Kimberling, Missouri to visit Branson and see the sights.

While on this trip I started getting some tightness in my chest area on and off. I was thinking that it was indigestion or my reflux acting up on me. I had been having a reflux problem for the past several years at this time.

TRIP TO ARKANSAS AND MISSOURI MAY 2001

From the motel in Pilots Point where Jake was married, we made it down to Denton and then East of Denton. We made our way to Interstate 20 and headed East toward Fort Smith, Arkansas, and ultimately to Clarksville where Alice Jean lived. It must have taken us about eight hours to make the drive to Clarksville from Denton, Texas.

We were all happy to arrive at Alice's house and planned to have a good night's rest. For the next couple of days, we drove around and saw the sights in the Clarksville area. We looked at houses with property for sale in the area. After a couple of days, we were ready to go to our timeshare near Branson, Missouri. We were going to drive up and bring Mrs. Griffin with us. Alice was to drive up and meet us a day or two later. On the appointed day we departed Alice's house in the morning hours for Kimberling, Missouri.

MRS. GRIFFIN AND I WALKING DOWN THE DAMN STAIRS

We arrived in the late afternoon. This facility was on a damn mountain. We knew that we would have problems with Mrs. Griffin having to walk so many steps. I tried to get a different condo at the office but was not successful. There was no such thing as a ground-floor condo at this facility. The one we stayed in had about forty steps to get to from the top and seventy-five steps to get to from the parking area at the bottom. So, I let Mrs. Griffin and Sarah off at the top to go to open the door and then drove to the bottom to park the car. I started carrying our luggage up to the condo. I had to make several trips. I started having more chest pains throughout this ordeal. I still had not figured out what these pains really were. We spent three or four wonderful days there visiting Branson each day. Alice came up a day or so later and we really had fun after she arrived. We took in some sites and even had our picture taken in a 1957 Chevy convertible. All four of us in the front seat no less. We sat on stools. in a certain position. The girls took the picture and then placed us in the 57 Chevy with a computer program. It was a really cool deal. I was driving- of course. I believed we took in a show or two but at this time of writing, I cannot remember what or who we saw. Maybe it was too soon ago that we did this trip. If it was longer ago, I may remember. Perhaps in ten years, I will be able to recall what we did on this trip. My short-term memory is not as good as my long-term memory or so I'm told.

After a few days there, Alice and her mom headed back to Clarksville. Sarah and I stayed another day or so. I have yet to stay seven days at my timeshare. The most time that I ever used was four days. I just lost the other days. When we left, we went and visited with our friends, Mike and Denise Fields who live in Fairfield Bay, Arkansas. This is a really pretty part of Arkansas. Fairfield Bay is a retirement community in the mountains situated on the edge of Greers Terry Lake. Greers Ferry Lake is a manmade lake of just over 100,000 acres of surface water. It is a huge and beautiful lake. We go visit with Mike and Denise almost every time we travel to Arkansas. They are fun to be around and with. They live about two and a half hours from Alice's house in Clarksville.

While working for Huntsman Chemical Company, Sarah, and Denise became good friends. After Sarah and I married, we all became friends in Seabrook, Texas. Mike was working at the Phillips Chemical plant in Pasadena, TX when an explosion occurred. He was injured badly. He eventually received his disability and after they traveled around awhile, they moved to Fairfield Bay, Arkansas where they built a house.

MIKE AND DENISE FIELDS

We spent one night in Fairfield Bay then headed back to Clarksville. After one night in Clarksville, we prepared to come back home. I set the agenda. The time I wanted to be on the road so I/we would not have to drive at night. We planned to drive straight through without a Sleepover. Well, Mrs. Griffin had her own agenda and was not about to get herself ready to depart in a reasonable amount of time. She piddled and fumbled around so much that I made several trips to her room to see if she needed help. I wanted to take her damn giant suitcase to the car. I was getting impatient since we were now over an hour behind my scheduled departure time. She got aggravated with me and shouted for me to leave her alone. I shouted back for her to get her ass in gear-so to speak. Now she could not remember if she took her damn pills or not. Now she was upset, and I was upset. She fumbled around to try and figure out which medicine she took and which she did not take. And it was all my fault for rushing her. I got the news. This lady has not been rushed in her life and was not going to be rushed by me or nobody else. She was the damn boss and wanted to be sure that everybody knew it.

We finally departed. I drove the whole way. I had chest pains off and on but damn if I was going to show it or stop driving to take a break or let anyone else drive. I was in charge of the trip. Well, maybe I fooled myself into thinking that I was in charge. I did not talk very much, which is really unusual for me. I only talked when asked a direct question. I was pissed off the whole day and then some. It took us eleven hours to drive straight through. I only stopped for gas, and we ate while riding - I think. Oh, yes, I had to stop a couple of times so they could pee. I drove in the dark for the last hour or two. I did not like it one damn bit. We made it in one piece. I unloaded the car and then went to bed without much conversation. My chest was bothering me. I could feel the stress and tension in my body. I do not remember how I slept that night. But if it was the way I usually sleep, I did not get much. I usually wake up five or six times each night. I guess that is good enough because it means that I go back to sleep four or five times per night. As time went on, I started communicating with Mrs. Griffin again, and everything was alright- almost. One thing that I like about Mrs. Griffin is that she could blow up at you and get over it quickly. I did not know her to carry a grudge. I wish that I could be like that. There is much more than this one thing that I like about Mrs. Griffin. It may take another book though to tell it all.

MRS. FRIEDA GRIFFIN

WORKING FOR HABITAT FOR HUMANITY

As part of my E C & T from Nova Chemical Corporation, I volunteered to work for the local Habitat of Humanity branch in Dickinson, Texas. Their house-building location was just a few miles from my League City home.

The deal was that I had to put in twenty hours of work a week with Habitat and receive one-half of my former salary from Nova for one year from my start date. After the year was over, I would receive my severance pay and would be done with them and they would be done with me except for my health insurance.

Habitat shared a house trailer as an office with another unrelated charity. There was one lady working part-time for Habitat taking care of expenses and doing all the paperwork required of an organization such as this. She had a small storage room next to her office. We made room for me in storage room. I did not need much space to operate in.

I started working for Habitat in July of 2001. while in the office I would spend my time looking, and researching for property for Habitat to acquire to continue building houses in this area. I decided to go to entities that collected taxes throughout Galveston County. I would research Sheriff's sales and other tax-delinquent properties that may be available at auction.

In many cases, I drove to the property in my car and looked it over.

On Wednesday and Saturday, I went out to the building site and swung a hammer. A volunteer group under a construction leader did all the building of the houses. There was a group of older men who were known as the framers. They really knew how to work together to get the frame of the house up in a short time. These houses are well put together. Everything is braced and re-braced. These houses are built to withstand a hurricane with winds over one hundred forty miles per hour. This is really good.

I worked on everything involved with building the houses. As one house was being completed, I would work with the layout man on his day of choice. The plot of land that we were building on had room for about five or six more houses. This volunteer group builds four houses a year or more. So, acquiring additional land was always a priority. On laying out the plat, I would walk out the tape measure so far and place a stake in the ground. After we had a square, so to speak, the boss would double-check the measurements then we tied a thick twine from one stake to another until we surrounded the square. We would measure off the walkway, porch, driveway, and place for the air conditioner/heater unit, etc., etc.

All the houses were set back from the street at an equal distance. All houses were uniform and in a straight line. Porches were alternated from left side to right side of every other house so as not to have porches on the same side of a house that was side by side.

There were only a few designs for houses. A two, three or four bedroom which was a little larger but not very much. The four bedrooms had a smaller living and bedrooms. All houses had two bathrooms. All Habitat houses came completely furnished with appliances bathroom fixtures and all lighting. When completed, they were in move-in condition. All appliances were brand new and came from the manufacturer. All that was needed was furniture. In some cases, furniture was included. So, folks who turned down certain items could pick an item that they wanted, and it would be included in the house.

As already mentioned, all Habitat houses were built by volunteers. All appliances were donated by large companies. Some of the labor to build was supplied by inmates or juveniles working off fines or sentences. This was a very good program and taught young fellows a trade in the process.

One had to qualify for a Habitat house first. You had to be poor and have a regular income. Applications were filled out for a house. Many questions were asked. One of the jobs that the lady who worked in the trailer had to do was check and follow through on all applications. Folks who lied or otherwise were cheating, were disqualified from ever getting on the house list. The approved waiting list for a home was very long. There were always folks waiting for a house. All that I know about were black or Hispanic.

One of the great things about Habitat was a person could get a ninety thousand-dollar house for less the forty thousand dollars. Six hundred dollars a month for a normal purchased house would be less than two hundred fifty for a Habitat house. One could NEVER get a house and then sell it for a profit. This stipulation was in the contract. You also must keep the property up. Cut the grass, pick up trash, no junk cars, etc., etc. Habitat did not build garages with their houses.

They built living space only. A storage shed was built in every back yard.

One of the main requirements besides an income to pay the note was the requirement of SWEAT EQUITY in your/or another house being built.

One had to put in many hours of work on a Habitat house. Their work was monitored and kept up with by the foreman and the lady in the office. If you were infirm and could not work, other members of your family and friends could volunteer to work for you. This meant participation by many folks on a project.

During the year that I worked, one HABITAT home couple got into a bad car wreck. When they finally settled with the insurance company, they received a large settlement. They purchased a larger house elsewhere.

Before they could sell their Habitat house, they had to contact Habitat to give them the first choice of getting the house back. Habitat took the house back. They repainted everything, replaced all the appliances with brand new ones, and offered it to the next person on the list. Most of the time, some beggars ARE choosers. They did not want this house; they wanted a brand-new house. In this case, there was a plan. If you do not take this house - we will give it to the next person on the waiting list and you will go to the BOTTOM OF THE LIST. If this is the case, it will take years to get a new house. I do not remember for sure, but I think they took the house.

Another very important thing that the lady who worked in the office did was to keep up with all the homeowners and their payments for their houses. Like who was up to date, who was behind, how far behind in the notes, etc. She had to send out registered letters to the owners who were way behind on their notes.

One of the things that I did while working there was to attend the Habitat board meetings once a month. The lady who worked in the office did that also. The meetings were held in a local church meeting room at night. No, no meals or drinks were served. Just as every other organization, every chapter of Habitat had a President, Vice President, Secretary, Treasurer, someone to write minutes of the meeting, etc. Each committee leader would give an update on their committee actions for the past month.

The lady was the only employee making a wage. I was on a special program, so I was not a voting board member. She got paid when she went, and I got three or so hours credit toward my twenty hours per week. She had to give the board a rundown of all the business. I gave the board an update on the information that I was getting searching for property that may be available in the area.

I could talk with the property owner and even negotiate with them, but I could not close a deal. This was for the board to decide. The treasurer would give their report. The money donations were really good for us and Dickinson was in great shape financially. At the meetings were other chapters from Texas City, who had a shit pot full of money, LaPorte, Alvin, and maybe one more.

The Alvin chapter had plenty of money also. Habitat National had a problem with the Alvin chapter. They were building brick houses. Beautiful brick houses. They had a donation of mega bucks and enough land for a subdivision in the City of Alvin. They had requirements to meet because of the city. The donation of land and money stipulated that they must build brick houses or not maintain ownership of the land or money. This was a violation of Habitat for Humanity's National by-laws. They were to build good quality WOOD houses and not anything as expensive as brick houses. At the time when I finished my year, Alvin representatives were not attending the monthly meetings and the talk was that Habitat National was going to expel them from the organization. In other words- kick them out. I think that Alvin was planning to go it alone. I cannot blame them. They had most of what you need to make it work. They would have to get donations of building materials, appliances, and everything else to make a go of it. They had a great supplier of bricks already and all the volunteer workers they needed. Hell, Mr. Baseball, Nolan Ryan who owned half of Alvin could have handled that by himself. I do not know for sure if Nolan helped with this, but I think that he and Ruth, his wife, would have.

I finally found some property across the street from where we were building houses. This property would give us enough room to build twelve more houses when the current plots were filled. I negotiated with the lady who owned the land, and it went quite well. She came down on her original price a bit because of the good that Habitat was doing in the area. At our next board meeting. I had everything pretty much settled and turned it over to the officers of the chapter. The deal was soon completed, and papers signed, and I was running the paperwork to Galveston to be placed into the proper records files.

There was a large section of property across the street from the houses already occupied. This land was owned by New Mexico Power

Company. IT was their right of way for the large utility poles and electric lines supplying the city of Dickinson with energy. I could envision a very large park for the kids in this area. I met several times with the local Managers of New Mexico Power about this subject matter. I had great success. They thought it would be great publicity for them. Hell, they would have furnished all the playground equipment and upkeep as well.

I felt really good when I brought this up to the board in our next meeting. But the timing was just bad. There was much talk in the news lately about high-power lines causing cancer and everything else under the sun. So, the board poo-pood it. In other words, they shot it down. It would not have cost us one red cent. But that is the way it goes. I called the folks at the electric company and thanked them for their time and efforts and explained that it was a no-go.

One of the first things that I noticed when I started at Habitat was, not long after a new family moved into a house we built for them, the old raggedly ass car they had when they moved in was gone. In the driveway was a newer and sometimes brand-new car. As you drive down the street in front of the Habitat houses almost all houses have a new car, SUV, or pickup truck parked in the front. I talked with the lady in the office about this. She had noticed this also. She started checking her files just to see who was behind on their house payments. I did not find out if there was any correlation there. But what was happening here is the folks saved so much money on the house payments compared to the rent they were paying before that they had this EXTRA money. They were also saving on electric and gas bills because of the newer energy-efficient appliances and the insulation in their house. My guess is that they were saving three to five hundred dollars a month. Well, what would you do with this extra money? Why buy a new car of course? Save it- hell no-are you crazy. We gonna get a new car. If we try to save it the government might want it. We cannot have that shit happen. I happen to agree with that part.

This situation was brought up at our next board meeting. Before long the whole Habitat organization was working on having classes training new would-be homeowners on finances. I think that they would have to make it mandatory to get these folks some of the training needed to take care of their finances. I departed there before they got the program started. But I do know that they had professional finance people getting lined up to have classes.

Working with the Habitat folks was a great experience for me.

Can I build a house now? HELL NO. Can I build a shed now? Same answer. I can drive a nail into a soft piece of wood, sometimes.

MEMORIAL WEEKEND
HEART ATTACK

Two weeks after the Arkansas/Missouri trip, Sarah and I were spending the weekend at the place. We were working in the yard raking and burning leaves in the yard all morning. I was not feeling well at all. Sarah helped me get into the house. I sat on the sofa in our living room. Sarah asked if I wanted her to go into Cleveland and get some Rolaids. I never answered her.

She almost left several times but did not. The pain was getting worse. Now my arms and checks were hurting as well as my chest. I could not rest on the sofa and was trying to lay on the floor. Sarah hurried to me and grabbed a hold of my arm. I could not get up by myself. We made it to the truck and Sarah drove toward the Cleveland hospital that was about thirteen miles away. I was hurting the whole way. It even hurt when I took a deep breath.

I had been burning limbs, leaves pine needles, and cones since the early morning hours, so I was really dirty and smelly. I had on an old tee shirt and black jeans that I cut the legs off with scissors. I was all sweaty and smelled like smoked leaves and worse.

Sarah droves right into the emergency room entrance area. She helped me walk into the emergency room. I sat in a chair with other folks waiting to see a doctor while she went and talked with a person who took down the insurance information. Within a minute I heard on the loudspeaker the following announcement. Attention doctors:

We have a 58-year-old male with severe chest pains. Within seconds I was taken into this room nearby. A doctor and two helpers started hooking up things to me. I took off my tee shirt. After the guy told me to take my shirt off, I was reluctant to raise my arms over my head. He repeated several times to take my shirt off. I remembered my old boss and friend, Harvey Burgoyne, telling me that he watched as a doctor attending to his brother who had a heart attack had him raise his arms so he could pull his tee shirt over his head and Harvey's brother died on the spot. The stress from raising his arms over his head gave him another heart attack and he died suddenly. Although I wanted to still think that I was having a case of severe reflux. I did not want to raise my arms above my head just in case. The guy nurse told me again to take off my shirt NOW. So, I did and thank God I did not die. I was feeling bad about not being cleaned up the way one usually does before he goes to see the doctor.

Now they had monitors hooked up to me. The doctor had his back to me. I told him that I think I was having a severe case of acid reflux. His response was, Mr. Raffray, you are having a heart attack. I almost shitted right then and there on the table. I did not want to hear this. Not now. Not today. Not any day. I had too much to live for. I had not accomplished anything yet. I was still waiting for God to lead me so I could accomplish something great for Mankind and Womankind. There is no way that this could be a heart attack. But alas it was.

Now they had an I V, going into my arm and a drip of some kind going into my hand and other gadgets hooked up to me. Before long I could not feel the pain anymore. I thought that this was good, and I should be able to go home soon. I became very cold inside my body.

The stuff that they were putting into my arm or hand, or both were making me shiver on the inside from the coldness. I announced to him that I was very cold. I was covered with a hot blanket. It felt so good. But I was still cold. They put another hot blanked on me and continued to do things around me. They were scurrying all around me. Sometimes as many as four folks doing things around me. I asked for another blanket and got it post haste. I remember all too well the freezing and shivering from inside my body. I was not feeling cold on the outside but my insides were damn cold. I had never experienced this before. I do not recall if I had three or four blankets covering me when I asked for another. I was informed that another one would do no good. I guess I already had the maximum that could be handed out at one time.

Those warm blankets really felt good.

They started inducing nitroglycerin into my veins. I started to react to it. I felt very bad and was losing consciousness. I told them so. I heard someone say, his blood pressure is fifty over thirty. I yelled; I was passing out. Someone yanked the I V from my arm or hand and stopped the flow. My blood pressure started going up again. I became more alert. Then they placed a pad on my chest. I thinks it was the same medicine as was in the I V. It was supposed to absorb into my system this way. I started fading again.

I was passing out again. I again heard the announcement of my blood pressure being down to fifty over thirty again. Then someone pulled the patch from my chest. My color came back, and my blood pressure went up. The doctor said to try such and such. I do not remember what it was that they tried but it worked. He stabilized my blood pressure and got a good pulse rate from me. I asked the doctor why I was allergic to the other stuff. He said that I was not allergic but that I just had a reaction. Duh! It seems like the same thing to me. I never did get a satisfactory answer to my question.

I was in the Cleveland Regional Hospital for about two hours after they stabilized me. They made arrangements with Saint Luke Hospital in Houston to take me as a heart patient. The Cleveland Hospital did not have the proper facilities to handle heart cases. I thanked the doctors and nurses several times for stabilizing me before I was transported from there. When the two girls came to get me in the ambulance to transport me to Saint Luke, I saw my doctor outside taking a smoking break. He was about five feet six inches tall and well over 200 pounds with a heavy beard about six inches long. I thanked him again.

During the time that they were working on me, Sarah droves back to the place. She had to put out the fires that we left burning and make some telephone calls notifying my sons and family and her family members about my situation. She left a message for Jacob and his wife whom we expected in, to go to our house in League City and spend the night. For some reason we had gone to our house in the woods in separate vehicles. We each had our trucks there. Perhaps Sarah had class to attend and came up a day or so later than we - but I just do not remember for sure. Anyway, Jake's coming down for the holiday really helped because Sarah made arrangements with him to drive my truck back to our home in League City where she met with them later.

Sarah made it back to the Cleveland Hospital well before the ambulance arrived to take me to Houston. I kept telling her that I loved her. I did not know how much damage was done or how much time I had left on this earth, and I wanted her to know how I feel about her.

Sarah told the two ambulance attendees that she would follow us to Saint Luke Hospital in Houston which is about sixty miles from Cleveland. The girls placed me in the back of the vehicle on a stretcher and strapped me in and latched the stretcher down on its wheels and took off. And I do mean took off. This seemed like a three-hour ride. I was vibrating and shacking all over that stretcher. I was scared to death the whole time. I thought that the driver was going over a hundred miles per hour. She was doing seventy-five to eighty is what Sarah told me later because she had to go that fast to keep up with the ambulance.

We finally pulled into Saint Luke's. Sarah had to find a place to park. When Sarah got into the emergency room receiving area, she found me and the girls in a hallway against a wall. It seemed that we were there for almost one hour before they processed my paperwork and let the ambulance drivers go. Shortly after that, they wheeled me into a room where we waited to see a doctor on duty. I was sent to a ward where heart patients go before procedures are done on them. Before long a young doctor working in the emergency section of the hospital came to talk with Sarah and me. He explained some things to us about the conditions of the heart. He answered all our questions in a calm and direct manner. He really put me at as much ease as I could be put under the circumstances. He also said that since this was the first day of a long holiday weekend, I would have to probably wait until Tuesday to find out what procedure would be performed on me to see how much damage had taken place. All of the doctors were off except one and all of the service personnel who assisted the doctors were off for the holiday as well.

As it turned out I did not have to wait that long. The next day in the early morning a six-foot-six-inch doctor with a large white cowboy hat came through the curtains and into my room. He had both hands on his hips and looked around the room, grabbed my chart from the foot of my bed, and stepped back out to see the nurse on duty without muttering a word to me.

He looked like Cheyenne Bodie of the old TV western series from the 1950s and '60s. Cheyenne was a good-looking, rugged, big cowboy who rode this horse about the countryside doing good for folks who needed good done for them. He was played by the actor Clint Walker. This doctor reminded me of Cheyenne Bodie.

The doctor came back into my room and told me that his name was Dr. Card, and he was a Cardiologist and that he was the ONE on duty for the holidays. I said something like I guess I will have to wait until Tuesday before I know what is going on with me. He said, not unless you want to, I can get a team here in two or three hours. I told him that it would be alright with me to do so.

This all happened before Sarah had arrived in the morning. When she came, I told her that I met Dr. Card and that he was going to do something today. We just waited to hear back from him.

I do not remember what time was that I was wheeled into the small operating or whatever it was called room where the procedure would be done on me. Beside Dr. Card, there were three other persons in there. I think one person left after he shaved my groin area. I was really careful not to move at all while this procedure was going on. That left Dr. Card and two others to do the other procedure.

He was going to take a look at my insides. I had already signed all the necessary paperwork for open heart surgery if that was necessary and/or any other procedure deemed necessary. I watched on a TV screen as he sent this wire up into my blood vessels from the inside of my right leg. It was really weird. He would tell me and the others what he was doing and what we were seeing. I saw two major blockages and a partial blockage. He then ran a balloon or something that pushed open the vein a little in the more important blockage and then placed a stint into that area. It had about a seventy percent blockage. He said that I could get along without the other vessel which was about eighty percent blocked. That I did not need it so he left it alone and it would completely block before too long. I think he ballooned the thirty percent blockage and said that there was no need to place a stint in it. All of my partial blockage was on the side of my heart that did not have my main arteries. I was very lucky indeed. To think that I have been having chest pains for almost a month and did not do anything about it until now. He then put another stint in there somewhere. I've got two stints. It just shows to go you.

I had started taking blood thinners in the Cleveland Hospital emergency room and continued when at Saint Luke Hospital. I went through the procedure with flying colors and felt alright about everything, except. They have the harness thing that they strap around your lower body and draw the straps really tight. It is designed to cover the spot where the doctor cut the inside of your thigh and inserted the wire thing to check for blockage in the blood vessel. The blood is now thinner, so this apparatus was placed there to put pressure on the incision and keep it from bleeding. Well, the damn nurse that first put this contraption on me pinched my skin on my inner thigh. It really hurt and I complained about it to each nurse on every shift for the two and a half days that I was in the heart ward.

None of them would undo the strap and reposition the damn contraption. I am told that they normally take really good care of you in the recovery room here. This was my only complaint except for the nurse that had an attitude. She was a minority of some sort and carried a chip on her shoulders.

Just before I was released from the hospital, they removed the contraption, and I had a large blood blister where it pinched my skin on my lower belly. This spot hurt me for two more weeks and took over a month to heel after the cut had long been healed. Then the dead skin peeled off and it took a long time for new skin to look normal again.

After about two or three months, I had a follow-up appointment with Dr. Card at his regular office. I went with a lot of excitement and wanting to hear that I was doing good and to thank him again for what he did for me. After sitting in the waiting room for an hour, the helping nurse took me to a room to await Cheyenne Bodie er I mean Dr. Card. After another half-hour or so, this guy with an all-white smock or coat type thing came into the room. He was dressed like a doctor. He was about five feet nine or so. This is shorter than me. He looked to be about 200 pounds. A little heavy for his height. He was BALD HEADED. He put out his hand and said, "Hi, I am Doctor Card." I almost shitted right there. What in the hell happen to the Cheyenne Bodie look alike guy. This guy had changed one hell of a bit in just two or three months. How can that be? Boy, what really bad genes. I could hardly believe my eyes. I may have missed some of what he said because of the problem I had believing this was the real Dr. Card. Oh, I was also disappointed in his handshake. It was kind of wimpy. But I do realize that this guy had to protect his right hand. And I did appreciate that because that right hand may have helped to save my life. This thought made me feel very good about him.

I went on a strict diet when I got home. Only nonfat food for me from now on. I lost a little more than twenty pounds and kept if off for almost a month. Over the months when you think that you are going to live, you start going back and eating the same old shit that caused your problems in the first place. The majority of folks revert back to their old ways and either have further heart problems or die from them before very long. I really want to eat better just as everybody else does that went through this sort of thing. It is just hard to do.

There was no heart damage is what I have been told by several doctors that I've seen. I feel very good about that. If I could get rid of this damn severe reflux and not have to take that purple pill every damn day, I would be much better off. I am only taking three medicines related to my heart problem at this time. I started out taking six different medicines. I am doing OK.

BEING SEVERED
BY NOVA IN JULY 2001

As we were approaching the end of June 2001, my time working at the Habitat for Humanities was coming to an end. My one year of working 20 hours per week for one-half of my former salary was about to come to an abrupt end. I did enjoy my time there very much. I was also enjoying being paid for being there.

During all this last year, I could have worked part time doing something else. I chose not to. I guess I just did not accomplish much except what I did for the Habitat. By working to help build houses, I helped the Habitat acquire more land to build more houses on. I worked on several properties but the first one we purchased was across the street from where the first Habitat house in Dickinson was built. There is enough land to build 12 more homes for folks who really need them. I attended meetings with the local water authority folks, the mayor's office, the Commissioner's and others to be sure that the location was a good one and included the services needed after houses were built on the land. An estate owned the land we were trying to purchase, and it took many months of dealing with their representatives, which was a bank in Galveston, to accomplish the purchase.

After, AFTER RAISING SUGARCANE

I left all paperwork and contact names and telephone numbers for three or four other properties nearby that I had worked on in a folder for the next Habitat volunteer to continue to work on in the future.

After July 1, I received paperwork from Nova restating the conditions of my release and severance pay. Since I had completed my requirement with the Habitat for Humanities, my assignment was complete. The half-pay checks stopped coming. Arrangements were made for me to start paying for medical and dental insurance by mail. Since I declared that I would retire from Nova, Sarah and I would continue to be covered by Nova's retirement insurance plan. During the time that I was being paid one-half pay, the monthly charges for our insurance were deducted from my paycheck. Now I had to send the money to the agent handling the insurance coverage for Nova. We later did the necessary paperwork to put this on an automatic payment plan at our bank. Nova set a requirement that scared the shit out of us. Their restriction was that if we were late with the premium payment, they would cancel the coverage and we could NEVER get it reinstated again. This is what I call screwing folks in their old age. This is why we put the monthly payment on an automatic payment plan with our bank. If our bank did not transfer the funds in time and we got canceled, I would have a case against them. Nova was hard-nosed about this and probably canceled several coverages each year.

All the time that I was with the Habitat, I was a non-voting board member. I attended all of the meetings and made a report on the progress for acquiring additional property at each one. This board had to approve any deal that I made. They actually approved the amount of money that I offered for the property and the good faith amount also. Everything went through the board of directors. Because of company transfers there were three different board presidents in the year that I volunteered. The president usually served a two-year term.

The Bay Area Habitat for Humanities had thirty homes built when I volunteered. We built three and one-half houses the year that I worked with them. This group averaged three houses a year. They had a great team of older retired guys that did most of the work. The future homeowner needed to work a minimum of 300 hours for Habitat with about half of that on their own house. Habitat calls this "sweat equity". Each Habitat homeowners must but in sweat equity or they do not get a house. Any member of the family working on a house can gives credit hours to the homeowner. This way if the homeowner is in a wheelchair and cannot work, the sweat equity hours are made up by a family member.

After all my ties with Nova were cut, I was on my own. Before long I received my 42 weeks' severance pay in one lump sum. They look out more tax than I expected. My net was still over $85,000, which was not too bad.

Before my heart attack in late May, we knew that our days getting pay from Nova were numbered and I did not have any prospects of another job, so I decided to sell the League City house and move to the property in the woods near Cleveland, Texas - with Sarah's approval of course. We did this to cut expenses and get some more money in the bank because I did not want to go to work for the man again. I figured that we could live cheaper in the county than the high tax area of League City. Property and other taxes were lower in San Jacinto County also.

After we put our house up for sale, several folks and a few realtors came by to have a look. We planned to sell it ourselves. We made flyers and placed them in the for-sale tube we purchased and placed it in the front yard.

The flyers went like hotcakes.

As I was recovering from my heart attack, my time with Nova and the Habitat was coming to an end. The day that I decided to take the for sale sign down, a lady and her husband came to my front door. They were interested in the house for her father who was 85 years old and pissed off at the complex he was living in. His son lived in the house behind ours.

As it turned out, we sold the house to Mr. Jordan, "the old man", for one hundred thousand dollars and no realtor's fee. I paid off my balance and put the rest in the bank. We moved to The Place in the Woods in September of 2001. It was our home now.

Since Sarah was still in college and now attending the University of Houston at Clear Lake, we had planned before the move that she would spend two or three nights a week at her mom's house in Texas City each week while attending classes. This would save a lot of travel time and money for gas going to and from classes. We now lived about seventy miles from the university one way. This would work out fine for a while.

Sarah's mom had been after us to move in with her. We really thought about it but finally decided that it just would not work. Her mom was set in her ways, and I was set in mine. When we went for a visit, we could hear the television before we turned into the driveway. Mrs. Griffin was hard of hearing and did not care for or want to wear a hearing aid. Maybe they just did not work for her. Anyway, there were other reasons we could not live together at this time.

We were now living in the Sam Houston Forest, 12 miles from Cleveland, Texas. We were mainly living off of our savings which were made up of my severance pay and the sale of our League City house. We also received one-half of Sarah's former pay while she was in school. We were also reimbursed expenses for books, fees, and course costs as long as she maintained a passing grade. Sarah never made less than a B in any of her classes. And the A's outnumbered the B's by far. It was less expensive to live in San Jacinto County than in Galveston County. We now had one less house note and property taxes to pay. This felt good for a short time. Things would change fairly quickly.

SELLING THE LEAGUE CITY HOUSE IN 2001

During the latter part of 2001, I decided to sell the League City house and move to The Place near Cleveland, Texas. The Place is what we named the property in the Sam Houston Forest that I purchased in 1996 before Sarah and I married. We did about ten to twelve thousand dollars of repairs and repainting on the League City house getting it ready to sell.

Sarah really liked it there in League City. We were in a great location and a really clean subdivision. We had a homeowner's association that kept everyone on their toes and their property in tip top shape. The main problem I had was with the property taxes. I was laid off and retired by Nova Chemical Corp, but with NO retirement income. It was a small three bedroom house. It had about fifteen hundred square feet of living space. This was really small when compared to the house I had on the Taylor Lake Village side of Clear Lake. It was over twenty-five hundred square feet of living space with four bedrooms, three bathrooms, and a two-car detached garage with a walkover cover and a large, covered patio.

The Taylor Lake Village house was in Harris County which contains the city of Houston. My League City house was in Galveston County. The taxes were supposed to be less in Galveston County. Well my property taxes were over twenty-five hundred dollars a year. Another way of putting this is that my property taxes was over two hundred twenty-five dollars a month. So, I knew that I would owe this amount each month even before I spent a single cent on anything else that we needed to survive. I just could not see paying this just to live in League City. Mr. League created a great city, but shit it was just too damn expensive for me.

After several months of having the for-sale sign in my yard, I decided to pull it up and just place it the garage for a while. The day after I picked up the sign, I had a knock on my door. When I answered it, I found a man and woman and he ask me if the house was still for sale. I said yes, won't you come in. These folks live on the street behind me and had seen the sign a day or two ago while driving around the neighborhood. The lady was looking for a place for his dad and my house was really close to their home.

I showed them through the house and answered all the question that they had. Yes, I told them the price. It was five or six thousand dollars less than I had in the paper for the carpet and any other minor repairs. The lady asked if her father could look at it the next day. No problem, said I.

The next day when Mr. Jordan looked around the house, he wanted it. There was no haggling about the price. It turned out that he was living in an apartment complex about two miles from me on the same highway that we were on. He got pissed off at the complex because they went up a little over one hundred dollars a month for rent. He said it was the principle of the matter. They wanted to screw him, so he would screw them by moving out. We made the deal on the spot. I hired an agency to complete all the necessary paperwork. I owed about eleven thousand on my house. When I purchased it, I paid sixty-seven thousand dollars for it.

I sold it twelve years later for one hundred thousand dollars. I had put over thirty thousand dollars down on it when I purchased it. This amount was half of the Taylor Lake Village house that I sold in 1990. My ex-wife Valerie got the other half.

A short time after I purchased my League City House, I refinanced it for a lower interest rate and was paying one-half note every fourteen days. This meant that I paid an extra monthly note a year. This paid the interest down much faster than paying monthly notes. I netted about eighty-nine thousand dollars and put it in an interest-bearing savings account. Since I did not have any income coming in on a regular basis, I was drawing three thousand dollars a month from my savings account into my checking account to pay the bills. There were months that I earned over three hundred dollars in interest. After selling this house, we went to live at The Place near Cleveland, Texas.

RECOVERING FROM HEART ATTACK FOR BALANCE OF 2001

After my commitment was over with Habitat, I concentrated on selling our League City house and just piddling around working on the house and not doing much of anything else. Sarah was looking after me during the summer then went back to college full time in August.

I sat around, boxed some items for our eventual move, and did a little yard work. I did not do any heavy stuff. I was really careful in what I did and what I ate as well. I lost twenty pounds after my heart attack. I stopped eating fast foods altogether. As the months passed, I went back to eating everything that was bad for me. Consequently, within a year I had gained the twenty pounds back and then some. I now try to stay in the 205-to-210pound range. I should shoot for the 175-to-185-pound range but I am what I am.

I stayed in the house a lot and did not venture too far from it, especially when Sarah was at school. I was scared to do anything by myself. I did and do have this tendency to overdo things. I usually try and do it myself instead of asking someone for help.

I visited with my neighbor more than normal because I was at the house more than normal - I guess. Dan had a real heart problem. He worked at NASA for a contractor I believe. He would be home because he just could not go to work because of his health. I think that he needed a heart transplant. He had a pacemaker implant in his body that would shock his heart and get it going again when it stopped. He called it a defibrillator or something like that. He has been stuck in meetings, and even when giving a lecture in other states, he would pass out or otherwise had to be rushed to the nearest hospital to be worked on. He spent a lot of time in hospitals all over our country. Dan could not even cut or edge his grass. He did not have the strength and was just not healthy enough to do it. He faired a little better in the wintertime when it was not as hot. But he still could not enjoy outside activities. He is a very nice fellow and would like to do things around his house but just could not. I am very lucky to not be in the shape that Dan is in. I wanted to help him more but just did not know where he needed the help. He never asked me for help either. I could not overdo it either and did not want to take a chance of taking on something that I could not finish. Things like repairing or replacing a section of his wood fence in his backyard. It was just too large a project for me to try at this time.

While I was recovering, I did repair a section of my wood fence and my main gate entrance. On the west side of my house where the back yard fence came to a left angle L and back to my house were a lot of banana trees. I had to cut some of them down and get in there and replace wooden boards. It was tight working among the huge banana plants. After completion of the fence, I felt really good at completing the project and was still alive which was a plus for me. But that damn fence leads to a major problem. When it rained, the fence was so tight that it held the water in the backyard. The water could not flow out fast enough and caused me concern and stress that my house may get flooded. So, I came up with the bright idea of making a gate out of part of this fence section that I just replaced.

The hard work that I had put into rebuilding and replacing boards on my fence was child's play compared to the work I had to do to make a gate there. I worked for over two weeks to make this damn gate. I thought that I could cut the top and bottom two-by-fours holding the pickets, place two hinges on the outside of the fence and a latch on the other end and I would have a gate. This should have been easy to do, right? Wrong! It was a hell of a lot harder than that. I had to saw and cut and trim and cut and trim and saw some more. I used three hinges and had to set in the ground two four-by four anchor post to support this heavy ass gate. It was a bitch. I did a lot of this work in the mud and soggy ground because of all the rain we had every damn day.

I should have mentioned before writing all of this that when I was repairing and replacing fence pickets I nailed the new pickets on the inside rails and did not remove the pickets that were already on my fence. My whole backyard had one hell of a picket fence. In fact, you might say that it was a double picket fence because that is exactly what it was. The older pickets were on the outside of the picket support runners and my new pickets were on the inside of the two-by-four runners. When I first started rebuilding my fence before my heart attack, I had to replace several four-by-four anchor posts with treated four-by-four posts and also replaced several sections of two-by-four runners with treated two-by-four runners as well. I used a level to keep the pickets straight and the fence looks good when completed. It was also very strong. It was a good looking strong six-foot-high treated wooden fence. The only problem with it was that when we had those heavy rainfalls, the double set of pickets would hold in the damn water. All the water from my backyard flowed toward the street. It would build up to over four inches deep in the backyard after I finished the last section behind the banana bushes.

Before I started on the gate, when I noticed that water was being restricted from the natural flow toward the street in front of the house, I dug out under the fence and moved dirt and grass. The water would go under the fence into the hole and then overflow toward the street. The problem was that it just did not move fast enough to keep from accumulating. Then after the rain stopped, our damn dog, Rue, would crawl out through this hole. I tried to block it off, but the dog would eventually break through it. So, I had to try and build a gate that I could open when it rained and close after the rain stopped. During the rain, the dog stayed in her doghouse. She was afraid of bad weather and would only come out of the doghouse to come into my house. In the final analysis, I did accomplish what I started out trying to do although it took a lot out of me. Because of getting tired quickly, I had to stop working on this project several times to take long rest periods sometimes days. But I persisted and lived through it.

HOSPITAL STAY IN NASSAU BAY, TEXAS

During 2002, I felt that I was fully recovered from the heart attack, Sarah was still attending college full time. We were living in the woods near Cleveland, Texas. Sarah was going to classes two days a week. On the days that she had class, she slept at her mom's house in Texas City. It was much closer to the campus than where we lived. After her two days of classes, she would come home and spend time with me in the woods.

I had several episodes of chest pain and underwent more medical tests throughout the year. One time I spent two nights in Saint John's Hospital in Nassau Bay for chess pains. They ran many thousand dollars of tests on me for my heart. I even did a nuclear stress test. I told the doctor that it may have been severe chest pains resulting from the acid reflux problem that I had. He just wanted to run the test on my heart. My heart checked out fine - again. However, I received no help for my acid reflux problem.

Many months earlier, I had completed months of stress tests with exercise equipment and other types of equipment. My heart is strong. It is just the blood vessels and arteries that go to my heart that is the problem. If I can keep the blood flowing, my heart will be alright for a long time to come. I need to be careful of the many other diseases that can kill me.

VISITING WITH FAMILY

During the year, Sarah and I made trips to Denton to visit Jake and also to the Fort Worth area to visit with Nathan and Ricky Griffin, Sarah's brother, and his family. We also visited with her Uncle Bunyan and Aunt Evadeanne while in Fort Worth several times. We visited with my sons a few times and with my brother and my sister in Louisiana. There must not have been any exceptional trips where things happened, or I would have written about them. They were just run-of-the mill trips.

CASINO IN MARKSVILLE, LOUISIANA

After one such trip we headed toward Louisiana to visit with my brother and sister and their families. We departed the Fort Worth area and made our way to the Interstate 20 for a trip to Louisiana. We went through Shreveport and Bossier City and headed for Marksville where we planned to spend the night. Upon arrival in Marksville, we located the huge gambling casino where we were to spend the night. I could not wait to check in and get into the casino and lose two or three dollars.

We went up to our room, threw down our bags, looked around the room, said, "This is nice" and headed downstairs to go into the casino area. We had been on the road for five hours or more and realized this after seeing the restaurant on the walkway between the hotel and the casino. "Let's eat", Sarah remarked. "Alrrrrrrrrright", I exclaimed. There were several eateries in a row. We looked them over and chose one. I sat where I could see into the casino. I guess I was not paying very much attention to Sarah because she mentioned it several times. She also said that my eyes lit up each time I looked toward the casino. She could see in my face that I was more than ready to lose my two dollars. I wolfed down whatever it was that I ordered and waited for Sarah. In due time she was done eating. We paid and headed into the casino.

I just love all the lights and sounds (noise) that a casino makes. It is just exciting. We walked and looked around for a few minutes before deciding where we were going to lose our money. We decided beforehand that we would each lose twenty dollars. This seemed like a large amount to me. After all, I was retired without any income. The truth of the matter is if I was still making six figures in salary, twenty dollars would still be hard for me to throw away. This is just the kind of guy I am- tight to the bone.

We each found quarter slot machines where we deposited some money. I cannot remember if we had to turn our money into casino slot money or not.

Some casinos let you play with real money, and some want you to use their imitation money. I do not know why this is but that is the way it is.

It did not take us long to lose our first twenty dollars. We each got another twenty and started moving around the casino and playing the slots here and there. We piddled around until about eleven pm, then went upstairs to our room for the night. Yes, we each lost another twenty dollars. But we had fun doing it.

The next morning, we went down for breakfast and found it to be very expensive. So, we drove to McDonald's and ate breakfast along with several other folks that we recognized as being from the casino. After our cheap breakfast we went back into the casino and lost about ten more dollars each before we checked out of the hotel and headed south.

It was hard to believe that we lost this amount of money here. This is the very first casino that Sarah ever gambled in. The casino was much smaller at that time. Before we married, she won money from every slot machine that she played. She was overjoyed until it came time for us to divide up the money. She gave it all to me. I found out several years later that she wanted it all and got pissed off at me for wanting my share. Since I financed the gambling money and told her that we were playing on halves BEFORE we even started playing the slots, I thought that I should get my half. This makes sense to me. Anyway, on that trip she won over one hundred dollars in quarters. From that first time in a casino, she thought that you always win like that. She has had a rude awakening since that day. I believe we lost every time we went into a casino since, except for the one in Niagara Falls, Canada, where she hit a small jackpot. Now that was really fun. We also won a little in Colorado somewhere.

THIRD CRAWFISH BOIL AT THE PLACE

During April 2003, Sarah and I gave another crawfish boil at "The Place". I only purchased two sacks of crawfish for this one. We had about the same number of folks as in the past but since some of them did not eat boiled crawfish, we were having hamburgers and hot dogs and chips and dip and such for the non-bug-eaters or anybody else who wanted some. This kept us from having a lot of boiled crawfish that we had to peel and put up after everybody left.

Our usual group, my department, Sarah's department, my sons and their friends from Austin, Sarah's son, and guests. At this time, we had Stephen McKenna who had joined my department and his family, and Beverly Curtice from our Lab and her family. There may have been a couple of others.

Stephen McKenna and his wife, daughter, and two young sons. The McKenna boys were really outgoing. They fought with each other and were into all sorts of sports. They ran all about my place - the twelve-plus acres. It came to pass that we could not find them after a while. We started shouting for them and walking and looking for them. They were nowhere to be seen or heard. Susan Ambler and her husband, Curt arrived a little later than most of the other folks. Susan mentioned to Stephen that as they were approaching my entrance, they saw two preteen boys down the road a bit. Stephen knew that it was them. He got in his car and took off. A little later he was back with his sons. They were just exploring the area. My twelve-plus acres was just not enough for them - I guess. Stephen thanked Susan for the tip and they had a good conversation.

CURT AND SUSAN AMBLER AND CAROL BEESON

This worked out very well for my department. Stephan had been with us for several months and did not get along with Susan very well. When we needed some extra help, my boss, Brent Turkington started worrying about me. I was giving him some hell about being overworked without enough pay and other problems. So much so that he was getting worried about me. My attitude was really bad.

He probably thought that sooner or later I would just quit or that he would have to fire me. He needed someone that had a lot of experience that could take over the whole operation. Stephan McKenna was that someone. He was really good and knew his stuff.

Stephen was the backup for whatever happened to me. His hire was fine with me. I liked Stephen very much and had worked with him for years when he was with Tauber Oil, whom we did much business with over the years. I only wished that we could pay him more at the time when he was hired.

We all had a very good time at this get together and became closer and had a better working relationship in the future.

I regret to say that my friend, Stephen McKenna, committed suicide some years later. He became troubled and felt like he had too much pressure because of being out of a job and having a family to take care of. He had transferred from my department to Huntsman's head office in Houston. After a year or two, he left there for a much better paying job in the barge industry in New Orleans. Then the barging industry turned bad, and he was out of a job again.

The odd part of all this mess is that he called me when I was having a mental breakdown myself. I was off work for a couple months after Nova Chemical purchased the business from Huntsman. We talked for a long time. We both told each other to hang in there that things would get better. Maybe he was trying to tell me goodbye. This was my last conversation with him. The pills I was taking to treat me and still taking today, helped me greatly. Stephen's pills that the doctor gave to him did not help him. I still cry over the guy from time to time. Such a waste. He was one of the really GOOD guys. I loved him.

STEPHEN MCKENNA

GRAND ISLE LOUISIANA TRIP

It was late in the year after our first Marksville casino trip that Sarah and I went to Louisiana for a visit. During this visit, my brother and his family had made arrangements to spend a night or two in Grand Isle which is on the Louisiana coast. It is the only saltwater beach in Louisiana. It is not a very pretty place. If Galveston is a ten, which it is not, Grand Isle would be a five or less. Anyway, we had fun crabbing in the surf. We did not catch many crabs, but we had a lot of fun trying. We all spent the night in a cabin. The next morning Sarah and I planned for an early getaway. My brother had his truck all loaded down and ready to go. Just before we said goodbye, his daughter, Jill, came running up and wanted a crab net because crabs were running up on the beach. A storm was coming our way which is why we were all leaving this early in the morning. After Jill left with one net another one came and asked him for the second crab net. Sarah and I departed as my brother was bitching about having to dig the crab nets out from under other stuff in the back of the pickup.

Sarah and I decided to come home along the Louisiana and Texas coast. We departed and finally made our way to Baldwin, Louisiana where another Indian Casino was located. We stopped to lose a few dollars there. I offered to finance our gambling and go on halves for any winnings, but Sarah said, "hell no", to that suggestion. She wanted to keep all her winnings. She remembered the first time she ever gambled and won all those quarters. Well, this time she lost. It did not take long for her to lose everything she had. Her money burned a hole in her pockets. She could not put it in the slot machine fast enough. She felt really bad after she was broke and came to me with a very sad face. I gave her ten more dollars which she promptly loss also. I then said that that was enough, and we left the casino. This was her sixth or seventh time in a casino since her big winning spree and she finally realized that her winning a few years ago was a fluke. We became pretty much selective on our casino gambling after this time.

Since the second Marksville casino trip, before we entered a casino, we determined the amount we were willing to lose. We usually stop after we get to the amount set which is usually twenty dollars each. For the most part, we are still sticking to this amount. Sometimes we go up to thirty each if we lose the twenty too quickly or are still having fun.

Sarah's money always seems to last longer than mine. I do not know why this is, but it is.

MRS. GRIFFIN'S HEALTH PROBLEMS

Late in 2002, Mrs. Griffin started having serious health problems. As she got older many small health problems became larger problems. She also had trouble with her hearing and eyesight. Sarah had been taking her from one doctor's appointment to another for the last year or so.

Eventually, she started having left leg problems. Sarah took her to several specialists. It seems that nothing was diagnosed for some time. Mrs. Griffin started to have trouble getting around. She bought a new walker and used it in the house. She started having problems getting out of her sitting chair. Sarah spent a day with her shopping, and she purchased a large chair from Star Furniture. This was not just any chair. This chair had rollers on it. It also came equipped with hydraulic equipment that lifted and tilted the chair upward and backward. This made the chair adjustable and easier to sit in and stand up with the aid of a walker. When you leaned the chair backward the footrest came out automatically when you pushed the correct button. The cost of this chair was a little over $800. This is a high-cost chair. Mrs. Griffin wanted it covered with material she picked out so the chair would be delivered several weeks later. As it turned out, this material was not the best kind to have a chair upholstered with. The flower print looked good, but it also looked lumpy and was not cushiony. We were disappointed with it, especially when the cost was considered.

Sarah was taking more time to look after her mom. We were spending a lot of time in Texas City. Sarah's brother, Ronnie, would help out with his mom too. He had moved back to Texas City from Arkansas some time ago. He was living in Mrs. Griffin's rented house. So, she was not collecting rent payments anymore. As we got into the new year of 2003, Mrs. Griffin started having more trouble with her leg. The Texas City doctors could not seem to find out what in hell the problem was.

We were down in Texas City visiting and helping out again when one night after Mrs. Griffin was in bed, she started yelling in pain. Her left knee was hurting so much that she just could not keep from yelling. She yelled and hollered. We ran to her room. After checking on her, Sarah called 911 for an ambulance to take her mom to the hospital. Which in due time they did. I do not know what took them so long. They took her to UTMB in Galveston. Sarah and I followed the ambulance. We notified Ronnie and he drove to the hospital to meet us there. This was after ten p.m. Sarah filled out the paperwork as the medical staff on duty was attending to Mrs. Griffin. We sat in the waiting room with Ronnie for five or six hours just waiting to see if a doctor would come and tell us what is going on. We finally left in the morning nearing daylight. We were in bed less than an hour when the hospital called and asked Sarah to come in for an update.

After Sarah's consultation, we still did not know very much. They had Mrs. Griffin sedated with drugs. This started a seventeen-day ordeal with this hospital. Sarah's sister from Arkansas and her brother from Fort Worth, came to sit in the hospital at different times to visit with their mom and give Sarah and Ronnie a break. They stayed with us in Texas City when they came down. The hospital had Mrs. Griffin so drugged up that someone had to feed her. The family took turns when we were there. I fed her on several occasions.

After several days, a young doctor wanted to know if the family wanted to just let her die. We all said, "HELL NO." She was not that bad off. I do not know what the hell he was thinking. She may have looked like it at the time because they had her so drugged up. The doctor said that she had cancer. The family wanted them to do more testing. Things in this hospital were not going as they should have. They were saying some preposterous things. We were not getting the service or medical care that Mrs. Griffin deserved to get. There were a number of meetings with doctors.

One day Sarah looked at her mom's chart hanging on the end of the bed and looked over it. She found out that her mom had fallen out of her bed one morning when she was all drugged up and left unattended. We surmised much later after she was getting treatment at M.D. Anderson Hospital in Houston for leg cancer, and that was when she broke her leg. She did not go into UTMB with a broken left leg, but she surely came out with one.

Somewhere during the discussions with doctors in Galveston about proper treatment for her mom. Sarah mentioned that her lawyer brother in Fort Worth was coming over for the weekend visit. Well - the shit hit the fan now. This was not a threat but just for their information. They did not want to treat her anymore. They wanted her out of this hospital in the worst way. They were going to send her home. Sarah made some telephone calls, and she was transported to another healthcare facility.

From this point on it was visits to M. D. Anderson and back to nursing homes. I think that three or four different nursing homes were utilized in the next four or five months. Mrs. Griffin started CHEMO at M.D. Anderson. She had several doctors there. One was for her broken leg, another for the cancer and another for blood and I do not know what all. She was also a diabetic which did not help matters. She also had other medical problems as well.

After her first visits to doctors at Anderson, they put a leg brace on her left leg and instructed us all that the leg was not ever to bend and for her to not place any weight on it.

For some of the first treatments, she was placed in a nursing home in Houston where other treatments could be done for her. An ambulance would transport her to M.D. Anderson for the three or four-hour CHEMO treatment and then back to the nursing home.

Sarah was relieved by her brother, Ronnie, who lived in Texas City, and her sister, Alice Jean, who lived in Arkansas. Alice started flying down from Arkansas every two weeks to give Sarah a break. She would spend two weeks down here then fly back to her home then come back two weeks later, etc., etc.

We would go home to Cleveland, Texas and Sarah would try and rest but even when she was off, the telephone calls continued to come. Sarah was the youngest in the family, but the main decision maker and she was always called by Alice or Ronnie or Ricky when they were looking after their mom. This is just the way it was. Sarah knew more of what was going on and had to be consulted by her brothers and sister before they could make any decisions concerning their mom.

Mrs. Griffin's leg/joint/bone doctor intended to operate to fix her leg after the cancer was treated and cured. All doctors at M.D. Anderson thought this type of cancer was very curable and she should be able to beat it. They planned to place a metal plate in the leg and said she should be able to walk on her own. Things were a far cry from the doctors at UTMB who wanted to pull the plug on Mrs. Griffin and let her die by starving her to death. This was a curable sickness. Galveston Hospital played a major role in Mrs. Griffin's health problems. What a bunch of putzes they are.

Eventually, Mrs. Griffin was well enough to come home and be transported back and forth for CHEMO treatment. Also, Medicare was coming to an end for the nursing home stays, and hospital stays while awaiting treatment. Each time she went to Anderson for treatment, she was discharged from the twenty-four-hour care facility and Sarah had to recheck/register her all over again. This may be one reason she moved from place to place during this time. Another reason was the care in the facility was not good at all and Sarah and her family found another one to try out.

This had become a very time-consuming event in the lives of the Griffin children. Sarah decided to become the full-time caregiver for her mom. She did not attend college in the first semester of 2003 to care for her mom. She did not get paid from Nova at this time either. Sarah set up a bed on the ground floor to better hear and care for her mom twenty-four hours a day. And boy was it twenty-four hours per day. Although her mom could get around in a wheelchair, she wanted to be waited on hand and foot. She would not even get herself a glass of water, which she was very capable of doing since it would be next to her. She was getting walking and exercise therapy from a lady who came by several times per week.

Before long she finished doing the CHEMO treatments. After a couple of weeks, she started the radiation treatment. I think that she had sixteen weeks of radiation treatment. The arrangement was made with Ronnie to drive his mom to the hospital three times a week to give Sarah a three or four-hour break from waiting on her mom's hand and foot. Alice came down for two-week intervals for Sarah to have some time off.

After experiencing what Sarah went through, we all have a better appreciation for the hell that a full-time care giver goes through.

During the time that Mrs. Griffin was going through her treatment regimen a strange thing happened. Her broken leg just under the knee had healed. It seemed the lower bone had fused with the upper bone. The x-rays showed the bones to be impacted and heeled. She got word from her leg doctor that there would be no need for an operation after all. Things were starting to really look up. Mrs. Griffin was even trying to use the bathroom again on her own, Things were really looking up now. We were seeing the light at the end of the tunnel.

During the summer of 2003, Alice came down to care for her mom. Sarah and I took a trip to Louisiana to visit my brother and sister and their families. I do not remember anything exceptional about this visit, but Sarah did get several telephone calls concerning her mom. When we were away, she was not really away. Her thoughts were always about her mom and what was going on back there in Texas city. It is like a five-hour trip and the day you arrive you get a phone call asking when are you coming home. You know what I mean Vern?

As the situation looked to be much better, Sarah made plans to go back to college for the fall semester. Her mom was well into the radiation treatment, and we had received word that she was cancer free. The doctors wanted to complete the sixteen-week radiation treatment though.

Sarah's mom was getting around much better although she did not want to rid herself of the wheelchair. She was getting around really well using the walker. Everything was looking good, and Sarah started looking around for a part-time care giver to replace her on weekends. After less than two weeks of classes, we decided to go up to our house in the woods for the weekend.

I had been spending most of my time there in Texas City with Sarah. Mrs. Griffin made her last trip to Houston with Ronnie on Thursday. This was the last scheduled trip for radiation treatment. We were so happy. As we were preparing to leave for the weekend, we had Jo Ann come by and visit with Mrs. Griffin to see if she was acceptable to her. She was. But Mrs. Griffin was not happy about it. Before we left, while Sarah was finishing the dishes at the sink, her mom rolled up in her wheelchair and told Sarah that she did not want to linger on if something bad happened to her. We wondered later if she knew or if she felt something would happen. I believe that Jo Ann was with Sarah's two aunts when they died.

Sarah hired the lady who looked after two of her aunts. Jo Ann came in on Friday afternoon and was going to stay with Mrs. Griffin until Sunday when we were coming back. Early Sunday morning about two a.m., we got a call from Jo Ann saying that Mrs. Griffin was making a fuss. We both thought that she was sun-downing again. This is something she had done the whole time of her illness. This is when folks make a fuss all night long. They get enough sleep during the day and cut up all night because they are afraid of closing their eyes. It is referred to as "sun downing" by the medical folks.

Sarah asked to talk to her mom. Jo Ann got the telephone near the bed to Mrs. Griffin. She told Sarah to come check on her. Sarah told her that we were at "the place" in Cleveland and it would take over two hours for us to get back there. She then told Sarah to come when you could and then handed the phone back to Jo Ann. Sarah talked with Jo Ann for maybe another minute or so then hung up. We did not know what to do. In a short period of time, Jo Ann called again. Mrs. Griffin was really cutting up, then got quiet. We could hear her over the telephone. Sarah asks Jo Ann to get her mom's attention. Jo Ann tried and said that she thought she was resting. She went to check, and she was not breathing. I think Sarah called 911 - maybe it was Jo Ann. After the first call, Sarah called Ronnie and asked him to go check on their mom.

When Ronnie arrived the emergency response folks were there working on Mrs. Griffin. Ronnie did not like what he saw. In the meantime, we had gotten dressed and were heading toward Texas City. By cell phone, we found out from Ronnie that their mom had passed away. We were in shock. Everything was going so well. It was just hard to believe. After such a long fight and now that she was cancer-free and had a healed leg -we just could not understand it.

We arrived between five and six a.m. We talked with Jo Ann who was still at the house, and she filled us in on the things we had missed out on after Ronnie came over. He was still there. Ronnie and Sarah went to the hospital where the emergency response folks had taken their mom.

Several hours later when they returned, contacts were made with other family members. We think she died from a blood clot. We are not absolutely sure of this because no autopsy was performed. It is still hard to believe. Sarah said that she physically fell on her mom's leg, which had cancer, and it was still very warm.

It is now mid-August 2003 and she started fighting this thing in late 2002. Mrs. Griffin was going to be 83 years old in November. The date was August 17, 2003.

MRS. GRIFFIN'S FUNERAL

Sarah made most of the arrangements for her mom's funeral. Her brothers and sister helped out where/when they could. The services were held at Emken Linton Funeral Home in Texas City.

Since there were several families from out of town, Sarah and I rented a room for a day or two at a local hotel. We let Ricky and his family from Fort Worth and Alice Jean and her family from Clarksville, Arkansas use our house to stay at for a few days. Some of the other younger members. of the family stayed at the same hotel that we stayed in. Mrs. Griffin's brother and his wife stayed there also.

The morning of the funeral my three sons arrived at our hotel to meet us. They used our room to change clothes. Kent and Todd lived in Austin, Texas. Lane droves down from Washington, D.C., where he lived, to attend the funeral. I was really happy and glad to see them there. We gave my sons directions to the funeral home and went to the lobby of the hotel to talk with Sarah's son, Jacob.

Just before we left the hotel, we saw Wes and Justin Griffin, Ronnie's sons, come into the hotel also.

NATHAN AND JACOB ELLIFF, LANE, KENT, AND TODD RAFFRAY

Sarah and I went to the funeral parlor and shortly afterward folks started coming in to view the body. There were a large number of chairs for us near the casket. Mrs. Griffin had four kids and a number of grandkids and great grandkids and one older brother still living.

The day before the funeral services, family members had a meeting with the preacher that they wanted to do the services and went over info they wanted to be said and songs that they wanted to be sung by a long-time friend and 1st Baptist Church member and choir leader. A number of things were discussed. Mrs. Griffin's brother and his wife were in attendance but did not add any suggestion that I can recall. The preacher was informed that Mrs. Griffin's father, Henry Peters, was a Baptist minister and the leader of the Spanish Mission in Texas City for many years. He could speak seven different languages. The next day at the time for the service to begin, Mrs.

Griffin's brother, Uncle Bunyon Peters, and his wife, Evadeane, were nowhere in sight. We waited for several minutes. We found out during the wait from Wes that he talked to them at the hotel as he was leaving to come to the funeral parlor that they were just getting in from a trip to Galveston to see the giant turtles and had to change clothes before heading to the funeral home. This pissed me off and other family members also. They were looking to Sarah to make the decision to start the services. Sarah was the go-to person in charge of everything. Just when she was about to have the service start, her uncle and aunt came strolling in. We were getting started fifteen minutes late because of them.

BUNYON AND EVADEANE PETERS

Uncle Bunyon did not know where to sit. He walked past the chair that was placed for him and started up the aisle of the chapel. I called out to him and started after him. He turned around and came back before I reached him. I got him seated in his chair. The services finally started. Within five minutes, Bunyon was sleeping in his easy chair. He was eighty-four years old then and in bad health and Evadeane had been dragging his ass all over the place. He slept through much of the service.

As the preacher was talking, he brought up Granny Griffin, who was Mrs. Griffin's mother-in-law. That lead to a response from one of the pall bearers that "Granny Griffin" started it all. Very shortly afterwards loud thunderclaps sounded outside. All of us family members looked at each other and we all had the same thought. That it was Mrs. Griffin saying that this is "my day" and NOT Granny Griffins. Talk about Frieda Peters Griffin. I do not remember much if anything mentioned about Reverend Henry Peters and his being a teacher and over the Spanish Mission in Texas City for many years.

The day was gloomy, and it rained on and off all day. We all went to the graveyard in Hitchcock and paid our last respects to Mrs. Griffin. An announcement was made there that food and beverages would be served at the 1st Baptist Church on Palmer Street in the meeting room behind the church. Many of the folks came and joined us. We heard some good stories about Sarah's mom from her first cousins who are older than her and her brothers and sister. Sarah's dad was about fourteen years older than her mom and did not marry until he was in his mid-thirties. So, most of Sarah's first cousins are twenty years or more older than she is. Her dad was the favorite uncle of many of her first cousins. Her cousins knew her dad longer than she or her brothers and sister did. I get the feeling that some of her first cousins were jealous of Sarah and her siblings. Maybe that is not the case, but it is the feeling I get.

After the family get-together at the church meeting room, many of the folks came back to Mrs. Griffin's house with us. As we were sitting in the living room talking, Uncle Bunyon stated that the 1st Baptist Church was where Mrs. Griffin's dad preached his last sermon before he died. We all looked at him with our mouths open. Where in the hell was, he when we had the meeting with the preacher who did his sister's services when we were going over things for the preacher to talk about? He could have brought the subject up then- damn it. Perhaps he was asleep at that meeting also. We were all pissed off. Henry Peters was a Baptist Minister, teacher, and scholar who spoke seven different languages. He was an educated man and gave back to every community he went to. He ran the Spanish Mission in Texas City for years until his death at the age of fifty- eight. Yet, Bunyon sat at the meeting and did not say one damn word.

Mrs. Frieda Peters Griffin was a religious person also. Being a lifelong Baptist and teacher of Sunday School for adults as her husband, Mr. J. D. Griffin did also. She was also one of the founding members of the Church of Houston a non-denominational church that preached the teachings of Witness Lee and Watchman Nee who were Chinese Christians in the communist country of China. Watchman Nee was in prison for many years because of his Christian beliefs and teachings in China. Witness Lee brought their teachings to America.

After visiting for some time with my sons, they departed for Austin. Sarah and I thanked them again for coming. Some of Sarah's first cousins who met and talked with them were impressed with them- or so they told me later.

We enjoyed seeing them and wished them a safe return home.

Ricky, Sarah's lawyer brother from Fort Worth, had to get busy settling the estate now. Sarah continued on completing her college work and received her bachelor's degree in May of 2004. Her sister, Alice Kotter, and nephew Raun Griffin, and I attended the graduation ceremony. I was very proud of her for accomplishing this goal as was the whole family. She never did think that this was a big thing, but it was. I think that it is a very BIG THING to complete at her age. After all, she was not a spring chicken anymore - you know.

At the same graduation from the University of Houston at Clear Lake was a friend of mine. He worked in the plant as an operator. For the life of me, I cannot remember his name. Shame on me. He had some health problems but beat them and came back to work and got his bachelor's degree also. He is a really good guy. Sarah and I looked him up before they went on the stage to sit and wait for their names to be called to go up and get their degrees. I gave him a little present that I purchased for him and met his niece who was with him for the graduation. He and she were so proud - as they should be and so were Sarah and I.

AFTER MRS. GRIFFINS DEATH

In late 2003, Sarah and I moved into Mrs. Griffin's house to live until Sarah finished college and received her degree in May of 2004. While living there a we started discussions with Sarah's brother, Ricky and sister, Alice Jean, about purchasing the house from the estate.

There were actually four heirs to the property - Ricky, Ronnie, Alice Jean, and Sarah. Ronnie had been living with his family in Mrs. Griffin's rent house for several years at this time. Some years after Ronnie's divorce from his first wife with whom he had three sons, he married Judy. They had two children, a girl, and a boy. At the time of Mrs. Griffin's death, Ronnie's sons from this first marriage were grown up and had their own families. In fact, there were several grandchildren who were years older than his last two kids.

Since Ronnie was living in one of his mom's houses and had no other place to go-and could not afford to pay rent if he did, the family decided to give him the house that he was living in and Mrs. Griffin's car. This meant that the house Sarah and I were living in was for Ricky, Alice Jean, and Sarah. We all agreed to a price that Sarah and I would pay for the house. Since Sarah owned one third of it, we paid two thirds of the value that we agreed upon to Ricky and Alice Jean. This was a good deal for Sarah and me. This was an older two-story two-bedroom house with two toilets. We figured about how much we would have to pay for repairs to the house and deducted that amount from our offer. Sarah's brother and sister accepted our offer. We purchased the house in June 2004. We spent a little over twenty thousand dollars on repairs and other updates to it. The foundation and new driveway were the most of the expenses along with a new garage roof and plenty of plumbing work and repairs to ceilings because of water pipe leaks. There was always something that needed to be repaired. It was an old house - but still a good deal. Sarah's mom did not pay any property tax on this house.

After we purchased it at the price we did, our taxes for a couple of years were very reasonable -but it was soon to raise up and up and up.

TEXAS CITY HOUSE

THE FIRST 1ST COUSIN DIED

In September of 2004, the first of Sarah's first cousins died. His name was Leroy (Buddy) Griffin Jr. He was raised and lived in Yorktown, Texas. It is located west of Texas City and down the coast of Texas. Yorktown is closer to Corpus Christi than Texas City. Sarah's dad, Jacob Griffin, was thirty-eight years old when he married her mom after he came back from WW II. His brothers and sisters had all been married for many years at this time. This is why many of Sarah's first cousins are over twenty years older than her. Sarah, Ronnie, and I drove down to Yorktown for Buddy's funeral. The last time we had seen Buddy was at Mrs. Griffin's funeral. Buddy and his youngest son, Andy, came to pay their last respects to her. Buddy had nine grown-up children. When Buddy's granddad, old Jake Griffin, left Southwest Texas in the very early nineteen hundreds, he moved to Texas City where he became City Marshall for a period of time. There were six or seven children that made the move with him and Granny Griffin. When Leroy, Buddy's dad, got old enough, he left Texas City and moved to Yorktown where he raised Buddy and his sister. At their yearly family reunions in Texas City, I still remember Sarah's aunts and uncles talking about their brother Leroy, as the one who got away. All the rest of Jake's children raised their families in the Texas City area.

Sarah and I had made several trips to Yorktown in the past. On one trip we took her mom with us and visited with Buddy who was retired then. We also took Ronnie with us one time. In the area near

Yorktown is the Griffin Cemetery with a lot of Griffin and other family members buried there. Buddy was not buried there. I do not know why. There is an Asher family cemetery nearby with Griffin's relative buried there also. One of Sarah's great, great aunts is buried in the Asher Cemetery. She was Granny Griffin's aunt and was married to John Wesley Hardin, who was considered an outlaw in some areas of Texas and other states. The family story goes that Granny Griffin used to sit on Wes Harden's lap when the families got together.

There are many books written about John Wesley Hardin. The one that I prefer most is the one that he wrote while in The Texas State Prison in Huntsville, Texas on a murder charge. I purchased the book at the prison museum on one of our visits there. My Cleveland area property was only about twenty miles from Huntsville. We passed by there every time we went to the Dallas/Fort Worth areas. John W. Hardin became a lawyer while in the state pen.

After Buddy's funeral, we met with his whole family and sort of got acquainted with them. Sarah's dad and mom did not visit Yorktown as two of Leroy's other siblings did. Ronnie and Sarah did not know any of their second cousins, Buddy's children. I never did find out why her family did not stay close to Leroy's family. It could be that Leroy liked to have a good time and left Texas City to get away from the Baptist anti-drinking brothers and sisters. Buddy married a Catholic woman and is buried in the Catholic cemetery in Yorktown. I may be wrong on this, but it may have something to do with Buddy raising his children Catholic. As for Sarah's folks, they would not go near a Catholic church for any reason.

I remember visiting with Sarah's mom one Sunday. We were at her house when she came in from her Baptist church services, threw her purse on the table, and stated, "I am NOT a Baptist". I told her in jest that perhaps she should become a Catholic to which she shouted, "MY GOD-NO". We left it like that. I did not make any more comments. I knew where she stood on Catholics.

KENT AND MELISSA'S WEDDING

My their eldest son, Kent, and his girlfriend, Melissa Poenisch, who had been going together for a number of years decided to get married. So, they made the plans.

The big day was set for October 2, 2004. It was to be held in their backyard at their home in Cedar Park, Texas. Cedar Park is located just a little north of Austin.

They had the yard all decorated and a tent set up in case of rain and chairs and drinks and cakes and everything else that one needs for a wedding. They were ready to get it on.

All of our family attended. There was Sarah and I, Sarah's son, Jake, and his wife, her other son, Nathan, and his girlfriend and my two other sons, Lane and Todd, and their mother, Valerie, and her dad, Al Stoltz, who lives with her in Cedar Park. There were a number of Kent and Mel's friends and co-workers in attendance also. Mel's parents and their spouses were there and Mel's siblings as well. It was a great day, and everyone had a good time.

Sarah and I spent a couple of nights in a local motel. Her boys spent some time with us. The night before the wedding, there was a dinner that all the family members were invited to. Yes, all family members - this meant the in-laws and the out-laws were there.

It had been raining throughout the day. A number of us were at the restaurant when Valerie and her dad drove up. I had not talked to or seen Valerie in a very long time and her dad an even longer time. I went outside to help her get her dad out of the car in the rain. As I was helping him get inside, he said thank you, sir. After we got settled at the table, I sat next to him, and Valerie told her dad who I was. He shouted, "Barry, how the hell are you?" I told him that I was just fine. He invited me to come visit them sometime. This is the first time that I was invited to see them in over twenty years. Did I go, you ask? You bet your bippy I did.

Kent and Mel's wedding got Valerie and me communicating again. Over the years, we would visit each other when visiting our sons.

TOP: MELISSA AND KENT RAFFRAY
BOTTOM: NATHAN AND JACOB ELLIFF,
MELISSA AND KENT, AND LANE AND TODD RAFFRAY

RITA HURRICANE

During September of 2005, Hurricane Rita paid us a visit. At least she was supposed to pay us a visit. The forecast started with her coming ashore near Galveston, Texas. Since we were living in Texas City about five miles from Galveston Island, as the crow flies, we decided to batten things down in and around the house before we hauled ass to Dallas or Louisiana.

By using the route of Interstate 45, Galveston Island is about twelve miles from our house. But as I mentioned above, it is a much shorter distance across the bay to get to us. From the Texas City Dike, about four blocks from our house, one could see all of the East end of Galveston Island.

We packed everything that we thought we would need for the trip. We had three dogs and a cat. We left the cat in the house with several bowls of water and food and two 'cat boxes' for bathroom needs. We placed several dog cages in the back of the pickup, our bags, and took off.

We left the house and came around the loop, took a right on State highway 146 heading North to Mont Belveiu where we could either continue going straight ahead to Dayton and on our way to Dallas or take another right on Interstate-10 East to Louisiana. We went less than one mile and came to a stop in traffic. There was a double line ahead of us as far as we could see. I figured that was this way all the way to Mont Belvieu or about thirty plus miles. I said, "shit on this."

We turned around and came back home. All I had to do was cross the medium and head back to Texas City. There was no traffic at all heading back. We unloaded the dogs and spent that night in our house watching the television news for updates on the hurricane.

The next morning, we took off again. It was clear highways until we came to Seabrook about twelve miles from our house. This is all she wrote. We were bumper to bumper with the other evacuees. According to the radio, Rita was still heading our way. It took us over four hours to get to Interstate 10 at Mont Belvieu, about twenty miles or so from our house.

We thought that we would make better time heading to Louisiana then continuing to go bumper to bumper heading North. So, we took the right at Interstate-10 and headed toward Beaumont and my brother's house near Plaquemine, Louisiana which is about eighteen miles below Baton Rouge on the West side of the Mississippi River. In a very short time, we were stuck in bumper-to-bumper traffic three lanes wide. In the meantime, Rita was projected to hit a little east of Galveston Island. We were stuck in traffic and there was no way to get out. As we slowly proceeded east more cars were trying to get on the interstate from the side roads. As the hours past, Sarah was getting really car sick. There was not enough room in the truck for her to lie down. We had our 1997 Toyota T-100 extended cab, but it was just not big enough to put her front seat back because of all the stuff we had inside of it. We had water for us and the dogs but that did not help her. I started to worry about if we had enough gas and finding a gas station that was open on this trip. I was worried that we would run out on the highway. Then we would be gone pecans. This was September but it was still very hot weather. I had turned off the air conditioner some time ago. We had all the windows down, but it was still very hot. The dogs were feeling it also but there was nothing that I could do. This hotness is the primary reason that Sarah got overheated. I felt sorry for her but would not turn on the air conditioner. Yes, you are right- I am a no-good bastard. But a bastard that will hopefully keep us from running out of gas in this mess. There was no way that anyone could get gas delivered during this mess. We had seen folks in distress. along the way with no way for them to get help.

By the time we reached Anahuac, about fifty miles from our house, Rita had moved more to the East. When we were approaching Winnie, Interstate-10 was still bumper to bumper with more folks leaving their homes that were east of Galveston Island. We noticed that the highway to Port Arthur was wide open so instead of staying on Interstate 10 toward Beaumont we continued straight ahead going to Port Arthur. Well, another stupid move by me. I was hoping to catch the ferry near Port Arthur and head to Cameron, Louisiana then head north to get back to the interstate deeper into Louisiana. We were making really good time with a lot less traffic until we came to a roadblock in Port Arthur. The damn police had blocked the highway and were diverting all the traffic into the middle of Port Arthur. We got behind school buses carrying old folks from old folks' homes, big rigs carrying freight, and many, many cars. We were all diverted onto this small street and again we were bumper to bumper. We lost another few hours trying to work our way out of Port Arthur and were moving backward toward Beaumont and not the Louisiana border. It was a long ride to Lake Charles. There was not one gas station open along the way.

Rita had shifted even more to the east and more folks from Port Arthur, Beaumont, Cameron, and Lake Charles were trying to get on Interstate-10 heading East- damn it.

Several more hours later, the traffic started thinning out as we neared Lafayette, Louisiana. While passing through the Lafayette area, I noticed a number of cars pulling off the interstate. We were really low on gas at this time. It was very dark outside now. I could see the lights at a gas station off in the distance. I had been driving a long time and now nightfall had caught us. We pulled into the gas station. There were about eight pumps and twenty or more vehicles trying to jockey for position. I took notice of where I was in line when I pulled in. There were two cars ahead of me. I wanted to be sure that I followed the second car to the pump. Other cars were arriving, Sarah got out of the truck and starting taking each dog, one at a time, for a walk so they could do their business. After each was finished, she bought drinks and snacks for us. The car that was ahead of me and the other two there before me finished filling up and worked his way away from the pumps. He backed out instead of driving straight out. This left me next in line for the pump. I was the only vehicle that could get to the pump- so I did. I set the pump to fill up my tank and went talk to the next driver that was there before me. He could see that I had no choice but to move into the pump spot. I told him that I was going to drive out in a way that he would be next. And I did. Our tank was on fumes when we pulled into the station. We had over four hundred miles on this tank of gas. I could not believe it but we used a lot of gas not going anywhere. We made really good time the rest of the way to my brother's house.

All toll it took us eighteen and one-half hours to make this trip which we usually did in four- and one-half hours. We slept really good that night.

Rita finally made landfall near the Texas/Louisiana border. When we returned home a couple of days later, we saw a lot of damage between Lake Charles, Louisiana and Winnie, Texas. When we arrived home, everything was in fine order. My neighbor, Felix, across the street did not even leave home. As he waited to make his decision about heading toward Austin, Texas, he heard the broadcast that the storm was moving eastward, and he decided that he had no reason to leave. Felix kept an eye on our house and the other houses that the owners left that are on our street. He was a good guy.

HURRICANE RITA EVACUATION 2005

ME AND GERALD

"BIG BEAR" PACKARD

After living in Texas City for some time, I met this man who lived a few blocks from us. His name was Gerald Packard. He drove a big red diesel pickup with the name "Big Bear" written on it. If we were in the house, we could hear when he was coming around the corner onto our street.

Because he used our street so much, we knew that he must live in our neighborhood. One day I went for a walk about the area. I noticed his truck parked on the side of an older two-story house. The yard had items all about it as displays. It was a very unique place.

In Texas City, all of the older residential areas have back allies behind/between the houses. Past our backyard, was an alley which was behind our backyard neighbor's house as well. The alley is where the garbage/trash trucks used to pick up the refuse. I walked in the alley behind Big Bear's house. Through the cracks in his wooden fence, I could see chickens. He had a fenced-in area for them. This is where the rooster crowing that we sometimes hear in the mornings, is coming from. I am doing some good detective work here.

There were also several older cars, and a really old pickup and an old panel truck in his back yard. I loved looking at them. I like old cars and trucks. I found out later that he had owned some of them for many years. Folks wanted to buy some of them, but he was not willing to let them go - just yet.

On the walk back to my house, I realized it. After seeing what was in his front yard, then walking his alley an seeing what was in this back yard, I came to the realization that Big Bear was a COLLECTOR-just like me. Not long after this we met each other in a grocery store and became friends. He is a few years older than me and also retired as I am. He loves to go to estate sales and flea markets, as I do. He has a 4440 Winchester carbine, as I do. He recently purchased a 1936 Buick, four door touring sedan that looks very much like my 1936 Oldsmobile, four door touring sedan. We both had heart problems but that did not slow us down very much at this time. We are birds of a feather, so we started flocking together from time to time.

As a younger man, Gerald spent years working in South Louisiana in his trade. He made many good friends in my home state, and he told me that he enjoyed his time there very much. He learned many customs of the Cajun folks while there and had many a good times.

We would visit each other from time to time. After he started having a friend of his working on his old Buick, he decided to sell the other old vehicles he had. He said that he just did not have the time to do anything with them. He cleared them out of his backyard. He kept the chicken that was giving him fresh eggs for breakfast every day. He would not part with them.

Gerald would go to Nacogdoches from time to time and visit with his family there. They often went camping or fishing and hunting trips. They would spend time at Sam Rayburn Lake and Toledo Bend Lake. He did NOT let his heart condition slow him down by one iota. He is always on the go. I miss seeing and visiting with him since I moved from Texas City. We do talk on the telephone from time to time to stay in touch.

CRAWFISH BOILS AT KENT AND MELISSA'S HOUSE

For a number of years, Kent and Mel would have a crawfish boil around Easter weekend at their home. I would get three sacks of crawfish in Seabrook, ice them down in my big ice chest, and drive to Cedar Park the day before the boil. I brought the boiling pot and seasonings. Kent purchased the potatoes, lemons, sausage, garlic, corn, mushrooms (they love mushrooms), etc. to throw in the pot with the crawfish.

They invited several of their good friends to come over. Mel would bake cakes and cookies and have trays of food to munch on while awaiting the crawdads to be ready.

I did this for about four years or so; I really enjoyed doing it, but my hands started to give me trouble - arthritis - I just could not continue to do it. Everything I tried to do gave me pain.

One time we had an early Easter. I ended up boiling the crawfish in a hailstorm. Mel had to move everything into her house. I have NEVER had a crawfish boil in a house. I would never do it. Mel pulled it off though.

I was the only one outside trying to boil the crawfish in the hailstorm. The hail was twice the size of BB's. I was covered up pretty well, so they did not hurt me when they hit me; but I had a lot of trouble heating the water hot enough to boil these suckers. It took over forty minutes to get one batch done. A batch is one sack. The actual boiling time is six to eight minutes. This is after the water comes back to a boil. We always would let them soak for twenty minutes after turning the fire off so they could suck up the flavors from the water.

I have never boiled crawfish under these conditions before. I know that they did not come out as good as in the past, but I did not hear any complaints. Come to think of it, I may not have heard any complaints because I was boiling the second batch while everyone else was in the house eating the hot first batch. I will never try to boil crawfish again when the temperature is in the twenties, and it is raining ice. As it turned out, I am not able to handle the chore of boiling anymore.

After the first two years of bringing three sacks of crawfish, I cut it down to two sacks. With three sacks there was just too much crawfish left. Not everybody ate them, which is why there is always something else to eat from Mel's Kitchen.

After everyone left, a few of us had to peel the tails and put them in the freezer for later use. These mudbugs are just too damn expensive to throw them away. I would not have any of that shit.

The Christmas after the last time I boiled, I gave Kent a complete boiling outfit whereby he could do it himself. He has been doing it for several years now with some help from his friends. I do wish that I was still able to do it - I REALLY DID ENJOY IT SO.

TOP: JACOB AND I WITH THE SECOND BATCH
BOTTOM: NATHAN AND I WITH THE FIRST BATCH

TOP: MIKE SONGY (FAMILY FRIEND), VISITING WITH KENT RAFFRAY

BOTTOM: MIKE SONGY VISITING WITH TODD RAFFRAY

SELLING SARAH'S RENT HOUSE

In the year 2006, we put the Texas City rental house up for sale. We decided to sell it ourselves and save the real estate salesman commission. I had already sold my League City house successfully and thought that we could do it again. The next-door neighbor was interested in buying it. He lived there with his mom and dad. His dad died and the young man with one or two children wanted to be next to his mom.

We had spent many months working on the house to get it ready for sale.

We put in a new bathroom floor, re-carpeted the whole house, repainted all the inside, replaced some windows, etc. We spent several thousand dollars on it. I did all the work on it that I could do and hired folks to do the things that I could not do. We had a new roof put on after Hurricane Ike came through. The house had three roofs on it, and it cost us much more to put a new roof on than we got from the insurance company. Much of the extra cost was in labor to take the three prior roofing materials off before installing the new felt and shingles.

We told the neighbor the price that we wanted for the house. Well, he was interested but not THAT interested. This young man was starting to straighten out I believe. As a teenager he was the leader of the Brown Assassins - a TexMex group of young folks who had fights with the Crips and the Bloods - both primary black kids and other gangs. These gangs would ride in the neighborhood and shoot up rival gangs' cars and houses. When Sarah and her two young sons lived here, her car got bullet holes in it by stray bullets. We do not know if her house was ever hit. These bastards could not even shoot straight. I think that the house got hit several times, but I could not find the bullet holes. I know of two times that the Brown Assassin's car got shot up. He would have it bonded up and repainted after each shooting. He did not like to ride around in a shot-up car. The boy did take pride in how his car looked and he also did not want to give any advertisement to the Crips or Bloods. When he got older, he went to work at Amoco's plant in Texas City as a contractor. There was a big explosion there and folks got killed. The boy got injured out there during the explosion. While recovering, he did some things that got him arrested and went to prison for several years. When he got out, he moved back in with his mom. I do not remember if his dad had passed before he went to prison or after he got back. During the time that his dad was sick, he used to drive his dad to the end of the Texas City Dike and sit there and watch the ships heading into Houston and back out again and drink his Pearl beer. His dad was white, and his mom was Mexican. His dad retired from the post office. His mom was married before and he had at least one older brother that I met. I used to yard-visit with his dad a lot. I never got close to his mom. We knew each other and said hi to each other but never had the conversations that Sarah and I had with his dad. His dad caught the cancer. He was the only person that we knew of who loved Pearl beer. There was one small quick shop that sold it in Texas City. After talking at the fence one day, he offered me a Pearl. I liked it and he told me where to find them. When I went to the store and asked for a six pack, they told me that they had one customer who bought Pearl from them. I told them that is how I knew that they had it. They checked to see what they had in stock to see if I could have a six pack. They wanted to be sure that they had enough for him if he came in before selling any to me. He was too good a customer for them to not have any Pearl beer when he wanted some. I really liked the guy. He had a cancer that there was no cure for. It just finally ate him up - but he was going to drink his Pearl to his last breath- and he did. We got closer to his son and the boy's mom after the boy got out of prison. We talked about his dad a lot. The boy really missed his dad a lot.

After a week or two with a for sale by owner sign in the front yard and no more interest from the neighbor, we called a local realtor. He was sort of a friend of Sarah's family. They walked through the house and property, took measurements, and pointed out several things that I should work on. They came up with a price to put it up for sale. We signed a three-month contract with them. They added the house to their list of properties for sale and published it in their next flyer. About a week or less after their sign was placed in the front yard, the neighbor boy came over to talk with me. He had taken one of the flyers and saw that the price was five thousand dollars more than I told him. Well, he was now interested again. He had received his lump sum from the chemical company's insurance for his injuries in the explosion. I do not know how much he received but believe that it was a hell of a lot more than fifty thousand dollars. He told me that he would now pay the fifty thousand dollars for it. I told him that I would have to check on it. You know when you sell a house there are a lot of other costs involved besides the six to eight percent realtor charge. After talking with Sarah, we went to talk with the realtor in person. We told them what happened and how we had given this guy a cash price before we hired them. Long story short – no hard feeling, they let us off the hook for the commission. We thanked them and told them that we would pay them to complete any paperwork that needed to be done to complete this deal. And we did.

On the day of the closing, the young man gave us a check from the Amoco Credit Union for fifty thousand dollars. We put it into the bank to spend later.

As you know, some folks can rent houses and make a good income doing it. We rented Sarah's house for about five years or so and never made one damn dime. We had renters tear up the house, some would not pay rent on time, or you could not find them to collect your rent, and on and on. It was always one thing or another. A sad story as to why they did not have the rent money. We had two or three bastards moving out in the middle of the night owing several months' rent. We had to pay for going to court to get non-rent paying bastards out of our house. We were just tired of all that shit that we had to take to rent a house. We felt so relieved after it was sold. Sad but relieved. Sarah paid notes for thirty years and had her house finally paid off. I may have helped a little for several years after we were married - but I was so proud of her for doing what she did.

The young man who purchased the house had some problems with the city. He started remodeling it. He was moving walls inside the house. He was redesigning it and then he gutted the inside to redo everything. Well before long he had a roof and foundation. At that point, the city shut him down. They said that he was now building a house without a permit. He needed to pay a fine and buy all kinds of permits. These things cost a lot of money. He may have gone to court against the city because his project was shut down for months. I do not know what problems he had with the city and perhaps the County also. I do know his project waited for many months. How it was resolved, I do not know, but he finally finished it. It looks a little different from the outside. I've never been inside to see the finished work. I just wondered if the city was trying to screw him for all the trouble that he caused when leading the Brown Assassins- I just do not know.

TRIPS TAKEN. DURING 2006, 2007, 2008 AND 2009

Sarah and I took numerous trips (vacations) over a period of several years. We had wonderful times during each and every one of them – to my knowledge.

One year we decided to go to West Texas and explore that countryside. I made arrangements to spend a couple of nights at my timeshare at Canyon City at Canyon Lake near San Antonio, Texas. It is located between Austin and San Antonio. It is on an eight-thousand-acre lake with beautiful scenery all around the lake. This is called the Hill Country. From where I come from, it seemed more like a mountain country. We took a back road called The Devil's Backbone to visit San Marcos, Texas. This is the city where the University of Southwest Texas is located. This is where Sarah's dad and mom took classes during the summer when they were not teaching in high school. It is also where my son, Lane, earned his master's degree in Public Administration. This is also where my youngest son, Todd, attended for a couple of years when he was trying to get his higher education. We all just loved this campus. The San Marcus River runs through it. The water is so clear that one could see their toes when waist deep in it. Southwest State University became Texas State University, and that name was put on Lane's Master's Degree.

After two nights at Canyon Lake, we headed further west to Marfa, Texas. There is a phenomenon there called the Marfa Lights. It is a mystery how that happens. Sometimes on dark nights, one could see darting lights in the distance. We were told that they put on a great show. Sarah's brother, Ricky, told us that he once saw them while visiting there.

There is a roadside parking area that the State of Texas built for folks to hang around to see if the lights were going to show up. It was very nice and well kept up.

We got a motel room not far from the rest area on the same highway. We drove around Marfa to check it out. It is a small town. It has mostly adobe type houses with stucco and tile roofs. Mostly Mexican Americans live there.

As evening approached, we drove out to the viewing area. People were already arriving. We met and talked with many folks while there. Some are from states far away. There were several serious sightseers with large cameras. The still and movie kinds. One was a professor from some university who said that he came out every year on his vacation to take photos. He had some first-class pictures.

We stayed out there until about two or three o'clock in the morning. NO - we did NOT see one damn thing. This is just our luck. We came all this way and saw zilch, nothing, nada, zero. I believe that these Marfa folks and Ricky are full of shit. We went on a wild goose trip and not did not see any goose; we also did NOT see any Marfa lights. They were all pushing our legs.

After a good morning sleep, we checked out of the motel and headed farther west to Fort Davis, Texas. We drove looking at the sites in the mountains there. There was not much of anything that I wanted to see. We stopped at the large motel and were thinking about checking in. There are cabins one could rent or stay in the lodge. The lodge and cabins were beautiful. They were like log houses. They were built using big-looking logs. The prices were high - in my opinion. We were thinking about a small cabin since there were only two of us. We decided to drive around and look at the cabins available. We had a map of the whole layout from the clerk at the lodge motel. Fort Davis is in the Davis Mountains. This is the largest mountain range in Texas.

As we were driving, we noticed a very large black cloud over the mountain to the west of us. We found a radio station that was giving warnings of a storm approaching. We got the hell out of there as fast as we could. We did not go back to the lodge, we did not pass go, we did not collect two hundred dollars, we just hauled ASS. We headed back to Marfa. The storm caught up to us, but we were on the tail end of it. At Marfa, it was not bad at all. Just rain and some wind. I know that in the mountains, they caught hell from it.

When we were driving around Marfa after checking in at the first motel, we noticed a very nice motel in the middle of the small town. It was of the type of construction one might find in Mexico. It was well built and had granite and terracotta tile floors and lots of flowers and small trees in and around it. It was a very pleasant atmosphere. We checked in there when we got back from Fort Davis. That night we went back to the spot to see THE MARFA LIGHTS. No fu er I mean damn lights again. Disappointed we went back to the motel earlier than the last time. Much earlier. This is bull shit, and I am not coming back this way again, ever.

While in the Marfa/Fort Davis area, we were very close to Mexico and Big Bend National Park but did not go there either. We were also close to Lajitas on the Rio Grande, but never went there either. I was selfish because I had already been to those places and did not care to go again. You might say I been there and done that and do not need to do it again.

After a couple of days there and no Marfa lights seeing, we headed up to Interstate 10 and headed back to the East. I made arrangements to spend one night at my Silverleaf Timeshare again on Canyon Lake. The day after the Canyon Lake stay, we headed for home.

BUYING THE 1936 OLDSMOBILE

Ever since I purchased "The Place" near Cleveland, Texas before Sarah and I married, we would go there to spend the weekends that I did not go to work. We really enjoyed our time there. We did a lot of work clearing brush and getting the house livable.

I hauled off over twenty-seven pickup loads of junk to the dump. The old couple who lived there were COLLECTORS - as I am. But it was just too much unusable junk.

We drove up Highway 146 from League City to Dayton, Texas. At Dayton, we took Highway 321 which took us through Cleveland. Out of Cleveland, we took FM-1725 for twelve miles to get to "The Place". It was about an eighty mile trip. After we moved to Texas City, in 2004, it became a ninety-five-mile trip.

About six miles before you get to Cleveland, we passed a residence that always had older cars and trucks for sale. The guy there was retired, and he would repair them and sell them. We stopped on a number of occasions and looked over what he had to sell. He was a nice enough fellow and over time I got to know and like him.

Once or twice, he had 1938 sedans in his yard. Since I loved older cars, I made sure to stop to look them over. He had a Chevy one time and a Ford another time. I did not care for either of these two brands. I just passed on them.

If any of you read my first book "Raising Sugar Cane", you may recall a story that I wrote about a ride I had with my mom driving our 1938 Plymouth four-door, humpback Sedan to Mrs. Olivia Falcon's house in the back part on Cedar Grove Plantation where I was raised.

This was an experience that I will never forget. It was the last time that I remember my mom driving a car. Although I was told by my niece, Kim Breaux, that Mom did try to drive with her when she was a little girl, I never knew of it. I believe that Mom quit driving after what happened to us on the mud road trying to get to the Falcon house.

Anyway, this vivid picture in my mind made me want a 1938 Plymouth four door Sedan ever since. Over the years, I have seen several of them but was not in the position to purchase one. Well at this time in my life, I was NOT poor anymore. Sarah and I even made a trip to the Dallas, Texas area to look over a 1938 Plymouth. I did not want to drive it because I told the guy that I did not want to buy this one. It needed too much work to make it worthwhile for me.

Well on this particular trip in early July of 2007, the guy near Cleveland had this black hump-back in his yard with a for sale sign on it. We had the pickup loaded down with our dogs and cat and enough stuff to spend nine days at "The Place". This was on our vacation that I planned for many months.

Nothing was going to stop this vacation. Not even work.

We made a U-turn in the middle of the highway and went back to his house. He greeted us upon arrival. We knew each other well at this time. Sarah and I looked over this car. It was not a 1938 Plymouth, but was a 1936 Oldsmobile, four doors, hump-back, Touring Sedan and only had 65,000 miles plus on it. I loved it right off the bat. We took it for a short drive up the highway and back. I still liked it. It is so much more car than the 38 Plymouth. This Olds was a Cadillac when compared to a Plymouth.

Sarah knew that I loved the car, and she encouraged me to buy it. She told me that I have been looking for a very long time, and I now have the money to buy the car. The guy gave me the price. I did not want to pay that price. I made a counteroffer and he said, "sold". I should have offered less, but a deal is a deal. We shook hands on the deal.

But now I have a problem. I told him that we were on vacation and on the way to our house twelve miles above Cleveland and I did not want to get the car right now. Truman said that was not a problem. I could give him a check for 'good faith' to hold it and when we are coming back this way complete the transaction then. So that is what we did.

I was all excited and the week of work and relaxation went by fast. I notified Truman that we would be passing back his way on a weekday. This worked out really well since his wife worked at the County Tax Office, she would handle all of the paperwork. As it turned out he had remarried a younger woman as I had. I do not know what that has to do with this story but I just wanted to get it in. It is my story, and I will put in what I want to - if it is the truth. We completed the deal on July 18, 2007.

Truman did two other things for me. He completely polished the car, and he delivered it to us in Texas City with his car trailer. I was really happy that he did that. He and his son arrived the next day. We had a little crowd in our front yard when they were unloading my new/old car.

The background on the car is that it was owned by a local banker from Splendora, which is just several miles away and he did not want it anymore. So, Truman got it. It was garaged and kept until Truman got it. But as it turned out, he did not keep it very long. It originally came from Cedar Rapids, Iowa. I still have some papers that show that.

We used the old car in parades and gatherings in League City and Texas City. We used to park it at free car shows about twice a month. We enjoyed all the older folks who told us that they had found memories of these types of old cars. We had many good times with this car.

P.S. As of this writing, I still have this car in my garage in Louisiana. Yes, it is for sale. It still has the Texas Bicentennial 1936 license plates on it. Those plate cost me over four hundred dollars to buy. It also meant that the name that I was going to put on the plates (in Texas there are two license plates), "Mrs. Josey", my mom's name, would not be used for the plates. The car is registered as a Classic/Antique in Texas.

ME AND MY 1936 OLDSMOBILE TOURING SEDAN

The Tommy gun was given to me by my good Texas City friend, Richard Daugird. The gun is real, but it shoots pellets. It makes a good prop for this car.

HURRICANE IKE SEPTEMBER 2008

In September or 2008, there was another hurricane brewing in the Atlantic Ocean. Its name was IKE. Ike was a bad one. We decided after first hearing about it that we would evacuate.

A year or two before Ike, we purchased a 1936 Oldsmobile Touring Sedan. It was always parked in our driveway and not in the garage. "Why," you ask? Well, I will tell you why. Sometime before we purchased this car, we had the driveway replaced. The cement was cracked, and big chunks were coming up.

The garage did not have a cement floor in it. It was dirt. When we contracted with this company to take out and replace our driveway, we wanted them to put a cement floor in the garage also.

When we were able to use the driveway again, the old car and my pickup could not fit through the garage door because of the height of the vehicles. They were too high to go through the doorway. The slab in the garage was about four or five inches thick. This raised the floor of the garage; hence we could not get the vehicles in it. I ended up with a two-car garage that I could not use for my car and truck. So, they just sat in the driveway.

Well here comes Ike. And he is aiming for us. Our friend, Lee Blanton, who is a jack-of-all-trades, was not going to let us leave town with our old car in the driveway with a hurricane coming.

ME AND LEE BLANTON

Lee is the guy who ran electrical wire from our house to the garage and put lights in it for us a year or so earlier. So here comes Lee again to bail us out.

He checked out what we had, then decided how he was going to do it. Lee cut above the doorway at an angle on each side of the doorway. Then he cut about eight inches out across the complete top of the entrance thus giving us plenty of room to drive the old car or pickup into the garage. Since we were going to use the truck to evacuate, the garage would be used for our 1936 Olds.

We also had a 2005 Toyota Matrix car that we drove near the garage and parked it. It was in the driveway, but I had more concern for the old car than the Toyota.

We were and are very grateful to Lee after what he did for us. He also worked on the old car for me from time to time.

We now had the old car in the garage. I would build doors for it after we got back. I did not have the time to do it now - we were running out of time to get away from Texas City.

We departed Texas City with our dogs and headed north to the Dallas/Fort Worth area where Sarah had relatives. Again, we left the cat with plenty of food and water in the house. We stayed with Sarah's relatives for several days before driving back home to Texas City.

Ike hit Texas City and did much damage. When we got home, we had a mess. There were huge oak trees down all over our yard. I did not mentioned that there were eleven large oak trees around our property. Five were in our yard.

When we turned from the street onto our driveway, we stopped quickly. There were limbs all over the place. I need to mention here that our cement driveway is twenty-one feet wide and ninety-five feet long to the garage. We could not see our little white Toyota in the driveway. There were too many limbs and brush to see it. We walked up fairly close and could tell that it was there under all the limbs/brush.

The front yard did not look too bad. The back yard was covered. The swing set was demolished, the hurricane fence between us and our neighbor was demolished as well. The house itself was alright as was the garage. We had our work cut out for us now.

After several weeks, we finally had everything cleaned up. I cut limbs and branches for days and hauled them to the front of the house for pick up by the City. I had a pile over ten feet high. If one was walking on our street, they could NOT see our house.

Several folks came by our house with trailers and cut smaller pieces of our oaks and loaded them. I helped several of them when I had the time. Texans love to BBQ with oak. They made a little dent in my huge pile.

We eventually got the yard cleaned up then I went to work repairing/replacing the fence.

By the way, we did NOT have any structural damage to our house or garage or my old car. As far as the Toyota car that was in the driveway – I could not believe that this car only had slight scratches on it. The huge limbs fell in such a way that they did not hit the car. It was just unbelievable. Well, you just had to be there to believe it.

SELLING THE TEXAS CITY HOUSE

During the year 2009 we decided to sell the Texas City house. I wanted to move back to Louisiana. Since I was now not working, I thought that we could live less expensive (cheaper) in Louisiana. The property taxes there are much lower in Louisiana than in Texas. Thousands of dollars lower.

We did some work on and inside the house. We did several thousand dollars of work on the foundation and repainted all the inside and outside to get it ready to place on the market.

We hired our family friend to appraise the property and do the listing. After some time, it was not getting any bites. The realtor had a niece who wanted to buy a house but could not/would not take out a long-term homeowner's loan. We made a deal with them to self-finance the house.

We agreed upon terms and conditions. They were to make monthly payments to us after a small down payment. One of the conditions was if they missed so many payments, we reprocessed the property. They would have to vacate and lose all payments and the down payment as well. They would pay us for a certain number of years at a certain rate and then have a balance due. They and I figured after this period of time that they could come up with the balance and pay it off in a lump sum or finance it at that time. It would be a much lesser amount to finance. This is what we did and received checks from them for years.

Of course, everyone hated to see us go. My three sons were/are living in Texas and so are Sarah's two sons. So, we started packing for the move to Louisiana.

I rented a large U-Haul truck and a ten-foot trailer to pull behind our T-100 Toyota pickup from the Galveston U-Haul store. This was during the Thanksgiving holidays, so we had plenty of loaders to help load the truck and trailer. Both of Sarah's brothers and their wives and kids were there to help and her niece and husband and her children. We were having a really good time loading the big truck.

Later in the afternoon, I realized that I did not rent a car carrier for my 1936 Oldsmobile. I called the Galveston U Haul place, and they had one. I told everyone that I had to go there for a car carrying a trailer. I thought that they would continue loading the truck. It took about two hours for me to get back with the car carrier. To my surprise, Ricky, and his family were pulling out of the driveway and heading back to Fort Worth. Nothing had been loaded into the big truck after I left. I was well pissed off. The whole group there was sitting around drinking beer. They did NOT know what or how I wanted to load stuff that was to be loaded, so they all just waited Sarah included, for me to get back. After I arrived other guests started leaving.

Within twenty minutes, everyone except Judy, who was Big Ronnie's wife left. Judy, Sarah, and I worked our asses off into the night to finish loading the big truck and the pull-behind trailer.

After spending the night and resting up the next morning I tried everything down in the big truck as best I could. I then hooked the car carrier onto the big truck, drove my old car onto it and tied it on the frame in front and back so it would not move. We had stuff packed into the old car as well. It is a four big door touring sedan and held a lot of stuff.

I took off heading to Plaquemine, Louisiana. Sarah was going to follow in the pickup and trailer later. Judy had come back to help her finish loading the U-Haul trailer. Sarah was also carrying the dogs with her.

It was a long trip for me. I did not/could not go over fifty-five miles per hour. I had a heavy load and towing my very heavy 1936 Olds made the pull even heavier.

It was really exciting when I got to Lake Charles. I did not want to go over the old narrow bridge, so I took the loop. The Interstate 10 bridge is not only narrow, but it goes straight up. I know that it is the shortest route but did not think that I could get up enough speed to make it to the top. Boy I was so right. A quarter mile before I got to the loop bridge, I floor boarded the truck. I had the pedal to the metal. By the time I got to the crest, I was going about ten miles per hour. I was cutting buttonholes with my go-go. I kept an eye on the traffic behind me. They all had the red ass at me because I could not get up the overpass doing fifty miles per hour. I was putting a crimp in their stile. They wanted to go. There is no way that I would have gotten up the Interstate 10 without coming to a complete stop on that bridge. While coming down the loop bridge, I finally got back to fifty-five miles per hour. I was really hauling ass then. The rest of the way to Plaquemine was smooth going but really slow.

I kept my Louisiana family appraised of my progress and they were waiting for me when I arrived at our new house to help me unload.

My sister and her husband and most of their adult kids and grandkids were there to help. My brother, his wife and several of their kids were on hand also. We unloaded the truck and placed the furniture in the house where I wanted it. It took us into the nighttime to empty the big truck.

It is usually a five-hour drive from our house in Texas City to Plaquemine. It took me about seven hours to make it with this load. It was a good thing that I left there early in the morning.

After everybody went home, Sarah pulled up with the trailer and our dogs. Sarah and I and my brother unloaded the pickup and trailer the next day. We had made the move A-OK. I was happy to be living back in my home state - for the next several years - anyway.

TRAGEDY IN MY FAMILY

My sister, Bobbie Jo, and her husband, Gene Bertrand, had six children. Their youngest and tallest, over six feet two inches, Mark, joined the Navy right after graduating high school. He served a number of tours while in the Navy. After serving six years, he received his discharge. He was out for some time then decided to go back in. He served another five years in the Navy.

Mark met his wife, Florence, while in the Navy and they married. It seemed then that they both wanted to make a career in the Navy. I do not remember how many missions that he and Florence did while on active duty, but I believe that they both had seen duty during the Desert Storm incident aboard ships off the coast of Iraq. This would have been in the Persian Gulf during the military action.

After his second five years in the Navy, Mark got out again. He works at a number of jobs on armed service bases for the next several years. Then he got the Cancer as they say down here. He had been out of the Navy for several years before he got sick. Florence had been sick for a number of years at this time also.

After some time of fighting this awful disease, Mark passed away on March 31, 2011, while living in Biloxi, Mississippi. He is buried in a military cemetery in Biloxi.

My sister, Robbie Jo Ann Raffray Bertrand, (she had one of those long names like I have), only lived another eight months after Mark passed away. This was totally unexpected, which was not the case with

Mark. Bobbie Jo had a stroke from a blood clot. She was conscious when she arrived at the hospital. She was given the "clot-busting" shot in the hospital where she passed away a little time later. It was just a sad situation and very hard to take.

My sister was seventy-two years and seven months old. For years she and us (me and my brother) wondered if we would live longer than our momma (sixty-six) and our daddy (seventy-two), when they died. We all made it past momma. Daddy was seventy-two and four months old when he died. Bobbie Joe made it past him by a few months. The ironic thing is that my sister passed away on the same date as our dad, December 14", but twenty-seven years later. So, 2011 was a very sad year for the Bertrand and Raffray families.

MARK BERTRAND AND HIS MOM BOBBIE JO BERTRAND

ME AND BOBBIE JO

ANOTHER TRIP

Sarah was into doing genealogy on her mother's side of the family big time. She was communicating with a distant cousin that she had never met in Kentucky. She also had family in Missouri. So, we decided to take a trip to do some research. On these trips we were taking, if I did not mention our dogs, that is because Sarah's brother, Ronnie, who lived in Texas City would look after them when we were on a trip.

We headed to Plaquemine, Louisiana where we spent the night at my brother's house. In the morning we departed for Mississippi. We spent one night there. We drove around several places to sightsee. We went through an old black college campus. We walked on a historical old wooden bridge. I forgot what the history was about it though. We saw other sites that impressed and depressed us. So much of the black folks history in this country is really sad. Although it may have been better than what their history would have been in Africa - this is something that we will never know. We did not spend a lot of time in Mississippi.

As we drove on Interstate 59, we departed Mississippi and drove through Harrisburg and Meridian, and we headed to Alabama and went through Tuscaloosa and Bessemer into Birmingham where we spent several nights. We enjoyed our time in the Birmingham area. Before we got there, we stopped for a tour of a Civil War Arms and Ammunitions facility. It was for the Confederate Army. The housing and smelting plant was interesting to see. This location was mined for lead that was turned it into bullets and other warring stuff.

In Birmingham, we stayed in a motel that was near the large Vulcan statue. This was a very picturesque statue with flowers and shrubby around the grounds. Vulcan seemed to be a hard-working man that worked in a steel yard. He had a large hammer type mallet in his hands - like for banging metal into shape. While driving about in Birmingham we got lost several times. We would stop and look for the Vulcan statue to find our way back to our motel. We passed by him a lot of times in our two days there.

One time while Sarah was driving, I was looking over a local map to find our next place to visit. When I looked up, I let out a scream that scared the hell out of Sarah. We were at a crest of a hill and I thought we were going over a cliff. Did I not tell you that Birmingham is a hilly city. It is a pretty place, but I would not live there in the wintertime. If they had ice or snow on the roads, one could go a mile coming off these hills without even trying. No way Jose would I live there.

Sarah and I had a good laugh about my reaction - sometime later – after my heart got out of my mouth and settled back down in my chest where it should have stayed. The only reason that I did not SHIT is because I forgot that I had an ASSHOLE. And as Edith Ann used to say on Laugh-In, "and that's the truth".

The second day there we purchased tickets to visit the Civil Rights Museum. We spent most of the day touring in it. They have a tremendous exhibit and display set up for everyone to see. I believe that anybody who visits Birmingham should go to this museum.

They would really have an appreciation of what the civil rights pioneers went through to finally get their human rights. There were no made-up stories or pictures there. As Sergeant Joe Friday (Jack Webb) on the old Dragnet television program used to say, "just the facts, mam, just the facts". It is sad and very informative for all who pass through it. If one does not feel bad after visiting this museum, they are not human. And that is all I have to say about that.

When we left Birmingham, we headed up Interstate 65 into Tennessee than turned left on a smaller highway to get to Tullahoma, Tennessee to spend two nights with Bully and Mary Jo Daigle. Bully and I went to high school together at White Castle High in Louisiana. We also graduated together in 1962.

Upon arrival, Bully met us in a drugstore parking lot. We followed him to his house. We had Sammy, our pug dog on this trip with us. He was a very good traveling dog. Sammy had to spend two nights in the Daigle's garage in his cage. The next day, Bully had arranged to take the day off from the hospital where he worked and took us to tour the Jack Daniels Whiskey manufacturing facility in the nearby town of Lynchburg. We spent quite a few hours there.

No - I did not drink any samples for free or otherwise. I cannot stand the taste or smell of hard liquor. I had to leave the tour at the Whiskey brewery vats and tour guide. It almost knocked me out, just the smell. I left the tour in a hurry at that point and waited downstairs for them to go into the other buildings.

In the old office area, they showed us the safe that Jack Daniels broke his toe on. The story goes that he was trying to open it and it did not want to open. So, he kicked it with his foot and broke a big toe. He always wore cowboy boots. He hobbled around on the foot for months. All of the pictures that we saw of him before he broke his toe, he had cowboy boots on. He must have had several dozen pairs of them.

Jack Daniels was a lady's man. He never got married and went out with beautiful women all the time. They were all chasing after him. He was a small man in statue. Even with his boots on in every picture that I saw, the ladies were taller than he was.

Jack started making whiskey when he was fifteen years old with an older man that taught him the ropes. He became a multi-millionaire off of whiskey. He died young- in his early forties, if my memory serves me right.

It seems that his broken toe never did heal. It kept getting worse and worse. They had to cut his foot off because of gangrene setting in. Sometime later, the doctors cut off his leg at the knee to try and save. him. And even some time later they cut his whole leg off, but to no avail. He finally died of gangrene poisoning. Such a waste. I think that Jack was hardheaded and always had to have it his way. They may have saved his life if he would let them cut more off the first time.

The ironic thing about this whole matter, when you think about it is, at any point after his toe got infected, if he would have put his foot into a vat of his whiskey, it would have killed all of the gangrene that finally killed him. There is nothing like alcohol to stop bacteria in it tracks. This just shows to go you. I meant to write the last sentence that way.

Jack left his whole estate and business interest to his nieces and nephews.

BULLY DAIGLE AND ME IN LYNCHBURG, TN

The next day, we said good-byes to Bully and Mary Jo, loaded up Sammy and left heading to Danville, Kentucky where Scott and Nita Reisinger lived. Scott was a good friend who worked for several barge towing companies that I did business with for many years. As is many cases during your life you meet and do business with folks and along the way you end up being friends for the rest of your lives. So is the case with me and Scott.

They had lived in North Houston but after retiring, they moved to Danville. They researched for a long time where they would settle down for retirement. This was it. Nita's mom lived with them. She was a very delightful and intelligent lady and enjoyed baseball, horse racing and other sports. During out several days visit, she kept us updated on scores of the baseball games and other hot news.

We rode around the area enjoying the beautiful scenery and blue grass and horse ranches of Kentucky. One day, we drove to Lexington, which was not very far from Danville. We went to a famous horse track there. I think that it was the Kentucky Horse Park. I am sorry to say that the

horses were not racing at the time. We toured the track and area and spent a lot of time at the gift shop.

Outside were statues of some of the great horses that won there. They have a lot of history there. One of the great horse statues was of the horse that won the Kentucky Derby in Louisville some years ago. There was a measurement area that showed the stride of this horse. I believe that it was the longest stride in history. It was just over twenty-five feet long. It was just amazing to see it marked off on the ground. What a site to see. I think that the horse's name was Secretariat. We enjoyed our visit with Scott and Nita and her mom very much. After a couple days it was time to move on.

TOP: ME AND SARAH AT KENTUCKY HORSE PARK

BOTTOM: NITA AND SCOTT RIESINGER

The next day we departed to visit with Sarah's distant cousin near Owensboro, Kentucky. She and her husband met us at a pre-decided place, and we followed them to their house in the countryside. They had several acres and a fishpond, a shop, and a large old barn that they were rebuilding. We spent six or seven hours at their house. They wanted us to spend the night with them. I just could not do it. I could not get a word in edgeways with the husband and I needed to flop my lips too. We had planned to spend the night in a motel in Owensboro. We all decided to eat supper at a restaurant of their choice in Owensboro. We followed them to the restaurant and spent the evening listening to more talk. During the visit, Sarah and her cousin traded information which helped Sarah in her quest to put her mom's family tree together.

As we were leaving the restaurant, a storm was brewing. They headed home and we went nearby to the motel. The weather got really bad.

Several tornados hit the area. I was praying that they got home alright. I was feeling bad for them driving to Owensboro to spend more time with us but very happy that we did not spend the night with them in their house trailer in the country. We called them the next day and they made it home O K.

During all the storm and stuff, the wind was howling and siding was flying all about the motel. I was scared shitless and Sammy the dog did not give a shit about anything. He just slept the whole time. If we would have had our pit bull with us, it would have been hell to pay. She is over eighty pounds and afraid of bad weather. The poor thing is a nervous wreck during bad weather.

We were traveling in our 2005 Toyota Matrix from Owensboro and crossed the Ohio River to go into Evansville, Indiana and drove to the Ohio River. I picked up a couple of driftwood sticks about five or six feet long and placed them in the back of the car. This car had a hatchback design and was a four door. We had the back seats down. This made plenty of room for our luggage and Sammy the dog. We then drove to Cairo, Illinois. At Cairo we drove to the Illinois River where I picked up a couple more driftwood poles from that riverbed and placed them into the back of the car. At Cairo, the Mississippi River, Illinois and Ohio Rivers are all very close. The confluence from the Ohio and Illinois Rivers flows into the mighty Mississippi River.

I loved this part of our trip. I had run barges up these rivers for many years and these cities were names and pinpoints on my large river maps on my office wall. From here we went to Cape Girardeau, Missouri where I picked up a couple more driftwood sticks from what is known as the Upper Mississippi River. Just above Cairo, Illinois is the dividing point of the Lower and Upper Mississippi River.

From Cape Girardeau we drove down to New Madrid, Missouri. This is the County Seat of some county or other. They had the records of folks from the area here. Sarah was able to go through the files and find some information on some of her relatives. This was just great to say the least.

From here we drove into Arkansas. Sarah had relatives near Jonesboro, Arkansas. The Jonesboro area was just beautiful. All the apple blossom trees were blooming. It was so pretty and smelled really good. We visited with them and spent one or two nights there with Sarah's mom's first cousin. Cousin Mildred and her sons and daughter and grandson were great folks. Mildred's dad and Mrs. Griffin's dad were brothers. The next day Sarah and I and Mildred and her grandson drove way out to the old homestead and property that the Peters used to own. They were business people and ran a mercantile store. One of those stores where you could get anything that you need or want. Someone was still running this store. They let us look all around inside and outside of it.

Mrs. Griffin's father's parents used to own and run this store. The story goes that Mr. Peters died and his wife ran the businesses for a while then she died. They were young. They also owned a lumber business. They would harvest trees and cut them into lumber to sell to build houses and such.

They had three young sons. Mrs. Griffin's dad, Mildred's dad, and Vivian's dad. Vivian is the other first cousin of Mrs. Griffin and lives in San Antonio, Texas. The boys were too young to care for themselves, so an old childless couple took them in and raised them to young teenagers. The boys left these folks as soon as they were old enough to leave. These boys had money from their parents' businesses but never saw a dime of it.

The old bastard that was supposed to care for them stole everything that they had. They had nothing when they left to go on their own. The businesses was gone, the property was gone, and the money was gone. Where it went to, nobody told the later generations.

The next day we took off to go southwest in Arkansas to go for a visit to our friend and co-worker al. Huntsman Chemical Company, Denise Fields, and her husband Mike. They live in Fairfield Bay on

Greers Ferry Lake. This is a beautiful one hundred-thousand-acre lake. We enjoyed it there every time we go. At one time we looked for a house to buy for when we retired. It is a great place to live.

After leaving there we stopped for several days in Clarksville, Arkansas where Sarah's sister, Alice Jean and her husband, Chris lives. Sarah filled Alice Jean in on our trip and the distant cousin that they had. As usual Alice Jean was not very interested in her family's history. We always enjoy visiting with them anyway. After leaving Clarksville, we headed back to Texas City. Overall, it was a wonderful trip with no car problems whatsoever.

AND ANOTHER TRIP

ME WITH THE STANLEY STEAMER AUTOMOBILE IN THE LOBBY OF THE STANLEY HOTEL

I received through the mail an all paid three nights stay in Breckenridge, Colorado. All we had to do was attend a sales session. We did not have to buy anything. They were trying to sell us a timeshare condo. There were a number of perks with the offer. It was to good too turn down. Their main question that they wanted answered was, could we afford to pay up to one hundred thousand dollars for a condo. "Why of course, said I." And I could - but I certainly would NOT. I already owned a timeshare on Canyon Lake, Texas and could not even give it away.

Sarah and I looked over a United States map and planned our next trip. There were some places that we wanted to go and see. We planned it all on paper. Then we made a schedule of the places to visit and time to spend at each place. In other words, we made a plan. I called them and got approval for our arrival date at their resort.

We started out heading West again on our trip. We spent one night in my timeshare at Canyon Lake. We preceded the next day to Junction, Texas. Since Sarah's parents had some relatives in this area many years ago, we had decided to spend a couple nights there. There is a State Park in Junction and we decided to utilize it. We brought camping gear with us. We found the park, paid a couple dollars to get in and set up our tent on a nice spot under some trees.

We went site seeing in the area. Sarah could not remember where the brother and sister who lived in the area lived. They both never did get married and lived all their lives on their parent's property until they each died. We did not know who the property went to after their deaths.

On the way to the park, we passed by a graveyard. We decided to just drive around in it. We got out and walked a bit and low and behold there was gravestones with their names on it. We could not hardly believe it. The old women's name was the same as one of Sarah's aunts on her daddy's side of the family. We figure that this was the person that she was named after or for. That never gets old. People just like to do that. It's in my family also. Sarah made some notes then we left there.

At our campsite was a clear water stream. We came prepared on this trip. We went in our tent and changed into our swimsuits and went into the stream. We played in the water for several hours. It was very relaxing. We met and talked with several folks while there. We were tired enough to have a really good night sleep after a roll in the hay. We kept hearing noises outside our tent all night long. The nighttime is when all the varmints come out. They scurry about looking for things to eat or just mess with. We kept our flashlight nearby and I was using it most of the night to see what was out there. I did not know if we were in bear country or not but. No bears show up thanks be to God. We enjoyed our time in the Junction area but not very much enjoyment when trying to get some sleep.

We left Junction heading for Carlsbad, New Mexico. I drove to Pecos, Texas and turned right on Highway 285 North and headed for New Mexico. We toured the cavern there. The Carlsbad Caverns at the national park are just wonderful and unbelievable. It took us all day to walk through them. We did not stay to watch the evening exodus of the bats leaving the caves as other folks did. We were told how exciting it was to be on hand for that. My thought was - HELL NO - I am not going to stand here and have millions of bats SHIT on me as they leave the cave NO WAY JOSE. I saw this on television and I would not have any part of it. Can you imagine if you were hanging upside down all day and could not shit because it would fall all over you because your ass hole is higher than the rest of you - what will happen as soon as you leave the cave. You are GONNA SHIT. That's it. You have no choice then but to let it go. That was not for me to witness or be covered by.

Next, we went to Roswell, New Mexico where we spent two nights. We did a lot of touring here. No - we did NOT see any spaceships from outer space or little green or gray men for that matter. Everywhere you go, they are trying to sell you alien shit. Well, not real shit but stuff is what I mean. Space alien stuff, fake stuff. It was very interesting to say the least. And the least is what I'll say on this subject.

After leaving Roswell we drove to Fort Sumner. This is where William H. Boney (Alias Billy the Kid) is supposed to be buried. On the way there we drove through long desolate areas with just white sand all around. It was so white that one had to squint one's eyes to look at it. If your car broke down on this over one hundred mile trip, you was up shits creek.

At Fort Sumner we visited a museum. It had a lot of Billy the Kid stuff to sell there. We visited the grave of Billy and several others while in Fort Sumner. This is another really small town that is hot and dusty or sandy or whatever. Perhaps the only reason that it is on the map is because Billy the Kid hung around there and is supposed to be buried there. Some folks believe that he was never killed by Pat Garrett. They were really good friends when they rode together during or before the Lincoln County Wars. Well, I do not know if he is buried there or not, but I did see the grave marker and read all the information about it there. By the way, there is an iron gated fence around the graves. There were two or three other graves there. I think one was the old man whose house Billy was at when Garrett supposedly shot him. Weeeeell that's enough on this.

After, AFTER RAISING SUGARCANE

ME IN JAIL AT FORT SUMNER, NM

We then headed to Santa Fe, New Mexico. We rode to St. John College were Ricky, Sarah's brother, attended for his freshman year. He later transferred to the University of Texas at Austin. We spent a night in Santa Fe. There was a big annual Indian native American arts sale going on. It was like a carnival in the downtown area. The streets were blocked off and venders selling stuff were everywhere. We also visited one of the oldest Catholic church west of the Mississippi River while there. They have the flee market every year at this time. We just happened to be there at the right time to see it. We met and talked with folks from other states who came here every year for this event. We enjoyed our time there. Santa Fe was a very pet loving city. Many of the vendors and store owners along the main street had bowls of water on the sidewalks by their locations for the folks who brought their pets with them. There were many pet dogs. Too many to count.

rom Santa Fe we drove to Salida, Colorado. We spent two days here. On the outskirts of Salida was a mountain. It was used for site seeing. It had a one lane road that circled around the mountain until you got to the top.

I could not tell if it was real, or man made. Driving up and down it you had to be very careful and watch for traffic coming from the opposite way. The road was very narrow. We parked at the top. There was a picnic area up there. It was very clean. From here you could see for miles and miles in all directions. It was the highest area in Salida. We passed a good time up there.

Back in the city there was a beautiful clean stream/river flowing through it. We walked the path along the river looking at the tubers and kayakers paddling down it. A stray black big dog who wanted a friend walked the path with me for a while. I gave him the last bite of my hot dog. He then left me. Ain't that just like man's best friend. You give him a treat and he leaves your ass to go looking to see what he can get somewhere else.

While back at the motel the weather started looking bad. It started to hail. I was worried about our car. The hail was a little bigger than BB size. Maybe twice the size of a BB. It hailed quite a bit. The street and parking lot was full of it. I was thinking about leaving and go onward with our trip but decided to spend another night while waiting for the hail to melt.

Somewhere along the way while driving in the mountains, we came to a little settlement. It seemed to me that this area was flatten out with heavy equipment. Several gambling casinos were built there. Never in a thousand years that I thought we would find this here in the middle of nowhere. Are you thinking that we passed it up? Well- think again. Hell no. No way. I turned into the closest one. We went inside and found the slot machines. We were there for only about twenty minutes when we hit a small jackpot. I told Sarah that it is now time to go. We left there with a little over three hundred fifty dollars of their money. We were very happy. On the way out we met a couple going in and I told them that we had ours and hoped that they get theirs. They just laughed.

We headed on out going to Breckenridge. We were driving through fourteen thousand foot plus mountains now. My car engine would miss every now and then. It was not used to this high altitude, and neither was I. I did NOT like it one damn bit. I had taken this route because it was lower than the one that had sixteen-thousand-foot mountains on it that I was afraid to go on. The highway must be better on the higher altitude route than this one. At one point we came to a complete stop and was in bumper-to-bumper traffic for several hours. I could not believe all the traffic we had going both ways in the middle of nowhere.

When I thought about it later, all these folks were on this highway because of the same reason that I was on the highway. It was lower to the real ground where I came from than the other route. The traffic was because the highway got down to a single lane where they were repairing it. Only one way traffic was moving in this area. I did not care for looking over the cliffs while driving. I knew then that there was no way in hell that we were coming back this way. I hate to not pass that casino that was paying off - but shit on that. I liked my life better than a chance for free money. Some folks in my family may not believe me when I say that - but I do.

It was amazing to see those huge white mountain goats jumping around on the cliffs like there was no tomorrow. It was like they had no fear of falling down the mountain. I believe that they were just showing off. I shouted out my window a few times calling them showoffs. I was a long way from them and know that they could not get to me those showoffs. I did keep an eye on them for a while. I did have the thought that my damn car would sputter if they started after us. Then we would be gone pecans if those goats would have pushed us over the cliff. Actually, with the small car we had, one mountain goat could have done it.

Since we got into Colorado, we could see the snow on the mountain tops. As we did not drive through any snow on our way to Breckenridge, we knew that it was last year's snow that had not melted yet. I think that high up that the snow never melts. I do not know for sure, but I would never live up there to find out.

We finally made it to the resort, unloaded our luggage and went sign in at the desk. After showing our identification and special papers that they sent to me, we were all set. The Bell Hop showed us to our room and told us about it.

We spent three nights at the resort. We had a number of free gifts. Like free dinners around town, free massages, free this and free that. So, we were busy getting our free stuff and site-seeing. We drove up to Frisco several times for breakfast/lunch and drove around that area.

We had to sit through a two-hour presentation of them trying their best to sell us a one hundred-thousand-dollar timeshare to use for one week out of the whole year. All we could say was No, No, No, No, No, etc. I do not like snow. I do not like to snow ski. I do not even like to make snowmen or snow angles or snow anything. They finally unlock the room and let us go. The lady and man there with their diamond rings and things acted like perhaps we could not afford a place like this. It seemed to me that they wanted to question why we came there. I did not let on that I knew what they were thinking but we sure in hell could afford to purchase one if we wanted one. At this time, we owned three houses in Texas with one that had thirteen acres with it in the Sam Houston Forest.

While walking the streets, I started having a problem breathing. I seem to not get enough air in my lungs. We made it back to the resort and I went to bed. Sarah started going through the brochures and pamphlets that we were given upon arrival. She found something. We went down to the lobby. It seems that they had this little portable oxygen container that you could take with you. You paid about fifty dollars for the oxygen and a fifty-dollar deposit on the container. When/if you brought the container back, you got your fifty-dollar refund. I coughed up one hundred dollars and started using that sucker right away. It worked. It was just great. Before we departed there, I got my refund for giving back the container. I was really happy that there was such a thing. I never had any more problems breathing on the rest of our trip in the high North.

SARAH AND I IN BRECKENRIDGE, CO

We left there heading to Estes Park even farther North. We went back to Frisco and took a right on Interstate 70 heading east toward Denver. When we are on our trips, I would usually drive for ten to twelve hours or more at a time. We drove east on Interstate 70 leading towards Estes Park. We had heard about Estes Park from Sarah's Aunt Evadeane who was married to Sarah's mom's brother- Uncle Bunyon Peters. Evadeane was talking about moving to an old folks settlement in Estes Park. So, we went there to check it out. We were this close and probably would never go back so why not. We turned off 70 onto Highway 72 leading to Estes Park.

Estes Park was another pretty place. It was a really clean city and not a large one at all. It was just the right size. There were elk running all over the place. They had the right of way. If you had a green light and an elk walked through the red light, you had to stop and give the elk the right of way.

Sarah and I were walking through a small roadside park in the city when I heard this awful sound. It scared the shit out of me. I turned around and this baby elk was running right at me. I made a step backward and he zipped by me. The height of his back was even with my neck. He was huge. He had lost his mom and screamed out to her. She was trotting toward me. They met about five yards from me. After getting over being scared, it was exciting, but too close a call. These elk were just everywhere. They seem to be tame or calm around people. Folks just stop their cars in the middle of the streets and take pictures much to the distress of the local residence, I'm sure.

Estes Park is famous for another thing - perhaps several others things. One is the Stanley Hotel. The Stanley Hotel goes way back to when there was not even electricity or running water in the buildings. Mr. Stanley was a rich man from back East. He was the inventor and owner of the Stanley Steamer automobile. This was a car that was powered by steam. Hence the name Stanley Steamer. He had nothing to do with the company that steam cleans carpet and other things. Although he did own other companies. He had the hotel built to move there for his health. He was not supposed to live into his forties according to the doctors, but he made it into his eighties. This is in the early 1920s.

A Stanley Steamer car is in the lobby of the hotel. We took a tour of the Hotel and enjoyed it. We went into a room where guests left in the middle of the night because of seeing ghosts at night. We also went into the billiards room where ghosts were supposed to hang out in the olden days. I am NOT buying any of the stuff, but I would not ever check into a room where ghost was said to be. I am just saying.

We were able to buy beers in the bar and go on the front porch. rocking chairs and look at the great plains from this mountain to we were on. It was a site to view. Of course, we drank the beers and more each after that one.

Rich folks from around the world would come to spend quite time at the Stanley. Many came to hunt the elk and mountain goats and mountain lions. For many years the Stanley would shut down during the hardest part of winter. It would be boarded up and abandoned for the winter. The only way to get there was by horse and buggy or the new fashion automobile. There were not good roads, and it was a very rough ride to get there. The Stanley became more well known or you might say became famous after the writer Steven King's movie "The Shinning" came out for public view. On our tour, we were told that Steven King, the book writer, was a teacher at the University of Colorado in Boulder. He came up during the last few days of his summer off from teaching, he was working on a novel and wanted to get away from Boulder and have more peace and quiet. As he arrived, the Stanley was in the process of shutting down for the winter. The cash register and all needed items had already been sent to Boulder for safe keeping as they had done for many years. King was told that he could stay if he had the exact cash in his pockets for the cost. He did and paid cash. The one person there cooked him a meal and told him that he would have to furnish his own meals after that one and departed after delivering the meal. Steven King stayed at the Stanley until he finished his novel- The Shinning. The book became a best seller and thus a movie was made several years later. Mr. King became a big celebrity afterwards and has written many best-selling books that became movies.

They actually did a short-lived weekly show for television. It did not make it two seasons. But the television folks spent hundreds of thousands of dollars fixing and painting it. Different scenes for the movie, The Shinning, were shot there also. The movie producers spent mega bucks painting all the inside of the Stanley white. I do not remember if it had any color on the wood before that time. I believe that running water, toilets and such and the old elevator was put in along the way as was electricity.

We did not stay in the Stanley- they were just too damn high-priced. And I was not going to take a chance of having ghost leaving their room with an axe coming to look for me. I am just saying. This does NOT mean that I am afraid of ghosts. I am afraid of the AXE. We stayed at a motel in town for about one third the price, where there were no ghost, but we went to the Stanley to hang out an walk the beautiful grounds every day. This was during daylight time when all ghost are supposed to be asleep to rest up for their night time roaming about.

While waiting for the bartender at the Stanley to get our beers, we started talking. I found out the he was from Baton Rouge, Louisiana. I asked him if he knew were White Castle, Louisiana was. He surely did. I told him that that was my hometown. We talked about things for a couple minutes then Sarah and I went on the porch to our rocking chairs to drink our beers. What a small world we live in.

One day we drove north of Estes Park to a national park. It was the Rocky Mountains National Park. State Highway 34 cut right through the park.

We were told that on a clear day/night, one could see San Francisco from there. I cannot see how that can be true. I only wanted to drive about a mile and come back I had nowhere to go up there. The park ranger wanted twenty dollars to do that. I said, "hell no- no way". Since I could not back up because of traffic behind me, I made a U turn around his booth and came back to Estes Park.

Looking at a national map, we were located just a little north of San Francisco but there was the rest of Colorado, all of Utah, all of Nevada and all of California to see before you could see San Francisco. They -whoever they are - are full of shit. There is no way a person's eyes could see it from here. Maybe Superman - but that may be stretching it.

On the fourth day we headed south toward Boulder, went through Denver (only a mile high- this ain't shit compared to where we'd been), to Interstate 70 and on the Highway 287. We drove on Highway 287 until I could not drive any more. I drove for about fourteen hours or more. It had been dark for several hours, so we started looking for a place to stop. We saw a motel, checked in and went right to bed. No roll in the hay tonight. It wasn't until when we checked out the next day that we found out that we spent the night in the Oklahoma panhandle. It may have been Boise City - but I am still not sure if it even was a town.

We kept on driving down Highway 287 and into Amarillo, Texas. We drove around Amarillo and took pictures of a building that Nathan, Sarah's son, helped to build when he was doing iron work. It was a special designed building. A great-looking building, Sarah took some pictures of it.

Staying on Highway 287 we kept coming southeast. We came through Childress, Vernon and into Wichita Falls. While on the drive we road behind an eighteen-wheeler empty flatbed truck and trailer for a bunch of miles. Highway 287 is a very nice four lane highway. Several of us had been riding together. I decided to pass the big truck. When I got on the side of the trailer, I noticed a piece of rebar (iron rod) about four feet long bouncing on the flatbed and moving near the edge of the trailer. Another bounce and it came straight at us. It hit my right fender and hood at the same time. It then hit the windshield and flew over the top of the car. The young couple in the car behind us rolled over it. We were so lucky that we were in our small Toyota car. If it was a larger car, I think it may have come into the car with us. I let up on the gas and got behind the trailer. The folks that was behind us got even with us and were asking if we were 0 K. I shouted that we were. I then got into the passing lane again. I was trying to get the truck drivers attention for him to stop. I was blowing my horn. He speeded up. I was going a little over eighty miles per hour and could not catch him. I know he knew what happened but would not pull over and stop. We came to a small highway to the right. He took it going too fast. As soon as he got on it, he floors boarded it again. He was not going to stop.

We pulled into a service station that was on the corner of this highway. We got out and checked out the car. We had a small groove cut into the fender and a dent on the hood. The steel bar had hit us broadside- meaning that it hit the windshield length ways and left a mark. Sarah's side had four marks on the glass and my side- the drivers' side, had six marks. This was the type of rebar that is used in construction. It looked like it has ridges on the whole length of the bar. It was these ridges that made the marks on the glass.

We called my insurance company and gave them the information that we had. I had gotten the name off the side of the truck. Nothing ever came of it.

After arriving home, several auto repair places wanted fourteen to sixteen hundred dollars to repair and repaint my car. They wanted to replace the whole fender. There are no REPAIR outfits today. They are REPLACE at five time the normal cost outfits. I forgot what my deductible was, but I said, "hell no". I did not have it repaired. I got a mallet and hammered my hood out and worked on the fender a little. I sanded it all down and bought some touch up paint from Toyota that matched my white car and touched it up. It was not perfect but good enough for us and still lasting until this day.

Back to the trip.

Before we got to Fort Worth, outside of some town that I cannot remember, we stopped to sightsee. This place was called the Cadillac Ranch. It was in a field that was planted with soybean or some other grain. It had a dozen or more Cadillac's buried front ends down in the ground and rear ends up in the air. They were buried about one-halfway down. They had a bunch of spray cans of paint for folks visiting to spray their names or whatever they wanted onto the cars. It did not cost us anything to get to see. You just park on the side of Highway 287 and had to walk about one hundred yards to get to the Cadillac graveyard. There were about twenty people out there looking and painting on the cars when we walked up. It was really something. All of the cars were Cadillac -no Chevys or Fords, just

Cadillacs. There was nothing for sale, nothing, to buy. As I stated, no charge to get in. I have no idea what that was all about. It was someone who just buried cars upright in the ground for folks to see. It was a site to see. I still do not know why in the hell it's there. Either the guy loved Cadillac's or hated them. Perhaps the dumb ass was trying to grow little Cadillacs. Who knows - I surely don't.

ME AT THE CADILLAC RANCH

We then drove into Fort Worth. We spent a couple nights with Sarah's brother there. We had a good visit and told them the things that we had been up to. After a couple of days, we headed back home to Texas City to rest up and decide where to go for our next trip.

We only went through four states but traveled over three thousand miles on this trip.

OUR FRIENDS JON AND JIM JOHANSON

Several years before we moved to Louisiana, a couple of guys from the Boston, Massachusetts area moved down the street from us. They did a lot of walking in the neighborhood. We would waive to each other as they passed by on their daily walks.

I do not remember the first time we actually talked with each other, but we eventually did and became very good friends from that time on. Jon was an engineer in Massachusetts. He retired and looked for a less expensive area to live than Boston. He had relatives in the Houston area and had come to this area a number of times. When he found the house down the street from us, he knew that he had found God's Country and purchased it.

Jim is Jon's son and those guys have traveled all over the world together. They could have lived anywhere in the world, but they chose Texas City, Texas. Besides traveling, Jon loves to cook. He can cook anything, but his favorite dishes are Italian. Sarah and I enjoyed many meals that Jon prepared for us.

Jim is into watching sports. Especially any teams from Massachusetts. He also became a Houston Astros Fan and he and Jon go to many games. Jim has an incredible memory. He remembers names of people and places that he visited many years ago. It is really uncanny.

Jon is also a walking encyclopedia. If you mention it, he knows something or everything about it. They have been to so many places around the world and met so many people and just sucked up the knowledge everywhere they went. When we moved from Texas City, Texas to Louisiana, we felt bad leaving our old friends behind. But Jon and Jim did not stay behind too long. Before long they were visiting us in our new home in Plaquemine.

Each time Jon and Jim came over, we went some place to tour. I learned more about my home state when they were here than I ever knew before. One time we visited beautiful St. Francisville, Louisiana, a really picturesque city. We also visited a Civil War Memorial graveyard in Port Hudson nearby.

Another time we went to Breaux Bridge for breakfast and dancing to Cajun music. After breakfast we traveled to Avery Island to tour the McILehenny Tabasco sauce company. I even tried a taste of Tabasco ice cream while there.

And another time we went to a Civil War Cemetery in Baton Rouge. It was off Florida Blvd., which is one of the main streets near downtown Baton Rouge. And I did not know that it even existed. We walked about the area. There were many graves of soldiers from Massachusetts there.

On one of their visits we went to Natchez, MS. We enjoyed a great time there visiting with our new friend Sherry, who served as our tour guide. We visited old graveyards and mansions. There is a lot of history in Natchez.

We did so much and learned so much every time Jon and Jim came to visit. We'll never be "Basta" when it comes to Jon and Jim.

JON JOHNSON

JIM JOHNSON AND ME NEAR THE MISSISSIPPI RIVER

BUYING THE HOUSE IN RANDOM OAKS (PLAQUEMINE)

In late 2009, we purchased the house in Random Oaks Subdivision near Plaquemine, Louisiana. I had been dreaming of coming back home for several years. Sarah was okay with it.

Sarah and I made a number of trips to South Louisiana to look for a place to live. We checked out houses in the cities of White Castle and Plaquemine. We also checked out places along the river road in that area. And also, the area of Samstown and a couple of other places. We did not really care for any of them.

My brother's neighbor started talking about selling their place and moving into the city of Plaquemine. They are Steve and Dee LeBlanc. Steve had a health problem and was starting to have trouble keeping the grounds up. They had almost an acre and a half of property. Dee was working full-time, so they wanted to move to a smaller home and yard. I told my brother to let them know that I may be interested in their place if they wanted to sell it.

Apparently, he did not, because one day I received a telephone call from him saying that they had listed their house with a realtor. I was sort of pissed off at him for not mentioning what I asked him to do. He is like that you know - OOH I guess you did not know. Well, you know now. But shit happens.

By the way, did you know that even shit is not dirty until it hits the ground. If you did not, you do now. This is a saying from my daddy, Newton J. Raffray Sr., in about 1966. I will never forget it. After a short time, I contacted Dee and talked with her about their house. She gave me all the information that I asked for. I told her that I would get back to her at a later date. Sarah and I were interested in the house, but I did not want to pay for or for them to pay the realtor's price or commission for selling it. I thought that they were asking too much for the property. I talked with Dee again and informed her that if their house did not sell during the contract with the realtor, that I may be interested in buying it direct from them. It so happened that several months later it had not sold while they had a contract with the realtor. Dee called: to let me know that they no longer had a contract with the realtor.

A couple of days later, after I counted all the money, we had available and could get, and called Dee back and made an offer. Neither me nor Sarah had been working for several years now so what we had is all we had. I wanted to pay cash and not borrow any money that would have me paying a note for years to come. I also did not want Sarah stuck with a house note in the case that I kicked the bucket, died-that is.

The LeBlanc's were not happy with my offer at all. I did explain since we are doing the deal without a realtor, they would be saving about nine thousand dollars or so right off the bat. Other costs to them were being eliminated. We would be taking the property as is. I would have to pay to fix things that need fixing later. Much later when I saved enough money to do it. I would not receive the mower and other equipment that they were throwing in with the property either. I also told them that they did not need to clean out the sheds and other storage building if they did not want the stuff. I would clean it out when I got around to it. Eight years later I am still working on that. Boy did they have some stuff and I have been adding to it with new stuff that I find on the highway or wherever folks throw it.

They waited a couple of weeks while still trying to sell the property at a lower price than listed but more than we could pay. That was certainly fine with me, I would have done the same thing in their place. I could not squeeze any more out of me. My offer was all we could do. They finally called me and accepted the deal.

When we first started talking, there was this house next door to their daughter in Plaquemine that they wanted to buy. It sold because we did not make our deal. Now another house just down the street from their daughter was up for sale and they need my cash as partial payment to buy it. So, our deal was made. Our closing was going to be in the first week of October 2009.

Now this is where I am at. I purchased a house that I had never been in. We did everything by long distance. My brother, who lived next door for thirty-six years has never been inside the house, but his wife has a few times. I did not know the condition of it at all. I did not even know how large it was. I know that the property had several outbuildings and a four-car carport because I could see this from my brother's yard. It had a screened-in back porch and a very small front porch that nobody ever used. The driveway went to the back of the house, and everybody drove to the back and went into the house through the back door.

Well, I can tell you that I was really surprised the first time I went into the house. It was huge. It had five bedrooms, two complete baths, a kitchen, dining, and a very large den/living room area. There are walk-in closets in four bedrooms and closets in the hall and den area. There is a walk-in washroom off the master bathroom for a clothes washer and dryer with plenty of room to hang clothes and double deck shelving.

Part of this house is maybe one hundred years or older and mostly made of cypress with oak wood-stained floors. The last two bedrooms were added to the house after it was moved to this location from the river road. Those two bedrooms are on a fourteen-inch-high cement slab. The rest of the house is on pillars and off the ground about twenty or so inches. This comes in handy when we get high water which happens in this subdivision way too often.

This house had belonged to the J. W. Bryant family and was located on their land near the Mississippi River. The Bryant family sold their land in the 1950s to a chemical corporation to build a plant on. They moved the house through the sugar cane field to this location. The house is now located almost two miles from the river road.

While on the river road, the Iberville Parish (County) Agent, Mr. Edward Burleigh and his family used to live in it and keep watch over the Bryant family cattle on his plantation. When they sold the land, the Burleigh family had to move.

Mr. Bryant's sons used the house as a camp after it was moved to Random Oaks.

Back in the 1950s, Mr. Vince Pizzolato purchased about fifteen acres from Mr. Bryant to create this little settlement. Mr. Bryant had to buy the land that the house is on back from Mr. Vince. I was told by a good source that he damn near paid as much for this one point, five acres, as he received from Mr. Vince for the fifteen acres. My good source was none other than Mr. Bryant's son.

Sometime after the younger Bryant grew up and did not want to use this place as a camp anymore, the Leblancs purchased it. Before that happened, Mr. Vince sold many lots, and houses were built and folks moved in house trailers to live here. My brother had his house built in the mid to late 1950s.

My brother remembers when the Bryant family moved the house to this location. As I mentioned earlier, it came from the river road through the sugar cane field. It is one point eight tenths of a mile from the river road to this house. I have cut through my back yard many times to drive on the headlands in the field to get to the river road. It is a short cut for me to do that when I need to go someplace on the river road.

Steve and Dee LeBlanc lived here for thirty-six years or so when I purchased the property from them. They raised three daughters here.

They wanted each one to have their own bedroom which is why they added on- I guess.

Dee's mom lived here for many years also. She had to use a wheelchair which is why there is a ramp to the kitchen door. After I purchased the house, Dee's mom moved with them to their new home in Plaquemine. She lived two more years and passed away at one hundred-two years of age. Talk about good genes.

Moving back here was the beginning of the end for us. After Sarah and I settled in we made numerous trips to see her sons and sister and brothers and my boys also. We had a wonderful few more years together in Louisiana.

Then we started prospecting with a new friend I just happened to meet. I introduced him to my Sarah the day we were prospecting and my new friend took my sweetheart from me. There is some plagiarism from an old song in the words above. Do you know it? No? It is The Tennessee Waltz.

Listen to it sometime when you get the chance. Sarah now lives in Texas, and we talk occasionally and stay in contact. *prospecting =

Hunting for treasure along the Mississippi River. It is amazing what can be found on the banks of this river. Things like antique bottles, rings, jewelry, silver, coins, civil war artifacts and bullets, beautiful driftwood, and many other valuable things.

JUST A FEW MORE PICTURES OF YOURS TRULY

ME AND A SOUTHERN PACIFIC ENGINE

ME AT THE PLACE IN CLEVELAND, TX

ME BEFORE

ME HALF WAY

ME ALL THE WAY

SHORT STORIES THAT I MADE UP

This is not part of my memoir. I just wanted to add some writing to add to the number of pages in this book. I wrote this story many years ago. But first I want to give the reader a little real history of my subject matter. This writing has to do with how the Acadians got to Louisiana.

Way back in the 1550s, France placed a colony of French folks near the Bay of Fundy in what came to be named Nova Scotia today. Over the years the colony grew and prospered.

Because of a treaty between France and Great Britten, France ceded all their lands in what is called Canada today to the English. The French Acadians lived under the English since 1713 and were treated terribly.

When Charles Lawrence became the Governor of the territory, he wanted to get rid of the Acadians. Although gone from France for some two hundred years, they thought that they were still French subjects and did not much care for the English.

On August 1, 1755, about two hundred years after arrival, the ancestors of the first French settlers were rounded up by English troops and deported from their homes. All of their property, animals, and everything that they owned was confiscated by the English. This is known as THE GREAT EXPULSION.

If you would like to read the actual events that led up to this event, get the book Louisiana's French Heritage by Truman Stacey - copyright 1990 by Acadian House Publishing Inc. This book is where some of the above information came from.

Now I will write my made-up story. Please keep in mind that some of my made-up stories are true and really happened.

HOW DEM CAJUNS GOT TO LOUISIANA (A CAJUN TELLING IT)

Well, I'm gonna told you a story about how Dem starving Cajuns got to Lusiana. It was way back in 1755- sometime like dat, dat dem English, Dey doesn't want da Acadians on dare land no mo. Dem wants to ship dem all out. All of dis happen because da Acadians don't sware to protect and defend them damn English from the French and the Indians and whoever was dared in Nova Scotia gave da English trouble. Dem Acadian's tink dat dey is still French after being dared for almost 200 years. Dey also could take care of themselves and dey don't need any stinking English troops to help them. In fact, dey was what you call self-sufficient and sold to da Engish what dey needed to survive. Da high-up English leaders don't like dat one lil bit.

One day, dem English, dey call for town hall meetings all over the provinces dare in Nova Scotia and got the word out dat all da Acadians including da wives and da children must come to the town hall for the meetings or da Law was gonna come after dem. You know dem Acadians, dey don't want any trouble with the Law, so most of dem went to the meeting places.

Dem English is so bad. Dey had a plan. Beforehand, they had lined up a bunch of ships. Dey put da Acadians on some small ships, hired some sailors dat work for cheap and told dem to took dees Acadians to Louisiana or anywhere else - just get dem outa here. Da said we don't want dem here no mo. Dey don't support us so take them away.

Man, dere was a bunch of dem ships full to the top with Acadians and after tree or two days, dey all took off for Lusiana, France, and anywhere else dat would take dem in. Many of the Acadians got separated from der family and love ones with all da co-motions going on. Dem English did not give a care, in fact, dey plan for it to happen dis way. Dey want to teach the Acadians who da boss is.

After som time on da ocean, som of dem sailors, dey got tired and pulled inta the Colony of Massatusetus. Da Govnor dare in charge say, "yall come on in here". Dat is why dare is Acadians in Massatusetus today. Dey talk different den the rest of us, but dey is still Acadians. When dey got to Massatusetus, dey don't got no money, so the Govnor dare made dem slaves til dey could work off der cost which took some folks two or five years to do. Den da became free peoples. Dem other ships. Dey kept going South and soon som mo sailors, dey get tired and they done already almost eat up all do food and drunk all do-good water dey had and dey decided dat dey had gone far enough. Dey got paid for the whole trip, but dey was some no-good sailors and wanted to stop in the Colony of Virginia. Dey had yeared about how good dat Virginia Ham was - I guess -and dey wanted som.

Well, da Govnor of the Colony of Virginia had yeared about dem Acadians on da ships and he did not want none of dem to land dare. He ordered his minute men to fire dar cannons on the ships and keep dem out of the Virginia Bay. Dey did and dey sunk some ships and kilt many Acadians peoples. So, da sailors don't try to come inta the

Bay no more. Dey kilt planty Acadians and dem other sailors on the other ship said we ain't stopping in der. We all gone to Lusiana.

Now, I can tell ya dat dem Acadians really wanted to go to King Louis da 14 lands real bad. Dey still tink da dey is French and wanted to be on French owned Land. Specially after da bad experience dey done had after dem English took over in Nova Scotcha. And HOW I know dey wanted to go to Lusiana so bad is dat day pass right by Nort Carlinia and Sout Carlinia where all dem beautiful golf courses is on da coast and da nice beaches too, and dey kept right on going. AND dats not all. When dey come by Flordia and dat Myima Beach and looked at all dem pertty gals playen beach bally ball in dem dare thong tings dey had on, dey did not even bat an eye - dey want ta got to Lusiana so BAD. Man, im gonna told you samtin. Dem peoples loved Lusiana and dey not even seed it yet.

Dis was a long trip. Dey had not invented no motors yet, so da trip was slow. Dey was getin hungrier, so da Acadians untwine some rope and made som long strings and put some fishhooks on do ends of the strings. Dey put som jerky on som hooks and som mashed up bread on som as bate. Den dey threw the line over the behind end of the ship. DIS IN NOW THE TROLLING BEHIND A BOAT GOT STARTED. Dey caught some fish and had themselves some fried fish right der on da deck of da boats. Dey all pass a good time and DIS IS HOW THE CRUSE BUSINESS ON A BOAT GOT STARTED.

Dem Acadians was very smart peoples, dey just don't got no money to start des businesses cause the English don stoll it all. Dat is why the sailors got da credit for inventin and startin doing business in da later years.

After, AFTER RAISING SUGARCANE

After som mo days, dey finally came to Lusiana. Someware round Intrcoastal City near Vermillion Bay, da boats dragged bottom and come to a stop before dey got to da dock. Wel, im goona told ya, dem Acadians, dey now become CAJUNS, and dey was so hungry dat dey jump off de ships inta da swamp, dey reach down in da mud and pull up som ousters, some crawdads, som shrimps, and som other stuff and said, "WE GONNA EAT YOU", and dey did.

Soon dey all come ashore and built some big fires and put som big pots with water in dem to boil. Dey spread out everyting dat dey fine in the mud and swamp, dey cleen it off and den dey throw dem in da pot. Dey are really hungry now. After about a couple hours, som of the people who were mo hungry dan da rest, dey would not wait no mo. So dey started eating what was in one of da pots. Som of the peoples who could wait a little longer - did and da ate about two hours later. After adding some rice dat dey found in the marsh dare into the pot. Dem was the first two CAJUN dishes cooked up after dey got to Sout Lusiana. The first people to eat ate what became known as GUMBO. It was juicy and had some gravy in it. Da second peoples to eat ate what became known as JAMBULIA. It was drier and didn't have gravy in it. Dis is how da two famus food dishs got started in Lusiana.

AND THE REST IS HISTORY - now you know.

Since the above is written in my native tongue, I realize that some of you folks may not be able to read my native tongue, so I will now write it in English.

HOW THE CAJUNS GOT TO LOUISIANA (ENGLISH)

I am going to tell you a story about how those starving Cajuns got to Louisiana. It was way back in 1755- sometime like that, that the English do not want the Acadians on their land anymore. The want to ship them all out. All this happened because the Acadians do not want to swear to protect and defend the English from the French and the Indians and whoever else that was there in Nova Scotia giving the English trouble.

The Acadians think that they are still French even after living there for almost two hundred years. They also could take care of themselves and do not need the English to help them. In fact, they were what you call self-sufficient and sold to the English soldiers everything that they wanted or needed. The high-up English leaders did not like that situation.

One day, the English called for town Hall meetings all over the provinces in Nova Scotia and got the word out that all Acadians must attend with their wife's and children, or the LAW was going to come and get them. The Acadians do not want any trouble with the LAW, so most of then went to the meeting places.

The English were bad people. They had a plan. Beforehand, they lined up. a fleet of ships. They forced the Acadians onto these small ships. They had hired sailors to work cheap and take the Acadians to Louisiana Territory or anywhere else. They just wanted them all out of Nova Scotia territory because they would not swear allegiance to the king of England.

There was a fleet of ships full from bottom to top with Acadians. After about two or three days, the ships departed for Louisiana and other places. Many were taken back to France where they were place in concentration camps until in the further when they would be relocated to Louisiana. Many of the Acadians were separated from their families and love ones with all the commotions going on. The English did not care, in fact they wanted it this way. They place the women and children on some ships and the men on other ships. They wanted to teach these folks who the boss was.

After some time on the ocean, some of the sailors got tired and pulled into the Colony of Massachusetts. The Governor allowed them to come into the docks. This is why there are Acadians in Massachusetts today. They talk different than the rest of us down in Louisiana, but they are still Acadians. When they got to Massachusetts, they do not have any money, so the Governor made them slaves until they could work off their cost which, for some, took five years. After their depths were paid off, they became free people.

The other ships just kept going South and soon some more sailors got tired they had already eaten almost all the food and drank all the good water and they decided that they had enough. They got paid for the whole trip, but they were some lazy assed sailors and wanted to stop in the Colony of Virginia. They had heard about how good the Virginia Ham was, I guess, and they wanted some.

Well, the Governor of the Colony of Virginia had heard about the Acadians on the ships heading south and he did not want any of them to land in his Colony. He ordered his minute men to fire cannons on the ships to keep them out of Virginia. They did and sunk some ships and killed many Acadians. So, the sailors stopped trying to come into the Chesapeake Bay anymore. After they saw the killing of the Acadians the sailors on the other ships, they said that they are not gone to try and stop here and decided to keep going to Louisiana.

Now, I can tell you that these Acadians really wanted to get to King Louis the 14 land. They still think that they are French and wanted to be on French owned land again. Specially after the bad experience they had after the English took over in Nova Scotia. And HOW I know they wanted to get to Louisiana so bad is that they pass right by North Carolina and South Carolina where all these beautiful golf courses are and the pretty coast and the very nice beaches and they just kept right on going. And that's not all. When they came to Florida and that Miami Beach and looked at all those pretty girls playing beach volleyball in their thong things they had on and they did not even bat an eye - they want to get to Louisiana so badly. Man, I am going to tell you something, these folks loved Louisiana and they have not even seen it yet.

This was a long trip. Motors had not been invented yet, so the trip was slow. They were getting hungry, so the Acadians untwined some rope and made some long strings and put some fishhooks on the end of the strings. They put some jerky and bread squeezed into a ball on the hooks, and they threw the line behind the ships. THIS IS HOW THE TROLLING BEHIND A BOAT GOT STARTED. They caught some fish and had themselves some fried fish right there on the decks of the boats. They all pass a good time and THIS IS HOW THE CRUSE BUSINESS ON A BOAT GOT STARTED. Those Acadians was very smart people. They just did not have the money to start these businesses. That is why the sailors got all the credit for starting these businesses in later years.

After some more days, they finally came to Louisiana, somewhere around Intracoastal City near Vermillion Bay, the boats dragged bottom and came to a stop before they got to the dock. Well, I am going to tell you something. All the Acadians became CAJUNS, and they were really. hungry. They jumped off the ships into the swamp, reached down in the mud pulled up some oysters, crawdads, shrimps, and some other stuff, and said, "WE GOING TO EAT YOU", and they did.

They all came ashore and built some big fires and put some big pots with water in them to boil. They spread out everything that they find in the mud and swamp, clean it off, and throw it into the pot. They are really hungry now. After about a couple of hours some of the CAJUNS who were hungrier than the rest and could wait no more started eating what was in the pots. Some of the folks who could wait a little longer did and ate an hour or so later after adding some rice that they found in the marsh into the pot.

Those were the first two CAJUN DISHES cooked up after they got to South Louisiana. The first folks to eat ate what became known as GUMBO. It was juicy and had some gravy in it. The second folks to eat ate what became known as JAMBALAYA. It was drier and did not have gravy in it.

Perhaps this was more understandable than the gibberish that I wrote above. Maybe I should not have put the above in writing. It may piss off some folks. I was just fooling around and do not mean to make fun of anybody's heritage so do NOT take it personally. If I poke fun, it is at me and no one else.

Now I have another made up story. I hope that you enjoy it.

MY CANOE TRIP ON THE MISSISSIPPI RIVER

Back in the early 1990s, I had a week's vacation coming to me. After twenty years with the company, we were eligible for six weeks of vacation per year. The plant union workers bargained and paid for the vacation, but everybody got it. When I moved to the Bayport, Texas location I (we) all lost one week's vacation.

This location was a NON-UNION location. After completing twenty-five years of service, we got that one week back. All employees kept the vacation accrued although the company was sold four or five times.

I always wanted to go to the headwaters of the Mississippi River and paddle down to New Orleans. I saved up my vacation to make one big trip. Ever since I was born and raised near the Mississippi River on Cedar Grove Plantation near White Castle, Louisiana, I had this erg to traverse the Mighty Mississippi. I added to this desire by working over thirty years contracting and scheduling barge transportation companies that traversed the Mississippi, Ohio, Illinois and Tennessee Rivers as well as the Intra and Intercostal and Tombigbee Waterways. Therefore, my desire grew with each new year. Well, I finally decided to do it. With the responsibilities that I had, I had to plan this trip very carefully. It took a couple years to plan it all out and to be away from the job for that long of a time. The day finally came.

I packed up my pickup with a canoe that I purchased and all the equipment and some food supplies that I thought I would need for the trip. You know you cannot get much stuff in a canoe. I did have a sleeping bag and lots of mosquito spray.

I left League City, Texas really early on a Saturday morning. It took me two days to get to Lake Itasca, Minnesota. I parked my truck and arranged everything in my canoe. I did have about six hours sleep before I arrived. There is a nice secure parking area there. I locked my truck, got in my canoe, and started paddling down the lake into the Mississippi River stream. I paddled to Itasca State Park and went right through it. There are many terrible places on the river. I stayed close to the bank as I could get while staying out of the backwash current. If you ever been on large rivers, you would know what that means. Really close to the bank of the river, the water flows backwards. If you are not careful, you could end up going back where you came from. If you stay out of the backflow, you do not have to paddle nearly as much. You use the paddle for steering the canoe/boat. The river current moves at a good clip. I traversed for about twenty hours the first day. Of course, I had a flashlight. A big one and extra D cell batteries also. One never should be on any waterway at night without lights. You must also always be aware of things floating in the water. Yes, I said things. All sorts of things that could take you down in an instant. You also must be aware of the world pools and eddies near the bank where small or large streams flow into the river.

Since I would not sleep while the canoe was moving, when I got tired and sleepy, I would find a small opening on the bank and tie the canoe to some willow trees so it would not drift off and nap for a couple hours. Sometimes I got on land with my sleeping bag and sometimes after tying the canoe secure, I would sleep in the canoe.

The river was flowing fast for this late in the summer. I passed Grand Rapids, Minnesota. I did not stop for and site sightseeing or anything else. I only had five weeks to completed this trip to New Orleans and back. The only site seeing that I will do will be from the river.

I would eat little snacks as I paddled downstream. I went through small towns like Hassman, Aitkin, Riverton, Brainerd, all little places that I never heard of. From the river, Brainerd seem to be a fairly large town as was Little Falls. St. Cloud was a large city but Minneapolis - St. Paul cities were huge. I passed between those two. I did not know where one stopped and the other started. You just could not tell from the river. They were really, really big.

It took me several days to get this far on the river. I thought that I was making a good time. There are many lakes that the Mississippi River flow through in Minnesota. Now I know why they call it the state of ten thousand lakes. Somewhere close to Point Douglas below the twin cities, the river runs along the Wisconsin border. It took me about a week to get out of Minnesota.

Minnesota also has a lot of National Forest and Parks. There is even a place called Detroit Lakes. I have no idea how in the hell Detroit got up there. And General U. S. Grant have a home there. I did not care to see him, so I did not stop. He tore up the South's asses back in the day.

One night I was resting on the bank. I was just about to dose off when I heard something in the brush. I turned on my flashlight to have a look. I should not have done that. I almost shit on the spot. I was looking in the face of a Grisly bear. It was huge. My light scared it as much as it scared me. It stopped dry in its spot. I hurried and grabbed my stuff and jumped into my canoe. I forgot to untie it, but that was okay because I drugged the small willow tree out of the riverbank to come along with me. It followed me as I was paddling double time to get out of there. It was a close call, but as you can tell, I made it. About a mile down river, after I settled down a bit, I realized that it was not a Grisly. It was a Black bear cub that was probably looking for its momma. I was very happy that his momma did not show up at the same time as he did.

I was making really good time now. I almost flew through La Crosse, Wisconsin. At Dubuque I entered Iowa. I also went through Clinton. This guy, Bill really gets around. Hillary needs to tie a chain to this guy to keep him at home. I had been floating for about two weeks now. I've got to speed up. I had Iowa on my right and Illinois on my left.

By this time, I am sure that you are wondering how I was making out when I needed to use the bathroom. Well, I will tell you that I made out quite well. I get number one and number two mixed up so I will use the words pee pee and poo poo. To pee pee was not a problem. I just pee peed on the go. If you have good balance, and I do, you could stand up in a canoe and just let it go overboard. The Mississippi River will not even know it is there. It will not make the river flood anybody out of their home or businesses. If your balance is not too good, you would kneel in the canoe and still get it over the edge. None of this is a hill for a stepper.

Now as far as the poo-pooing - that is another question. When I was on land, it was easy. I am sure that many of you have done it while fishing or hunting. So, you know that it is easy. I brought some supplies for just that. When drifting down the river, I did not want to lose a lot of time by heading to the bank each time the urge hit. It was not easy to hold the paddle and take a crap over the edge of the canoe. I could not afford to put the paddle down and take a chance of heading out further in the river or into the backflow near the bank either. There were times that the poop did not make it over the side of the canoe. Well shit happens. I only had to deal with the smell a short time. It was easy enough to grab it and throw it overboard. There was plenty of water to wash my hands each time it happened. As it was, I was losing weight because of not eating so much and that was a good thing. My canoe would start picking up speed as it lost more poundage in it. As far as handling of the poo-poo, as my daddy used to say, "even shit ain't dirty until it hit the ground". When poo-pooing from a canoe there was no ground to hit on the river, so my shit stayed clean all the time.

I had been averaging about four to six hours a night sleep. This seems to work out okay for me. I was still holding up well. As I am floating, Missouri comes up on one side of me and Illinois on the other. This is a long stretch and I finally pass through St. Louis. I take a really good look at their Arch. I used to think that the Arch crossed the river. But it does not. It is all on the St. Louis, Missouri side. It does not go into East St. Louis, Illinois. Now I am really moving again. I am coming to Cape Girardeau, Missouri then Cairo, Illinois.

It is three weeks now and I better get a move on. I now wished that I brought an outboard motor to hook on the back of my canoe.

Now I have Tennessee and Missouri, then Tennessee and Arkansas on each side of the river. There is West Memphis, Arkansas on my right and Memphis, Tennessee on my left. I can almost see the great state of Mississippi from here.

I am getting a little behind on my schedule. I start paddling harder and faster to pick up speed although the current on the lower Mississippi River was pushing me along. It seemed like I was doing over thirty miles per hour. Man, I was going lick it split.

Up ahead is Greenville, Mississippi where I visited once before. I had driven there on land where I visited with two brothers who ran a barge cleaning plant there. They are really nice folks. They stripped all of our styrene monomer barges when coming back empty from the Ohio and Illinois Rivers. Our upriver plants could not get all the bottoms out of the barges when emptying them at their plants. So, to keep us from having problems when reloading them, these folks stripped the bottoms out of the barges for them to be ready to reload upon arrival at my dock near Houston.

Hey there it is - Ferriday, Louisiana. If I had more time, I would stop and say hello to Jerry Lee Lewis. He was a great Rock and Roll singer in the late 1950s and 1960s. Then he went Country later on. He is first cousin with the preacher Jimmy Swaggart and that other country singer, Mickey Gilley. I have been to Gilley's in Pasadena, Texas. It was the largest dance hall in Texas until Billy Bob opened up in Fort Worth. I've been to Billy Bob's place also. Both of them by land- of course.

Well, I am rocking and rolling down the Mississippi River now. As I pass Ferriday, I am just about passing Natchez, Mississippi. I forgot to mention Vicksburg but since I did not stop there on the river trip, I have nothing to say, except that on another trip there, I hit the slots on a river gambling boat and enjoyed it very much.

Now I finally made it into the toe part of Louisiana's boot. It is actually the foot part of the state.

Hey, there is St. Francisville. There is a Civil War graveyard and monument here. There was a big battle between the North and South in this area. Many men died here. Too many damn good men. Most of the dead were from the North by a large margin.

I am getting closer to Baton Rouge. I will be passing Three Nigger Point soon, hey, there is the entrance to Devil's Swamp Canal. It is actually the Baton Rouge Industrial Canal on the East or right side of the river, but most folks know it as Devil's Swamp Canal. This is the entrance to get to the dock of Foster Grant Chemical Company/United Brands Company/American Hoechst Corporation/and Del Tech Corporation. I may have missed one- or two-name changes. I worked here for over twelve years before being transferred to the Texas Plant to handle the distribution, transportation, and traffic for that location.

I am now coming around Baton Rouge and wanting to get to New Orleans which is about another one hundred thirty miles away by water. From Baton Rouge to the mouth of the Mississippi River is two hundred twenty-eight miles. New Orleans is some ways up the river from the Gulf of Mexico.

It has been four weeks and two days since I started out from Lake Itasca, Minnesota. I have to be back at work in five days and it is a two-day trip after I get back to my truck if it is still there. I hope that it stayed there where I told it to. My truck always listened to me and did what I told it to do.

I do not think that I have time to even make it to White Castle - shit. I am so close to my hometown, well hells bells. I knew that I was not going to make it to New Orleans. So, I turned my canoe around and started paddling upriver back to Minnesota.

Oh, you are wondering if I got back to work on time. HELL YES, that was not a hill for a stepper. I went to work bright and early on Monday morning. But I will say that it had been nice pulling your leg. I just needed a filler to add pages to my book. So, I made this story up. Just so you know, some of the things mentioned in this story are true. The trick for you is to find out which ones are. To do that, you would need a national map and follow the Mississippi River all the way down from Lake Itasca.

After, AFTER RAISING SUGARCANE

ME AND MY CANOE "KAYAK"

If you want to read a real voyage down the Mississippi River, get Johathan Rahan's book, OLD GLORY. I read it many years ago and enjoyed it very much. It was copyrighted in 1981. He really did it.

Now if you already read any of my books, you may have some idea of where I stand politically. If not, continue reading my writings below. You will then have no doubt as to what I am about. These are some suggestions for our nation to get back on track and get out of the deficit spending that our politicians have been doing for way too many years now. The damn buying of votes has got to stop. What I have written many years ago could still be utilized to get our federal government to a balanced budget.

ULTRA CONSERVATIVE RIGHT-WING CONSTITUTIONALIST

MY BELIEFS

- PUBLIC EXECUTIONS For Capital Crimes by Hanging
  1. Use stadiums/Auditoriums
  2. Sell tickets to families
  3. Sell close circuit television
  4. Sell concessions - anything that the public will buy- (no liquor at all)

NOTE: All proceeds go into a fund for the victim's family and will be issued in accordance with the needs of the family

- SUNSET THE IRS AND Have Flat or Consumption Tax
  THE DEPT. OF EDUCATION, No income tax on less the $18,000 yr.
  THE DEPT. OF INTERIOR, AND OTHER DEPTS./AGENCIES

- WELFARE & ASSISTANCE RECEIVERS

Mandatory training for jobs. Off welfare/assistance rolls after two years, trained or not. Go into other programs if not trainable - see next item

- UNEMPLOYMENT COMPENSATION RECEIVERS

Must work 20 hours per week doing community service to continue to receive unemployment checks after the first check is received.

1. City residence will be assigned to keep street and sidewalks cleaned trash in front of residences or nearby locations as assigned.

2. Country residents will walk the highways/byways in their area and pick up trash to continue to receive a check

3. There will be work programs such as:
   Cutting grass by hand
   Using weed whackers
   Using lawnmowers (walk behind)
   Cleaning government offices
   Cleaning government buildings
   Maintain government grounds and structures
   Maintain government vehicles
   Etc., etc., etc.

When they get off the DOLE, they get off the work detail list:

NOTE: As more people are put to work under this plan, towns, cities, states, and federal workers will NOT be replaced as they retire. A much smaller force will be maintained to supervise the workers that is on the dole to check to see that they accomplish their tasks before they receive an unemployment check.

- ASSIST all citizens 25 years of age and over who work full-time and make less than $18000 per year. Help with grocery, clothing, and education
- OTHER GIVEAWAY PROGRAMS –

I.e. Commodities/assistance of any kind but medical

1. Will work 20 per week cleaning street, curbs, sidewalks, ditches, etc. in own neighborhoods or specified areas. Where their section ends, another person will start. They help to police each other.

2. Medical assistance receivers will be the overseers/leaders to check up an see that the work is being completed. If person does not have a good excuse for not putting in their 20 hours, their commodities/assistance will Be CUT accordingly.

3. When they get off the DOLE. They get off the work detail list.
- LAYOFF/RETIRE Maintenance workers (mentioned above) at all levels of government. The citizens living off the taxpayer will do their jobs.   for the assistance they receive without insurance benefits. This will   encourage them to find a job.
- UTILIZE abandon/shutdown armed services bases for prisons, government housing, hospitals, etc. DO NOT build new   prisons/government housing at taxpayers' expense. Take advantage of all under used "government property". Stop paying for guard services to watch abandoned property. Stop paying rent/leases to private property owners for property NOT being actively used.
- AUCTION all government surplus (all levels) to public. DO NOT pay rent to store or guard service to watch government surplus items. Monies for the sales goes into funds for assistance programs in interest bearing accounts.

- RESTRICT GOVERNMENT (all levels) from renting/leasing/buying property from political friends/family as scam to make money. No more Renting property that is not for a "good" purpose.

• CUT PRESIDENTS and Federal Congress pay in half and per diem. And the amounts for attending meeting, sessions, luncheons, dinners, etc.   Stop Free banking, limo rides to and from offices, and any other perks that are not allowed to the ordinary person.

• REDUCE PENSIONS for federal congress, federal judges and president and vice president. Congress and judges should have a least 20 years of service before receiving any pensions. And must be at least 55 years old before starting to receive it. It should be patterned after what the workers of America have. They should NOT collect anything for just 6 yr. of service.

• NO MORE FEDERAL JUDGES appointed for lifetimes

   1. Re-appointed every four years
   2. Check their work record/ethics before re-appointment
   3. Politics WILL NOT play a part in re-appointment

• RESTRICK COST of ex-presidents' private office to a maximum of $100,000 per year and any other ex-government official to zero.

• REDUCE SECRET service personnel on detail for politicians.

Reduce perk for congress and appointed officials of federal, state and local   governments. They tend to forget where they came from and what the   everyday person have to do just to get by.

NOTE: All politicians say they want to serve us. Well, I want to help them serve us and not serve themselves, their families, and their friends. After they get into office; they tend to forget this service to the people and too many of them become millionaires, it they weren't one to begin with. The ones that were millionaires before become multimillionaires on our back before they retire and die.

I now would like to add some writings that I did many years ago. It was a BLOG that I named SAM'S WOODS. This was when I was living in the Sam Houston Forest.

~ Barry R.

SAM'S WOOD

LS AND U - WHAT WILL THEY DO

The basketball gals of LS and U
Beat so many teams
That they did not know what to do
This is the first time they kicked in the door
They finally made it into the final four
But the struggle is not over
As everyone will see
Cause now comes Tennessee
Trying to watch the Vols on TV
The BP explosion interfered with me
I pulled for the Tennessee team to win so they could play LS and U again
The Vols beat the Tigers in their only game this season
The Tigers must win the next one for them get even
One thing is sure and for sure it will be
A Southeastern Conf. team will make the final on TV
It is the best basketball conference in the whole US of A
It may be the best in football and baseball that there is in the nation today
I will pull hard for LSU
As hard as can be
But it will not be easy
To beat the Vols of Tennessee

SHAKIN IN TEXAS CITY

Your may have heard the news last night
Everyone in Toxic City was in fright
Things at BP Chemicals just wasn't right
What happened next had all of T.C. in flight
It was near 6:30 pm when we heard the BOOM
Sleepy and I was so disturbed-we left the room
The sirens screamed and honked and blew
Most of the folks here did not know what to do
We turned the TV to channel sixteen
Impatient for news- know what I mean
About ten minutes past-then it flashed on the screen
"Explosion at BP Refinery" is what we seen
No one was dead, or injured or missing
This was great news as we sat to listen
After about a half hour or more
All network stations gave us the score
The fire at the scene was a site to behold
As most of the residence sheldered in place as they were told
Another hours past as we were on a needle and pin
The news finally made it to the great CNN
It was old news to us there is no doubt
But CNN had to tell everyone else what it was all about
Four hours later the sirens blew a long time
That was the all clear-everything will be fine or
Four hours later the sirens blew a long blast
We all felt relieved-they had saved our A--

PEOPLE DON'T WANT TO WORK NO MORE

Well today is another day in Chemical city
I've been sitting at my computer trying to look pretty
It is just not working, no matter what I do
This trying to look pretty maybe it works for you
I called a man to work on Grandma's house
When he called back he sounded as meek as a mouse
You must be weary of contractors who sound like that
When they leave the job your're left only with your draws and hat
It is hard to find a worker who will treat you right
One you can trust- perhaps its because I am so tight
There are several things here that must be worked on
If Sleepy in TC and I will make this our home
So all contractors, repairmen and repairwomen to
Please return my calls - we have work for you
It seams that workers are not as hungry as they used to be
They are living high on the hog in this land of the free
But the day will come when they will all beg for a job
When everything get tighter and its no longer easy to rob
That day may be here quicker than they think
Cause the world we live in is starting to shrink
butchrock

WITH SLEEPY IN TEXAS CITY

*Sleepy just went off to school today it won't be long
before she's home to stay
Tux the cat is sleeping on the bed with a "do not disturb"
sign hung over his head
Sammy the Pug is naping in his cage
he is snoring, snorting and grunting as if in a rage
Rue the big dog is guarding our yard outside
she barks and growls and sit on guard with pride
I went to the Chiropractor to have my bones crack
the pets and Sleepy were all waiting for me when I got back
I feel a little better now that it is done
when Sleepy get home we may go out and have fun
I can move about more, although I had to pay
this is the only blog that I will write today
butchrock*

BLUE'S IN THE WOODS

It is Blue's Sunday in Sam's Woods
I sure would like to be with Sleepy in TC if I could
KPRC will be playing the blue's all day
But Sleepy is out on the dike having fun on the bay
It is a big holiday for Big Ron down in T. City
After church today, he'll be at the dike- sittin pretty
You only get to go around once in this life
But Big Ron I think he went around twice
Happy birthday big fellow
I don't want to feelin like "old yellow"
You've now made it into your mid 50s
You're still here man - I think that is nifty
So to the dike you go to have some fun
Sleepy is there with the beer, the BBQ, and the sun
I wish you well as well as you can be
I get to TC tomorrow - you'll be the first one I'll see
Well I got to go now they are play my song
I am laid back in the woods - so long
butchrock

SICK COMPUTER IN THE WOODS

We got the bad news that our computer is sick
it cost so much to fix that I want to hit it with a stick
I get so mad that our computers don't work for long
it makes we want to write a real sad song
the repair guy called to see if we want to fix it
I told Sleepy to tell him NO- I just nixed it
I picked it up and brought it with me to the Woods
I am using it now I knew that I could
it will not last much longer- the hard drive is dying
I'll continue to use it until it quit trying
then put it in the back room - with the others that died
and think about buying a new one after this one is fried
butchrock

KEEPING COOL IN THE WOODS

Here I am again. Just keeping my cool in the woods.
Sam's Woods that is.
It is 47 degrees out and looks like it will be another
beautiful day in the woodshood.
I will hate to leave but I must make a treak to Chemical City.
Hey, maybe I will try and contact
Sleepy while I am down there.
I hate to leave, but I really must go
have to bring the computer brain back to the store
I am sick and tired of it making be feel like a clown
the damn thing have problems thats getting me down
It need fixen and fixen right cause its been the company I have at night
but pretty soon everything will be alright
I'll be back in the arms of my wife tonight
now I gotta go and get out of here
to be with my baby and hold her near thats all for now
butchrock

IT WON'T BE LONG-NOW (APRIL 28)

Sleepy went off to school today
it won't be long before she's home to stay
Tux the cas is sleeping on the bed
with a "do not distrub" sign above his head
Sammy the Pug is naping in his cage
he is snoring, snorting and grunting-as if in a rage
Rue, the big dog is guarding our yard outside
she barks and growls and sit on guard with pride
I went to the chiropractor to have my bones crack
the pets were all waiting for me when I got back
I feel a little better now that it is done
when Sleepy get home-we may go out and have some fun
I can move about more-although I had to pay
this is the only blog that I will write today
butchrock

CENTRAL SYSTEM FOR THE OLD HOUSE (APRIL 21)

Ely is coming-that he did
Ely is coming to give us a bid
on central heating and central air
we wanted a bid that would be fair
for this old house in Texas City
to be updated-but it is a pity
the price is to high- the cost to big
for a little hot and cool air-can you dig
we don't know yet what we will do
it may come down to depending upon you
when Ely left we had the bid in hand
we were scratching our heads and mumbling "man oh man"
I don't think we can afford it-just don't think we can
if Ely's to high- should we call another hand
NO they couldn't do the job as Ely could
they wouldn't complete the work as Ely would
perhaps $6200 is not too much to pay
for being comfortable on a hot or cold day
sweating in TC

U OF H CLEAR LAKE ALUMNI PARTY (APRIL 17)

The U of H Clear Lake Alumni sent a letter
inviting Sleepy and I to a get together
at the Haak Winery in Santa Fe
for wine tasting and star party on this day
we invited Ronnie, Judy and kids along
the kids rode with us and we sang a song
we tasted the wine but did not have any cheese
the wine taste good and made me sneeze
Mr Haak took us on a tour of his winery
we saw everything-oak barrels and steel tanks all in its finery
then listened to an astronaut talking about the space project
when the questions and answers was over-no on object
to going into the yard near all the grapes
and using the telescopes to see the starscape
Saturan was beautiful and a site to see
it was very bright-as bright as can be
you could see the break in the ring surrounding Saturan
I could hardly wait to have another turn
to view this planet that was so far away
this is something that I will remember for many a day
soon it was past nine in the p m
we said goodbye to the Haaks and left them
on the way home we stopped at Taco Bell for a bite
it was a great way to end our night
butchrock

57 YR. ANNIVERSARY OF TEXAS CITY DISASTER (APRIL 17)

It has been a week of ceremony here in Texas City
but 57 years ago on April 17, it was not very pretty
bags of fertilizer started burning in a ship's hole
people rushed to the docks for a site to behold
the Grandcamp was a French vessel moored at the dock it was the same
Grandcamp that blew up near 11 o'clock
nearly 200 people met their deaths
many hundreds more got sick as the explosions took their breath
businesses, plants, buildings and homes all disappeared
as the terrible explosion occurred that no one feared
the earth shooked in Galvestion and Houston and Beaumont-
where a large plume of smoke could be seen in the air
the seismograph checked and jumped in Colorado
they thought it was an earthquake just this side of Mexico
some folks thought is was Pearl Harbor all over again
but they soon found out- much to their schgren
that a ship had blown-up without any warning
although people say that the warning was there
the ship's metal was hot and smoke filled the air
as the hands on the vessel closed tight the hole
the pressure built up in the ship and made ready to explode
all but one Texas City fireman was standing on the deck
when the vessel went up-no one was left
it was a sad sight-a sad sight indeed
so much damage so many people in need

but as strong people do-they rebuild in time
they did not just sit around to weep and whine
within several years Texas City was back
bigger and better and smarter -in fact
butchrock

PHI KAPHA PHI INDUCTION (APRIL 16)

We left the house early so we wouldn't be late
Sleepy left the address on the kitchen table where we ate
we headed North on Texas highway 146
listening to rock and roll on the radio and gettin our kicks
driving and driving and driving we did go
where we were going-we did not know
we took a left off Red Bluff onto Alameda Genoa Road
Sleepy was worried and carring a load
into Baywood Cuntry Club we came to a halt
only one thing was known-it was not Sleepy's fault
I went inside Baywood to check and see
then rushed right out-it was not to be
lets go to Bay Oaks Country Club in Clear Lake
we headed for the highway-there was no shortcut to take
Sleepy's foot was heavy as we headed back South
made a right turn on Bay Area Blvd near the canal's mouth
we made it to the ceremony withnot a minute to spare
as we rushed in she was straighten her clothes and fixin her hair
we found a table and sat right down
we introduced ourselves and shook hands all around
soon the announcement was made that dinner is served
we jumped up-headed to the buffet-but was beaten-what a nerve
after the great speaker had been heard
the Master of Ceremony got up and announced the word
all the honorees come stand in a line
Sleepy got up and went-she was looking so fine

*the President shook their hands as he handed the pin
welcome into Phi Kapha Phi honor Society-now you're in
Sleepy got hers and headed back to our table
I could not help but think that she looked like Betty Grable
we said our good byes to the new friends we made
hope to see you all soon-now we're going home and get laid
butchrock*

NEW TEXAS CITY CONTAINER PORT (APRIL 16)

Big things are happening all around Texas City
when the Container Port is built-it will not be pretty
but 1000 new jobs there will be
and containers on Snake Island for everyone to see
the dedication was had down at the dike
folks attended from miles around-some came by bike
the Mayor, County Judge, US Representative, and State Senator too
made speeches and told us what the new port will do
like bring high paying jobs and construction projects to review
that will vastly increase Texas City's revenue
more tax money for the politicians to spend
for buying votes from their enemies and friend
the new port is coming was the yell if only it could do
something about the chemical smell the ceremony
was good and enjoyed by all it was a beautiful day-we thought it was Fall
the honored guess took the shovels and stuck them in the ground
and pictures were taken while they pitched the dirt up and down
we ate cookies and drank bottled water as many folks hung
around while others were lining up for the buses to take them
back to town
We shook hands with the politicians and told them they did and good job
then headed for buses checking for our wallets to be sure we were not
robbed
butchrock

THE EASTER THAT WAS

On Good Friday-we departed for Louisiana
not knowing if I would see my cousin-Anna
when we left Texas City-we knew we had a 6 hr. ride
Nathan was to meet us there-for which we felt pride
he was driving from Forth Worth-he had further to go
we figured we would arrive there many hours before
we both departed about the same time
but I drive slower that that stepson of mine
we pulled up to the house at six fifteen
thinking that Nate won't arrice til late-know what I mean
well a little after seven there he is-pulling in
he made the trip all alone and without a friend
we hooted and hollowed and was happy he arrived safe
then chastised him severely and got in his face
for driving so fast-which he had to do
to arrive right behind us-I'm telling you
we all made the trip down with no problems at all
got to my brother's house where we had a ball
on Saturday we piddled around for a spell
then went to gamble on the Baton Rouge Belle
this was Nate's fire time-so we want to teach him right
if we played the nickle slots-we could gamble all night
our ten dollars each lasted over three hours
this was a lot of entertainment for very few dollars
when this fun was over-we headed back to my brother
where we ate such good food we thought we would smother

then came Easter morning-it came with a bang
before long three sacks of crawfish and the whole riffraff gang
my brother did the boiling-one sack at a time
with potatoes, onions, corn, mushrooms, sausage, lemons and lime
we all ate and ate and ate-till we could not eat any more
than sat down and rested while some layed down on the floor
after everyone had rested and they all departed
Nate, Sleepy and I were ready for a party
over to the Bon Chance -a hot spot in the woods we did go
with our friends-Bell and Pete leading the way-I want you to know
some folks that I met there-I had not seen in years
we talked and visited and shared a few tears
Nate shot pool with everyone that came in
Sleepy had a few beers and sat there with a big grin
we piddled around and visited with relatives and friends
we all passed a good time and wished that it would not end
but alas it did- and we had to go
we headed to Pierre Part to see something I wanted to show
over to Shell Beach we went-I wanted Sleepy and Nate to see
where my family spent much time and where they brought me back to my
brother's house for one last night for on Monday morning we would make
our flight and leave God's Country with their very low taxes and head back
home to our beloved TEXAS
butchrock

BEEN GONE TO LONG

I guess you think I took a break
it surely looks that way- for heaven's sake
but I've been writing all along
not on my computer blog- it was gone
but Sleepy showed me how to get it back
and now I am catching up- getting back on tract
I have a number of these blogs to do
and sure hope and pray I don't drive you coo coo
butchrock

WAL-MART WOES (I got the)

*As we were leaving after breakfast in the "Big Thicket" we noticed folks
outside Wal-Mart carring pickets
we decided to turn in to see what was up
and got the scoop from the man who approached our truck
they were protesting many things that Wal-Mart did
that would never have happened if Sam Walton had lived
cheap products from China was heading the list
if Ole Sam was alive, Wal-Mart would not do this
low wages, less benefits, so much foreign made products
put the hurt on America's workers to sum up - it sucks
we have known for some time that Wal-Mart is not for the worker
the owners just act like the rich man and keep on a smerkin
with their 50% turnover in employees, you think they would worry
but as long as the money rolls in they are not in a hurry
to make any changes that would help their reputation
or to give benefits as Costco does or make reparation
to their employees for all the jobs well done
and more time off with their families to have some fun
if Ole Sam Walton was alive - would it be better or worse
I like to think it would be better if Sam was still on this earth
Butchrock*

BREAKFAST IN CLEVELAND, TEXAS

It was the past Friday we did depart
for our place in Sam's Woods to start
the weekend off and have a great time
where there is no rain and the sun doth shine
early Saturday morn we decided on breakfast in town
to the truck we went and started on down
we headed for Cleveland- twelves miles away
it was a pleasant drive and a very fine day
over toward the "Hot Biscuit" we did head
this was much better than staying in bed
the Biscuit is a landmark in this country
good food at a good price for everybody
I opened the door and we walked on in
and the first one we see- is our ole friend
Represented Nick Lampson is his name
I told him "howdy" he did the same
we shook each other hands and exchange pleasantries
as I reminded him of our last meeting at Habitat for Humanities
where we sat and talked and ate together
before his speech about politics and the weather
Nick was here to meet folks and get ready for another election
because the folks in Austin had changed his direction
he had lost his territory that was in Galveston
and picked up Liberty County now to run
he had to make new contacts all over the place
get out amoung these folks so they can see his face

*I wished him well in his next big election
as he went to a table shaking hands with people eating
confection
Nick is a democrate - although I don't know why
But if I was to ever vote for a democrate- he would be the guy
butchrock*

WHAT A TIMESHARE

*At the timeshare playing in the swimming pool overlooking the lake
enjoying the beautiful scenery- it was not a fake
enjoying the wonderful sunsets beyond the hills to the West
the thought crossed my mind- this place I like the best
on the 18th day of May it should be a national holiday
we went to Austin to wile the time away
for a visit with two of my sons and to go out to eat
because it was my birthday- this was their treat
we all passed a good time then we said our so longs
we hope to see yall again before to much time is gone
back to the timeshare and the scenery that awaited us
we arrived in due time without a very big fuss
after five days and nights in the Hill country seeing all
the sites and visiting with relatives and friends
we headed back to Sam Woods, where once our trips began
then off again to Corpus Christi to spend three days and nights
and a visit to South Padre Island and take in all the sites
another visit with relatives and to have a little fun
but it all went by so fast- it hardly had begun
then back to Texas City where we've been spending most of the time
to check on our dog Rue, and cat, Tux, who we had left behind
all was well when we got back, nothing went awry
we may leave for another trip soon which would make our pets cry
raffriff*

ON THE ROAD AGAIN

After Sleepy's graduation, a trip we did take to the Texas Hill Country
and a timeshare on Canyon Lake Sleepy and me,
with Alice Jean made three and Sammy,
Nathan and Marilyn- without a flea
made six of us heading to the lake
two vehicles full- with all we could take
a seventh one was awaiting our arrival there
it was Linda Kaye, with the very blond hair
Two bedrooms and a couch is where we would lay
except for Sammy and Marilyn- they slept on the hay
because they are two dogs who traveled with us
we enjoyed their company, they weren't a fuss
to San Antonio on Sunday to visit old cousin Vivian
for stories of ancestors-dead and several still livin
letters were read and pictures were past
then lunch was served and we all ate fast
to get back to the stories and tales of old
about several generations before us that was never told
we then drove about a mile down the road
to visit an old Spanish Mission and hear another story told
this mission was built in the year 1720
it was hard times for making a living and that is not funny
on the grounds was a great old church that we went through
I stopped in it long enought to say a prayer or two
then back to Canyon Lake we all went
discussing the events of the day and our time well spent, raffriff

ON THE MOVE

I've been away from my blog for sometime
perhaps you thought that I could no longer rhyme
not so- I tell you- not so at all
I've been catching my breath between Winter and Fall
A lot has happened since I last wrote
I don't know where to begin- no, I did not have a stroke
Sleepy graduated from college back in May
we took off for a couple weeks to play in the hay
It was a long haul and she came a long way
she now have that sheepskin that no one can take away
we rejoiced and celebrated as we drove from city to city
we really passed a good time, and Sleepy's now sitting pretty
for when she decides to go back to work
a higher salary she could command with a smirk
but for now is weighing her options and deciding what to do
before getting back in the workforce with all of you
raffriff

This is where I will stop my third book in this series. At this time, I do not know if I will continue to write about my life's story anymore. It is not as interesting when you live by yourself and is pretty boring, to say the least. So, this maybe it. Oh, I had some fun times with a lady friend for about three years, but I do not think that she would want me to write about some of the things that we did while going together. So, I will say that I love you all, and thanks for reading, Barry Franklin Anthony (Butch) Raffray.

This is the final end of this book. Thanks for reading it.

www.ingramcontent.com/pod-product-compliance
Lightning Source LLC
LaVergne TN
LVHW021220080526
838199LV00084B/4295